Assessing and Diagnosing Speech Therapy Needs in School

Assessing and Diagnosing Speech Therapy Needs in School is a unique text that offers practical guidance in pedagogical diagnosis of speech and communication difficulties within educational settings.

It outlines theoretical assumptions of the diagnosis process and presents hands-on solutions for pedagogical and speech therapy. Underpinned by theoretical knowledge and written by experienced practitioners, the book equips its readers with tools to understand the diagnostic process and make accurate diagnoses based on each child's individual circumstances. It starts by clearly distinguishing between pedagogy and speech therapy and outlines issues and theoretical considerations in diagnosing these disorders. To contextualize the theoretical observations, it goes on to present case studies, and touches upon crucial topics including readiness to start education, tendency toward aggressive behavior, aphasia and hearing loss. The authors also elaborate on a range of selected diagnostic tools to assess specific difficulties in speech and language therapy. Finally, a list of resources, including games and exercises that can target reading, writing and articulation skills to help children develop, are also featured in the book.

Highlighting the importance of practical and theoretical knowledge for those who work with children, this will be a valuable aid for teachers, special educators and speech and language therapists working within school settings. The book will also be of interest to students, teachers and trainee practitioners in the fields of speech therapy and special educational needs.

Małgorzata Przybysz-Zaremba is a habilitated doctor and professor at the National Vocational College of Ignacy Mościcki in Ciechanów, Poland. She is also a pedagogue, a special educator and a pedagogical therapist who works with children with special educational needs. She has authored over 200 scientific publications. Her research interests include social pedagogy, rehabilitation pedagogy, behavioral disorders, suicidal behavior, addictions and special educational needs. She aims to analyze these topics in the diagnostic, preventive and supportive (therapeutic) context.

Aleksandra Siedlaczek-Szwed is a habilitated doctor and professor at the University of Humanities and Natural Sciences of Jan Długosz in Często-chowa, Poland. She also heads the Center for Research and Assistance to People with Speech Disorders. Her areas of scientific interest are pedagogical and speech therapy aspects of education, teaching and upbringing. She has authored several monographs and publications of national and international scope.

Krzysztof Polok is a habilitated doctor and professor at the University of Bielsko-Biala in Bielsko-Biała, Poland. He is a linguist, and his research focuses on the influence of lesson plans with and without the use of the ICT tools on teachers and learners of language. He is the author of 12 books and more than 150 publications. He also works as a sworn translator of Polish and English.

Assessing and Diagnosing Speech Therapy Needs in School

Pedagogical Diagnostics in Theory and Practice

Małgorzata Przybysz-Zaremba, Aleksandra Siedlaczek-Szwed and Krzysztof Polok

LONDON AND NEW YORK

First published 2023
by Routledge
4 Park Square, Milton Park, Abingdon, Oxon OX14 4RN

and by Routledge
605 Third Avenue, New York, NY 10158

Routledge is an imprint of the Taylor & Francis Group, an informa business

© 2023 Małgorzata Przybysz-Zaremba, Aleksandra Siedlaczek-Szwed, and Krzysztof Polok

British Library Cataloguing-in-Publication Data
A catalogue record for this book is available from the British Library

ISBN: 978-1-032-40802-6 (hbk)
ISBN: 978-1-032-40798-2 (pbk)
ISBN: 978-1-003-35475-8 (ebk)

DOI: 10.4324/9781003354758

Typeset in Bembo Std
by KnowledgeWorks Global Ltd.

Contents

Figures

Tables

Introduction

The challenge of modern education is to help students in difficult situations, many of them being conditioned by environmental factors and/or individual developmental characteristics. Systemic changes in education that are introduced in individual countries contribute to the modification of the process of helping and supporting a student at school, which therefore requires taking actions related to diagnostic activities.

Diagnostics is a scientific discipline whose direct subject of research is a human (a kindergarten-attending child or a school student) functioning in the socio-environmental context (perceived and/or understood in various ways in social sciences). On the other hand, pedagogical diagnostics is a field of knowledge dealing with the theory and practice of diagnosis. It is thus a process integrally related to rational, educational and care-giving activity, its environmental conditions as well as its course and effects. The main task of pedagogical diagnostics is to show the need for its practical knowledge in everyday work, as well as in individual educational environments (mostly school-related).

Diagnosis in pedagogy, as well as in other scientific disciplines, such as speech therapy, for example, is a creative process that requires an individual approach to a specific case. It deals with the method of collecting data and their analyses, which is the basis for the assessment of the studied phenomenon (case study). It is a complex, multistage process, adapted to the abilities of the child/student (or the euphemistically treated patient), as well as the type of the discovered disorder in terms of diagnostic methods and tools. In the case of speech therapy diagnosis, the results of specialist examinations are also taken into account, which refer not only to the examined entity (i.e. the child/student or patient) but also to their family and immediate surroundings. Symptoms are established on the basis of observation and interview data, language trials and tests. Depending on the results of various supplementary tests (e.g. psychological, pedagogical, neurological, audiological, orthodontic, phoniatric), a qualitative and quantitative assessment of linguistic behavior is taken and appropriate forms of treatment are performed (Czempka-Wiewióra & Graboń, 2017, p. 151).

This monograph should be approached as a form of challenge to meet (and possibly cover) large gaps in scientific and methodological publications

DOI: 10.4324/9781003354758-1

in this area that were noticed on the British and European market. Hence, the authors of this monograph wanted to see it as an important didactic aid for practitioners, methodologists, speech therapists, therapists, teachers working with children in kindergartens and students of grades 1–3, specialists employed in schools in supporting students with special educational needs (e.g. special educators, oligophrenopedagogues, pedagogical therapists, etc.), as well as students of pedagogy who intend to work in primary schools in the near future. This monograph allows readers to broaden their knowledge of the theory and methodology of pedagogical and speech therapy diagnosis, as well as the practice of pedagogical and speech therapy. Its aim is to familiarize readers with the theoretical and practical assumptions of the diagnosis processes and to present pragmatic solutions for diagnosis and pedagogical and speech therapy for students.

The issues presented in the monograph have been divided into two specific areas of diagnostics: pedagogy and speech therapy. The theoretically analyzed issues are discussed in the first two chapters, which constitute the key foundations for the practice of the pedagogical and speech therapy diagnostics processes to be carried out at school.

Chapter 1, entitled *Pedagogical Diagnostics as a Key Activity in the Educational Process of a Child – General Theoretical Assumptions*, covers the issues related to pedagogical diagnostics, that is, a complex process, which in school practice requires the teacher (care-giving specialist, diagnostician, etc.) to have many competences and skills. The authors not only analyze the specificity, features and functions of pedagogical diagnosis, which are important in this process, but they also present methods, techniques and tools used in the diagnostic process. At the same time, they point to additional tools that can be an important source in collecting diagnostic material, thus making the process more complete, in-depth and even holistic. An important issue discussed in this chapter relates to the competences of the teacher-diagnostician. The authors indicate both key competences (recognized as absolutely necessary) and those perceived as additional competences, which are nevertheless still important in the implementation of the diagnostic process. The course of the diagnostic process conducted at school by a teacher-specialist (and additionally by a team of specialists at a psychological and pedagogical counseling center) is presented in detail. A patterned model of the pedagogical diagnosis process in school, which can be used in many countries, is outlined in the final section of the chapter, which concludes with an analysis of the problems and dilemmas related to pedagogical diagnosis.

Chapter 2, *Introduction to the Theoretical and Methodological Foundations of Speech Therapy – Speech Therapy Diagnosis and Speech Therapy Procedures*, discusses basic issues related to speech therapy as a scientific discipline; it also outlines interests among other sciences. It must be said right away that this interest has not been recognized as enormously important; the popular *Merriam-Webster Dictionary* (2020) gives a very short and not very telling definition of speech therapy, stating that it is a scientific discipline dealing with 'the treatment of speech impediments', while another widely used English dictionary, the *Oxford Advanced Learners' Dictionary* (OALD), does not even include the term *logopaedia* in its collection. Additionally, the term *speech therapy*, in the way it appears in Merriam-Webster's collections, refers its readers who are more interested in the subject to specialist medical literature. This arrangement of the issues clearly indicates that the authors of the aforementioned dictionary see speech therapy and – more broadly – all activities related to it, as up-to-a-point medical issues, almost equating speech therapy problems and other medical ailments that people may complain about (e.g. the 'treatment' used in COVID and/or other diseases). The authors of this monograph understand these types of issues in a decidedly different way. In our understanding, speech therapy is a scientific activity aimed at providing help to children and/or adolescents who have been found to show such speech disorders as – for example – lisp, rotacism, stuttering, hearing impediments, cleft and/or other such disorders, defects or handicaps. This approach means that any medical (or even meta-medical) aspect cannot be considered at all, as the aforementioned disorders cannot be considered a disease. The issues in question, which in a decisive way shape the quality of life of language users, are closely related to communication and – in general – to communication issues. OALD (2020) states briefly that the phenomenon of communication (and communicating) is used to define the entire process of information transfer from one source to another by the participants in the process of creating various types of phenomena that appear in the daily functioning of its users. It is therefore understandable that people with the aforementioned disorders will have various types of problems with both the transfer of information and its reception. Due to the fact that the communication process covers not only the issues of speech (i.e. the production of information) but also the issues of receiving information (i.e. the issues related to obtaining it and mentally processing it), various forms of disturbances directly related to any stage of communication will shape both the comfort of reception as well as the production of news. Therefore, the authors of this monograph analyze the development of linguistic competences, which to some extent are shaped by a child's educational environment. These competences – in short – define the ability to appropriate linguistic behavior (and thus also communicative and cultural behavior) of each of the users of the communication process. Such a definition results directly from the issue of understanding the concept of language, which Wittgenstein (1953) understands as a kind of game of 'meaning'; Chomsky (1965) as an internal, inalienable ability to express various kinds of thoughts and ideas; Hymes (1972) as a meaning-generating system; and Trudgill (1982) as a product of the cultural heritage of a particular group of people. All such definitions, however, result from the structuralist approach of de Saussure (1916), which recognizes language as an inventory of grammatical signs and rules that allow building complex signs from simple signs, which can refer each of their users to other objects or phenomena in three different ways: with indicators, icons and symbols.

From this interpretative approach, Hymes (1972) derives the division of competences into linguistic (i.e. knowledge of such rules of a given language that enable its users to both build new, grammatically correct sentences, and understand them) and communicative (i.e. knowledge of all these language rules that operate on the social platform). All such events, functioning within the phenomenon of communication, should be skillfully used by each of the participants of the communication act during the construction of their communication contacts, because each of them belongs to the internal and external inventory of the communication process (i.e. the situation of receiving and producing information by each of the users of a given language). People who show various types of problems during the production/reception of messages (e.g. stuttering, rotacism, lisp, hearing loss, amblyopia, etc.) require the help of a speech therapist or – in other situations – a diagnostician. Therefore, an important issue discussed in this chapter is the methodology of speech therapy diagnosis that takes into account, for example, a developed scheme of speech therapy examination, which is universal and can be used in the diagnosis of all speech disorders. The authors emphasize that conducting a reliable diagnostic procedure is the starting point for designing individual speech therapy.

The three remaining chapters constitute the methodical nature of the monograph and indicate its coherence and integrity around the content discussed.

Chapter 3, *Pedagogical and Speech Therapy Diagnosis – Exploration of Selected Cases*, presents examples of the cases of children who were diagnosed in the pedagogical and speech therapy areas. The pedagogical diagnosis includes two cases of examined children in terms of their readiness to start education in a public primary school at the first stage of education (early school education) as well as detected disorders in concentration and tendency toward aggressive behavior. Apart from that, the speech therapy diagnosis includes five cases of children diagnosed to suffer from aphasia, hearing loss and Asperger's syndrome. Each of the presented case studies contains conclusions and recommendations for further work with the child (learner). The analyzed case studies are the results of the original research, which is addressed to everyone interested in the diagnosis process. They can be a model for the practice of carrying out the process of pedagogical diagnosis in primary schools (or in 'zero' classes run in kindergartens) and for novice speech therapists employed in specialist clinics.

Chapter 4, *On the Application of Selected Tools Useful in Pedagogical and Speech Therapy Diagnostics*, presents proposals of tools used in pedagogical and speech therapy diagnosis. Apart from the proposed tools presented in the tables, the authors make a short description of them, indicating the type of dysfunction (or disorder) for which a given tool can be used. Information on who can use the tools in practice is also provided. This type of information enables the diagnosticians (teachers, speech therapists or other specialists) to choose the tool that, in their opinion, will be the best for the diagnosed disorder (problem). In addition, this material has been supplemented with notes and practical tips, which are an indispensable help in pedagogical and speech therapy practice for teachers (or other specialists) from various countries.

The last chapter presents proposals of exercises and games used in pedagogical and speech therapy for improving the development of children in preschool and early school age. The presented exercises and games have been planned in such a way that they refer not only to the diagnosed cases of children (i.e. the material that can be found in Chapter 3) but also take into account the specificity of pedagogical work of early school and preschool education teachers from various countries, as well as many speech-related specialists (therapists, speech therapists, neurologopedists, psychologists, special educators). The exercises and games have been carefully described, so that everyone who wants to use them in working with children/students knows what actions should be taken in them. In addition, the material has been provided with notes and practical tips, which hopefully make it more in-depth.

The reader who has reached for this book will receive reliable and, to some extent, broadened knowledge about pedagogical and speech therapy diagnosis, as a process carried out in many schools in different countries, as well as a methodical handbook of actions that a teacher-diagnostician and speech therapist must undertake in their everyday professional endeavors. It is about taking pragmatic actions related to the process of pedagogical and/or speech therapy diagnosis, the selection of appropriate diagnostic tools, the course of the diagnosis process and, on its basis, taking appropriate therapeutic interventions. The exercises and games in the last chapter of the book are a kind of inspiration for quite a large number of creative therapists (educators, teachers, speech therapists and/or other specialists) looking for new solutions.

The monograph authors believe that this book will fill the existing gap in the topical British and European publishing market.

Bibliography

Chomsky, N. (1965). *Aspects of the theory of syntax*. MIT Press.

Czempka-Wiewióra, M., & Graboń, K. (2017). Diagnoza i postępowanie logopedyczne w nauczaniu języka polskiego jako obcego [Diagnosis and speech therapy in teaching Polish as a foreign language]. *Postscriptum Polonistyczne* [Polish Postscript], *1*(19), 147–161.

Hymes, D. (1972). On communicative competence. In J. B. Pride, & J. Holmes (Eds.), *Sociolinguistics* (pp. 269–293). Penguin.

Oxford Advanced Learners' Dictionary. (2020). https://www/oxfordlearnersdictionaries.com (Accessed 02/09/2022).

Saussure de, F. (1916). In C. Bally, & A. Sechehaye (Eds.), with the assistance of Albert Riedlinger. *Cours de linguistique générale*. Payot.

The Merriam-Webster Dictionary of English Usage. (2020). https://www.merriam-webster.com (Accessed 02/09/2022).

Trudgill, P. (1982). *Introducing language and society*. Cambridge University Press.

Wittgenstein, L. (2001 [1953]). *Philosophical investigations*. Blackwell Publishing Ltd.

1 Pedagogical diagnostics as a key activity in the educational process of a child

General theoretical assumptions

Pedagogical diagnostics – explanations of the basic concepts related to diagnosis

Pedagogical diagnostics is a relatively young discipline in the system of educational sciences; it is constantly developing, providing various effects. Due to the complexity of the subject of interest of educational sciences, and thus the multitude of areas of diagnosis, its scientific paradigm (i.e. a set of commonly recognized theoretical assumptions, basic concepts, methods, techniques, etc.) in relation to only one area of diagnosis (educational diagnostics) has not been precisely defined yet (Wysocka, 2013, pp. 14–15).

In many European countries, the pedagogical diagnosis of a child is associated with the recognition of its level of development in terms of readiness to start education at school. For example, in Germany, Austria or Switzerland, before starting school education, children follow the expected core curriculum by attending a preparatory group or class, located in the nearest kindergarten or primary school, depending on the child's development level (Eurydice Unit, 2003; Mykyteichuk et al., 2021). In France, however, various forms of preschool integration with the first years of primary education are used. In practice, it is the case that children aged 4–5 who attend kindergarten most often participate in classes together with the children of the first grades of primary school, thus completing the so-called 'preparatory class' (Eurydice Unit, 2008). In Finland, this is done by attending a preschool group for 6-year-old children, and in Italy children are expected to attend the so-called 'schools for children' (this is the type of yearlong preparatory school to be completed before mandatory school education) (European Commission, 2010). In Poland, the first pedagogical diagnosis of a child in terms of readiness to undertake school education is carried out in the so-called 'zero-classes' for preschoolers. These are preparatory groups that are conducted in kindergartens – compulsory for children aged 5–6 – or in schools. Parents can choose where the child will complete the preparatory stage for school education (European Commission, 2010). This stage of education, during which the pedagogical diagnosis of a child is carried out for the first time in terms of its development, is carried out in almost all

DOI: 10.4324/9781003354758-2

European countries, through appropriate forms, which are defined by the legislation of a given country (Eurostat, 2013). Its effective realization conducted in various types of schools and/or kindergartens is extremely important, because it is largely recognized to be the focus (and proper guidance) of a child's education.

Diagnostic tests are very often used in empirical sciences and take the form of heuristic or verification tests. The first of these tests is aimed at discovering the phenomenon and determining its genesis, while the second checks the diagnosis. In pedagogy, an important place in empirical research has been occupied by pedagogical diagnostics. Each diagnosis and its results constitute an integral part of the purposeful procedure in practical sciences. Diagnostics, as a type of pedagogical procedure, should be considered in terms of methodology. The methodology of pedagogical research is the science of the principles and methods of research recommended and applied in pedagogy (Łobocki, 2010). The relationship between diagnostics and methodology seems to be very important, because without the knowledge of methodology it is impossible to properly design and conduct any research.

Basic terminology related to pedagogical diagnosis

The term 'diagnosis' comes from the Greek words *dia*, meaning 'through', and *gnosis* – 'recognition, cognition', and defines the ability to recognize an item on the basis of an analysis of the examined problem and its symptoms (Guziuk-Tkacz, 2011, p. 15). The introduction of the concept of diagnosis to the social sciences is attributed to Mary Ellen Richmond (1861–1928), who in the United States made an attempt to visualize and professionalize social work (Richmond, 1917). In Europe, however, this concept was popularized in Germany by Alice Salomon (1872–1948) (Salomon, 1926). The term 'diagnosis' is used by representatives of many scientific disciplines. One can speak about, among others, medical, psychological, pedagogical or speech therapy diagnosis, as well as diagnosis in rehabilitation. The understanding of individual types of diagnosis and the scope of activities undertaken by diagnosticians are slightly different. When explaining the term 'diagnosis', it should be noted that it is sometimes used in two senses. In the first sense, it means the diagnostic procedure. Thus, a diagnosis is the activity of a diagnostician (e.g. a psychologist) aimed at explaining the abnormal functioning of a child from the point of view of the causes, psychological mechanisms and effects of a given disorder. In the second sense, diagnosis is the end result of the activities mentioned, the effect the diagnosis is aimed at. It is a description and explanation of abnormalities by indicating their patho-mechanisms, which allows to prepare a suitable therapy plan. When analyzing the scope of the subject of diagnosis, two perspectives can be presented. In a broad sense, it can either be a comprehensive (holistic) diagnosis, and in this case it concerns the entire development and functioning of the examined person, or it can also refer to physical and motor aspects. In the narrow diagnosis approach, we are talking about a partial diagnosis (or a selective diagnosis) that refers only to a selected aspect of a child's development and functioning. Didactic, upbringing, caring and preventive activities constitute the plane of teacher-pedagogue interaction aimed at various groups of children and adolescents. The effectiveness of these activities is determined by the degree of identification of needs, which in turn is reduced to diagnostic work, preceded by educational activities. The didactic, educational, caring, preventive or developmental diagnosis thus covers pedagogical activities at every stage of education and in every type of school. Pedagogical knowledge, as the basic element of work in the educational area, is a complex task, requiring methodological, psychological and substantive preparation, along with the possession of appropriate personal characteristics by a diagnostician.

Many definitions of diagnosis have been formulated in the social and natural-medical sciences. Various proposals are available in which a transformation of their approach is visible. However, the definition most often cited in various scientific disciplines is the one offered by Ziemski (1973). According to him '[...] diagnosis is the recognition of a specific state of affairs and its development trends on the basis of its symptoms and on the basis of the knowledge of general regularities in a given field'.

When analyzing the concepts related to the diagnostic process in pedagogy, it is initially necessary to refer to its basic terminology. The objective scope of the cognition process is determined by the content of three basic concepts: diagnostics, diagnosing and diagnosis. Diagnostics is a science, the subject of which is the activity of recognizing and differentiating the phenomena and states of affairs needed to be analyzed. On the basis of the methodology of already developed diagnostic procedures, not only methods but also techniques and tools for collecting information and methods of their analysis are developed. When defining the rules and principles of the correct course of the cognition process, we include the rules of ethical diagnostic procedure (Wysocka, 2013, pp. 45–46). It should be emphasized that a diagnosis is not only the process of data registration but also the process of their processing, in which we distinguish two elements of cognition: experience and reasoning. On the other hand, pedagogical diagnosis is a process, the effect of which is the description of certain states of affairs made according to specific criteria (Jäger, 2007). It is the basis for all rational pedagogical activities, and its effects are used to plan and take preventive, therapeutic, aid, corrective, compensatory, supportive and rescue activities.

In colloquial use, the word *diagnosis* is often replaced by such words as 'assessment', 'description', 'recognition' or 'statement'; which are even recognized as its synonyms. In the Polish scientific literature, the authors (e.g. Jarosz, 2003; Podgórecki, 1962; Skałbania, 2011; Wysocka, 2013), when describing the processes of a diagnosis, mention the following distinctions:

- description – a compilation of research data against which purposefulness-specified proceedings are undertaken; otherwise it is recording, determining, stating facts;

- assessment – allows one to compare the collected facts and the state under study with these facts and postulated state, which helps to identify possible discrepancies;
- conclusion – defines the need (or lack of the need) to undertake purposefulness of the proceedings;
- translation – the explanation of the causes of the studied phenomenon;
- postulating – depicts states destined to be realized or reformed;
- making hypotheses – practically means identifying the relationship between the project and the causal factor.

As observed by Ziemski (1973), on the basis of pedagogical sciences, a full diagnosis (also referred to as comprehensive or holistic) consists of several (i.e. partial) types of diagnosis, which include:

- typological (classification or assigning) diagnosis, which defines what the studied phenomenon is and – based on the literature – classifies it as a known type or species;
- genetic (causal) diagnosis, which deals with explaining the phenomenon under study and looking for an answer to the question why it is so;
- meaning (purposive) diagnosis, which determines the impact of the identified state on the entire phenomenon under study;
- phase diagnosis, which consists in assessing the skills, efficiency or state of knowledge presented by the examined person;
- prognostic (developmental) diagnosis, which assumes predicting the further direction of development of a given process or phenomenon.

An example of a comprehensive diagnosis in pedagogy, taking into account partial diagnoses, may be the description of the situation of a child with speech and language development disorders.

Diagnostic activities necessary in pedagogical work are of great importance at every stage of a child's education, and are most desirable in relation to younger children due to the priority of equalizing educational opportunities. The diagnosis process based on theoretical assumptions, methodological knowledge and skills, along with the teacher's own research and creative attitude, should lead to the full knowledge of the student, taking into account the broad situational and environmental context. Cognition, as an element of pedagogical work, occurs in all areas that are the subject of pedagogical interest; therefore, there is a need to prepare future educators to conduct diagnostic proceedings in relations with the pupils, students or other caregiving youngsters.

Nowadays, the growing educational difficulties affect an increasing number of children and adolescents. The rational pedagogical procedure aimed at improving this state of affairs is diagnosing (recognizing) the students under charge and their life conditions, that is both the initial personality state and their psychosocial conditions.

In pedagogy, diagnosis is interpreted as getting to know a child with disorders and explaining their behavior in various life situations. In this monograph, the notion of pedagogical diagnosis concerns children and their readiness to start education in a public (i.e. state) school at the first stage of education (i.e. early childhood education). Thus, attention is paid to various problems and disorders of children, which most often appear as a result of the diagnostic process. In the third chapter, the cases of children undergoing a pedagogical diagnosis and their disorders are presented, which makes it difficult for children to be fully ready to start education at school, and later also to achieve educational success. Among others, selected cases of children can be found in terms of achieving school readiness (along with comments and practical tips for teachers and parents regarding actions to be taken to minimize the disorders occurring in a child), along with cases of children with speech therapy diagnoses. The children presented there are those diagnosed with disorders of motor dysphasia, motor aphasia, Asperger's syndrome, hearing impairment, hearing loss and motor aphasia.

In educational sciences, diagnostic tests are one of the most common, because they look for the causes of the phenomenon under study. They are used to forecast and modify didactic and educational problems, and thus contribute to enriching not only theory but, above all, pedagogical practice. Therefore, diagnostic tests belong to the group of practical tests.

Didactic and educational (pedagogical) diagnostics is a methodology of pedagogical diagnosis, which consists in the description and explanation of the methods of recognizing the didactic and educational situation of a student, especially the changes that occur in it under the influence of pedagogical influence (Niemierko, 1993, pp. 96–99). On the other hand, the diagnostics of caregiving needs require organized and systematic research activities with the use of multifaceted knowledge about people and their lives. It is thus a multifaceted and, at the same time, complex activity, because – as observed by Wysocka (2013, pp. 34–35) – it involves a multilateral cognitive process resulting from the diversity of the needs of individuals and human groups.

In pedagogical practice, you can also meet with social rehabilitation diagnostics, which deals with making accurate and reliable diagnoses for the purpose of social rehabilitation education of socially maladjusted people. In practical terms, it is one of the most difficult processes of diagnosing social maladjustment of an individual, because it determines the adoption of an interdisciplinary model of its assessment and involvement in the diagnosis process of a *[...] team of reflective specialists* (Wysocka, 2016, p. 199), along with taking into account two dimensions of diagnosis: individual and environmental.

The term 'diagnosing' describes the functional aspect of the cognition process, that is the nature and forms of actions aimed at recognition. On one hand, 'diagnostics' is a science, the subject of which are the activities of recognizing the phenomena and states of affairs analyzed. On the other hand, a diagnostic tool is the narrowest concept, limited in meaning to the technical side of collecting empirical data in the course of research (Wysocka, 2013, pp. 46–49).

In the development of pedagogical diagnostics, an increase in the scope and areas of diagnosis is observed, which influences its specialization, and therefore the emergence of specialist diagnostics (educational, social, psychological, caring, social rehabilitation, special, speech therapy), which differentiates the subject, and partly also the rules, principles and methods of cognition.

Closely related to professional diagnosis are terms such as 'diagnosing', 'diagnostic test', 'diagnostic cognition', 'diagnostic procedure' and 'the act of diagnosing'. A diagnostic test comes down to efforts to obtain reliable information and statements of true facts and phenomena; establishing the actual state and detecting real relationships between phenomena and processes (Apanowicz, 2005, p. 42). The starting point for this type of research is diagnostic cognition, which should be based on experience, collecting the starting material and reasoning, that is causal and purposeful explanation (Ziemski, 1973, p. 20).

A term similar in meaning to diagnostic cognition is the 'diagnostic procedure'. It means a procedure, which is a syndrome of research activities, consisting of assessing the existing problem currently under investigation in order to discover its causes. In a broad sense, it means research that is both cognitive and practical, while in the narrow sense – a research for practical purposes (Apanowicz, 2002).

The process of diagnosis includes stages of the research process that relate to the empirical side and nature of social sciences. The stages of the scientific cognition process are reduced to the full act of reflective thinking, consisting of such elements as experiencing theoretical or practical difficulties; their detection and definition; adopting possible variants of the solution; deriving conclusions from presumed solutions; and, finally, observations and experiments leading to the acceptance or rejection of the solution(s) made (Apanowicz, 2000, pp. 140–141).

By analyzing the concepts of the authors of various methodological studies (including Góralski, 1987; Kazubowska, 2020; Łobocki, 2011; Pilch, 2001; Skarbek, 2013; Węglińska, 2010, pp. 51–68), which refer to the pattern of the research procedure, it can be stated that the diagnosis in broad terms corresponds to the following activities:

1 formulation of the main and specific research problems;
2 formulation of the main and detailed hypotheses;
3 preparation of a research plan, that is collecting and analyzing activities stored up till then;
4 collection of research material, consisting in collecting the data after prior selection of research methods, techniques and tools;
5 analysis and interpretation of the obtained research material;
6 construction of research conclusions.

However, the narrow diagnosis process begins with the appearance of a problem and should end with drawing conclusions, which is:

1 a research process that begins with the emergence of practical problems and ends with recommendations;
2 the basis for preventive, intervention, aid and therapeutic activities.

In connection with the preceding, it should be stated that the process of diagnosis does not only consist of data registration but also data processing and interpretation, which requires the inclusion of not only the processes of perception but also the processes of thinking and inference. It is an emotionally and socially difficult process as an activity and a social situation involving the subjects of the relationship.

The importance of diagnosis in scientific research and practical activity plays an important role in establishing general regularities, along with recognizing the properties, conditions and/or development of individual cases. Accurate diagnosis in scientific research is the basis for recognizing what is typical, general, good enough for making a hypothesis. Diagnostic research is an indispensable component of all empirical sciences. A correctly formulated diagnosis is the basis for an effective, successful therapy; and, above all, it has the status of a preparatory activity for interventions and optimizing the educational reality.

The specificity, features and functions of pedagogical diagnosis

The pedagogical diagnosis is undoubtedly a difficult process due to the functions resulting from its decision-making character and the complex nature of the phenomena constituting its subject. The high degree of difficulty implies the need to reflect on the preparation of an appropriate diagnostic procedure, the formulation of specific rules of diagnostic procedure and the construction of specific methods, techniques and tools allowing for an objective assessment of the phenomena under study (Fernández-Ballesteros et al., 2001, pp. 187–200; Turner et al., 2001, p. 1099).

Pedagogical diagnostics is an independent discipline, but is guided by the general principles and methods of cognition developed in social sciences. The complexity and multifaceted nature of pedagogical diagnosis, related to the emergence of the subject of interest of individual detailed diagnostics, along with the development of the general methodology of cognition, are the basis for reflection on the basic dilemmas in the area of pedagogical diagnosis. The awareness of the existing problems related to pedagogical diagnosis is the basis for solving them, that is developing methods, principles and rules governing cognition. Diagnostic tests based on experience and reasoning refer to a comprehensive description of individual diagnostic features. In the diagnosis and methodology of pedagogical research, features are classified in the category of people's properties, problems, phenomena, things or events. Also related to the term 'feature' are terms such as 'state' and 'event/s/'. Properly conducted diagnostic tests for practical purposes are associated with a holistic diagnosis and assessment of the person examined and the subject of research. Such an assessment is made by determining a set of diagnostic features. The basic classifications of diagnostic features include the division into permanent and non-permanent features, while the fixed features describe the topic and subject of the research, that is they decide on including the diagnosed elements into a specific group. On the other hand, non-permanent features are those that – briefly speaking – make individuals different.

Features of the diagnosis

The complexity of the phenomena that is the subject of pedagogical diagnosis makes it necessary for the diagnostician to assume the overall nature of the diagnosis. The diagnostic process is an infinite one, therefore it seems impossible to precisely define the diagnostic way. The diagnosis cannot be made at once, but must be carried out systematically, and the formulated hypotheses must be repeatedly verified in the course of the cognition process and in cooperation with various specialists. Therefore, cognition is a continuous and endless process, and the acquired data should come from many sources. When using information from various sources, we must be aware that the obtained data are exposed to subjective distortions of the information provided by the examined person (García Medina & García Caicedo, 2021, pp. 248–257).

Pedagogical diagnosis should cover a wide area of the diagnostic process. It must concern not only symptomatology but also the causes and effects of problems and disorders in psychosocial functioning experienced by an examined person, in the individual, environmental and sociocultural spheres. The activities of pedagogical diagnosis, regardless of its ultimate goal, in many cases include recognizing the family environment of the examined person as the basic environment in which human (child) development takes place (Kawula, 2003, pp. 664–674; Przybysz-Zaremba, 2020, pp. 52–65). By diagnosing a child's school difficulties, behavioral disorders, difficulties in social adaptation of a child or other problems of an individual in a more or less precise way, we recognize the family situation. Researching the family environment allows one to search for a relationship between the analyzed state of affairs and its development conditions. It should be emphasized that the diagnosis of, for example, attention deficit hyperactivity disorder (ADHD) is based primarily on the analysis of the past of a given person, on the simplest of all procedures, namely, conducting an interview to reconstruct the history of the individual (Przybysz-Zaremba, 2013, pp. 63–76). Similar actions are also required in the child's speech and language diagnosis, which indicates the need to conduct an interview with the child's parents/guardians, which will provide information on their physical development, including help in directing the diagnostic process (Sochacka, 2014; Thal et al., 2000, pp. 175–190). In this case, the specialist diagnosis of the child is also important – in Poland it is carried out by speech therapists employed in schools, who cooperate with teachers and other specialists listed down by psychological and pedagogical counseling center specifications (e.g. a specialist teacher in the field of supporting a child during education, provided that such a child has a certificate of the need for special education) (Przybysz-Zaremba & Gołębieska, 2020).

Pedagogical diagnosis has its specificity determined by the subject of interests and goals of activity, which means that its features determining the overall diagnostic procedure include pragmatics and methodology. According to Wysocka (2013), the basic features of pedagogical diagnosis include the following types of features: practical, decision-making, comprehensive, evaluating, permanent, descriptive-evaluative, open (infinite), active, hypothetical, insightful, prognostic (developmental), dynamic, expanded (full), reflective, interdisciplinary and multifaceted features. A general description of the individual features is presented in Figure 1.1.

Functions of a diagnosis

The diagnostician's attitude toward the studied phenomenon and the examined person is very important, not only due to the nature of the phenomena being studied, along with the social position of the examined person, but also due to the specificity and complexity of the person's problems. In practical pedagogical activity, diagnosis performs various functions, which depend on the object of diagnosis and the way of presenting the diagnostic process. The basic function of pedagogical diagnosis is therefore not the identification of essential and constructive facts for the accepted understanding of the studied phenomena, but obtaining a multidimensional picture of the functioning of a given individual in all spheres, along with the features and properties of their social environment, which is carried out in a development perspective covering the past, present and future.

A professionally conducted pedagogical diagnosis is therefore applicable in:

- the process of education, upbringing and care;
- the process of shaping and teaching;
- counseling and pedagogical counseling;
- activities of institutions related to education, upbringing and social support.

The basic functions of pedagogical diagnosis, in which all detailed functions can be located, however, come down to its cognitive-practical meaning, that is the diagnosis seen as a cognitive and decision-making process. In the context of the decisive nature of any pedagogical diagnosis, it becomes necessary to evaluate the results of developmental and educational processes. Therefore, the diagnosis must fulfill the function of checking the effects of the designed process of pedagogical activity, and the diagnostician should

		practical	A diagnostic process is integrated with the overarching goal - the modification of reality.
		decision-making	A results of the diagnostic process are the basis for making decisions about the type of intervention.
		comprehensive	A diagnosis includes an assessment of the dysfunctions and strengths (positive and negative diagnosis).
		evaluating	A diagnosis is related to the assessment of the state of development of the unit made in relation to the adopted norms and standards.
		permanent	A diagnosis is a continuous process, cyclical in stages: assessment, design, operation, verification.
		descriptive-evaluative	A complete diagnosis consists of a description of the facts, explanation and interpretation of the obtained data.
		open (infinite)	A diagnosis not only precedes the intervention, but is also developed in its course.
		active	Analyzing the relationships between features previously perceived as independent and organizing them into a meaningful whole.
		hypothetical	A diagnosis consists in formulating hypotheses and their probabilistic verification.
Features of a pedagogical diagnosis	➡	insightful	Linking various facts (interpolation) and inferring about their consequences for the functioning of various systems.
		prognostic (developmental)	A diagnosis is the basis for forecasting the further development of the phenomena subject to assessment (forecast).
		dynamic	A diagnosis covers the entire biography of the individual, taking into account the interdependence of various phenomena and events.
		expanded (full)	A diagnosis should cover (identify) all aspects of the known object.
		reflective	The diagnosis must be subject to theoretical reflection (data analysis with reference to the adopted theory).
		interdisciplinary	A diagnosis is made by a team of specialists from various fields, analyzing data in various contexts.
		multifaceted	A diagnosis is a complex process concerning the assessment of all spheres of the individual's functioning and the environment of his life.

Figure 1.1 Features of a pedagogical diagnosis

Source: Authors' own elaboration after Wysocka (2013, p. 69).

refer to scientific knowledge not only in the field of human theory and its difficulties but also in the field of methodology.

Types and classifications of pedagogical diagnosis

In the literature on the subject, diagnoses are classified according to their types and smaller units, called subtypes, or even smaller than these, called varieties. The basis for distinguishing types of diagnoses is the adoption of a specific criterion of classification. For example, being guided by the type of the examined function, we can distinguish the diagnosis of intellect, auditory functions, visual functions, attitudes, personality and so on. Whereas taking into account the type of phenomena understood in terms of deviation from the norm, we can indicate the diagnosis of dyslexia and behavioral disorders. While referring to the field, one can distinguish psychological, psycho-pedagogical, pedagogical, speech therapy, medical diagnosis and so on. If the approach to diagnosis is adopted as the criterion, the diagnosis can be divided into psychometric, clinical, dynamic, and so on (c.f. Paluchowski, 2007).

By adopting the criterion of the scope of explaining the phenomena, a developed (complete) diagnosis, which requires the examiner to carry out many mental operations, is distinguished from a partial (shortened) diagnosis, where it is proposed to use at least two types of diagnoses (Ziemski, 1973, pp. 63–68). The types (aspects) of diagnoses can be defined as partial diagnoses where the following types of diagnoses can be found:

- **assigning** diagnosis, that is the initial stage of the diagnosis process aimed at assigning the examined problem to a specific type; it occurs in two types: as a classification diagnosis, which consists in classifying the examined state of affairs to a specific type, and as a typological diagnosis, which determines the relation of the examined phenomenon to one or more types;
- **genetic (causal)** diagnosis, establishing primary and secondary causes by breaking down the problem into prime factors;
- **purposeful (meaning)** diagnosis, consisting in explaining the sense of the problem under study, that is the importance of a partial factor on the global development of the state of affairs under study;
- diagnosis of the **(developmental) phase**, determining the stage of development of the examined state of affairs;
- **prognostic (predictive)** diagnosis, aimed at determining the direction of changes in the development of the analyzed state of affairs.

In turn, Krystyna Marzec-Holka (1990, p. 11) indicates other types of diagnosis and the corresponding criteria. Thus, the scholar distinguishes:

- **complete** diagnosis, including the diagnosis of the group or all spheres of the examined person;

- **comprehensive** diagnosis, relating to selected spheres of the respondent;
- **fragmentary** diagnosis, taking into account only one sphere of the examined person.

Among other classifications of pedagogical diagnoses, the bipartite classification functioning in the pedagogy of cognitive and decision-making problems should be distinguished. Hence, there appear two types of diagnosis – **cognitive** and **decision-making**. Cognitive diagnosis enriches the existing knowledge with new facts, while the decision-making diagnosis refers to specific practical actions, for example preventive or interventional. In turn, in the rehabilitation diagnosis, one can distinguish a **fact-concluding** diagnosis (which defines deficit areas and areas for development, along with the strengths of the respondent, and indicates potential sources of difficulties – an aspect of the etiology of the phenomena under study), **orientation** or **design** diagnosis (used to elaborate and/or develop a corrective/preventive action program, and implement it in everyday school practice) and the **verification** diagnosis (the stage of evaluation of the corrective actions already taken) (Pytka, 2005).

Guided by the needs and competences of a diagnostician, available tools and time, a **standardized** diagnosis can be distinguished, carried out with the use of standardized tools (e.g. tests, questionnaires, observation sheets), which are equipped with standards and equipped with textbooks, and **informal** diagnosis – carried out with the use of nonstandardized tools, prepared by a diagnostician for their own use. This type of diagnosis is an auxiliary material in the student's educational process (Niemierko, 2009, p. 30). On the other hand, assuming the object of diagnosis as the criterion, one can distinguish a historical diagnosis (its subject is an individual biography), a sociological diagnosis (the subject is the living environment), a medical diagnosis (the subject of evaluation is health), a psychological diagnosis (the subject is the personality of an individual) and an educational diagnosis (the subject is the learning process) (Niemierko, 2009, p. 40).

The literature on the subject and pragmatic pedagogical activities also indicates the diagnosis of the individual and the diagnosis of the group. Ewa Domagała-Zyśk et al. (2017, pp. 58–59), as part of the work carried out on the project entitled *Development of Instruments for Conducting Psychological and Pedagogical Diagnosis*, indicate the following types of diagnosis: positive, comprehensive, profile, developmental, prognostic and noninvasive. (This diagnosis should take place in the student's natural environment, i.e. at school or at home.)

Knowing the advanced diagnosis model, it is easier to read specialist diagnoses and plan one's own research activities. The awareness of the presence of many models of diagnosis allows for understanding the phenomena in the research perspective from the perspective of various specialists and allows for greater freedom in designing cognitive behavior.

In pedagogy, it is possible to use various structural and functional models of diagnosis that describe the diagnostic process, taking into account various theoretical assumptions that constitute the essence of the cognition process.

From the methodological point of view, diagnostic tests should be carried out in accordance with the adopted research model; this is because the method of its conduct, such as the purpose, object, subject, selection and construction of research methods, techniques and tools, along with the way of interpreting the results, are strictly dependent on it.

Methods, techniques and tools used in pedagogical diagnostics

Although currently we know various methods and techniques of pedagogical research, so far they have not been exhaustively and separately classified. The reason for this may be the unsatisfactory level of development of scientific research methodology in general, and pedagogical research methodology in particular. The methodology of pedagogical research plays a significant role in effective research proceedings in the field of pedagogy. Without methodological knowledge it is impossible to properly construct and carry out research. In order to be sure about the proper selection, creation, planning or implementation of research, it is necessary to know the methodology of pedagogical research. The selection of methods by which data is collected is used to assess the development of individual functions, so it requires an individual approach and its further adaptation to the problems of the examined person or phenomenon. Hence the necessity of the diagnostician's competences in the cognitive, emotional and social areas, necessary to create a multidimensional image of the examined case. We identify the research method with a certain type of research search aimed at discovering the truth, collecting data that constitute the basis for drawing conclusions and verifying research hypotheses.

Discussions around the process of pedagogical diagnosis concern the model of diagnosis, its scope, the application of research methods and techniques, and the practical use of diagnosis results. All research procedures, which include individual research activities, are referred to as a method. Technique, as a concept subordinate to the method, is a specific way of achieving the research goal (Pilch & Bauman, 2001, p. 70). The research method may, therefore, include several research techniques aimed at explaining the problem under study.

Basic methods used in pedagogical diagnostics

The extensive methodological literature describes many methods and techniques of pedagogical research used to identify phenomena related to the educational process either in the individual or group dimension. So far, in the process of pedagogical diagnosis, three main methods have been indicated, that is **interview, behavior observation** and **testing** (Skałbania, 2011, pp. 49–52). Currently, among the numerous systematics of the methods used and the pedagogical research techniques subordinated to them, the classification of Mieczysław Łobocki (2011), one of the leading methodologists in Poland, effectively helps one to be better oriented within the multiplicity of divisions. The author proposes a list of the following methods and techniques assigned to them:

- **observation method**, which includes (a) two standardized observation techniques, that is categorized observation technique and time sample observation technique; and (b) four nonstandardized observation techniques, that is occasional observation technique, observation diary technique, photographic observation technique and event samples technique;
- **estimation method** (grading scales), embracing numerical and graphic scales, adjective and descriptive scales, discrete and continuous scales, forced choice scales and others;
- **pedagogical experiment**, with the following techniques: parallel group technique, rotation technique, four group technique, singular-group technique and quasi-experimental research;
- **tests of school achievements**, which entail tests according to the measured feature of the participant's achievements, tests according to the reference frame of the test results, tests according to the degree of their construction advancement, tests according to their range of application and others, for example written, oral and practical tests;
- **sociometric method**: classic sociometric technique, a plebiscite of kindness and dislike, the 'Guess Who?' technique and a ranking technique;
- **document analyses**: (a) classic techniques of document analysis – internal and external analysis of documents; (b) modern techniques of document analysis; (c) qualitative, quantitative and formal analysis of documents; (d) analysis of essays, journals, drawings and other techniques of document analysis;
- **survey method**: (a) polling techniques with the use of a questionnaire – the technique of an auditorium, postal and press survey, including an anonymous and public questionnaire; (b) polling techniques with an interview, that is partially or completely free and structured or categorized interview, open and hidden interviews, along with individual and collective intelligence interviews;
- **dialogue method**: individual and group conversation, direct and indirect conversation, conversation based on passive or active listening;
- **biographical method**, with its two varieties: (a) the monographic method and (b) the method of individual cases (Łobocki, 2011, p. 31).

The methodological basis of diagnosis is defined as a research diagnostic procedure, which consists in collecting and combining methods, techniques and research (diagnostic) tools in order to:

- research and evaluation of a specific segment of the didactic and educational reality, for example of a given student;
- research and evaluation of a specific didactic and educational problem;
- performance of the scientific function – the results of diagnostic tests contribute to the development of pedagogy;
- implementation of the practical-utility function – the research results are used to make practical decisions (Guziuk-Tkacz, 2011, p. 156).

It is worth emphasizing, however, that even methodologically correct research methods and techniques do not always guarantee the knowledge of the studied phenomena, as it is also dependent on the fulfillment of many other conditions of methodological correctness, for example ensuring positive motivation of the respondents to participate in the conducted research, applying more than one method or technique of research, or even drawing wrong conclusions.

An important requirement in pedagogical research is the knowledge of the methodological principles applicable in them, necessary to be applied during all stages of the organized research process. The methodology of pedagogical research is the study of the principles and methods of research recommended and applied in pedagogy. By the principles of research procedure we mean the recommendations applicable in pedagogical research, and by the methods – research procedures (i.e. methods and/or techniques) related to their construction, along with the collection and development of research material. It must be remembered that the theory, apart from the appropriate orientation of pedagogical research, allows for deepening the interpretation of research results and drawing correct conclusions. It allows not only to explain the researched facts or phenomena but also enables forecasting. The mere knowledge of individual research methods and techniques without methodological knowledge is insufficient; it may affect their routine-like, stereotypical or poorly creative use.

The diagnosis in a broad-research approach requires the use of research methods such as pedagogical monograph, diagnostic survey, pedagogical experiment or the method of individual cases. In a narrow (practical) approach, the method of diagnosis should be understood as all diagnostic procedures, which include planning the diagnostic course; constructing, selecting and applying techniques for collecting and describing the features of the examined object; diagnostic reasoning, including the verification of the diagnosis, prognostic activities and the overall final assessment of the results of pedagogical proceedings (Lepalczyk & Badura, 1987, p. 45).

It should be emphasized that there are no ready-made methods of diagnosis to be used in a specific case; each time, the situation should be assessed and the most appropriate methods, techniques and tools should be selected, in this way using the methodological principles of research. In the case of diagnostic tools, a researcher (a teacher-diagnostician) often develops them on their own or searches for ready-made tools that have been prepared by specialists in a given field. For example, when identifying the individual needs and psychophysical abilities of a student, the teacher can use the **specialist tools** available for them. These include tools developed by specialists/experts. The selected (proposed) tools are presented here:

- Dyslexia Risk Scale for Children Entering School (SRD – 6) (Bogdanowicz & Kalka, 2011);
- Identification and Remediation of Year Zero Dyslexia, a New Opportunity? (Montgomery, 2017);
- The School Readiness Scale (Frydrychowicz et al., 2006);
- School Readiness among Preschool Children (Majzub & Rashid, 2012);
- Predicting School Failures and the Scale of Hess' School Readiness (Hess & Hahn, 1974);
- Teacher's Pedagogical Diagnosis in Kindergarten and at School (Chojak, 2021);
- Assessment of Dyslexia in Arabic (Elbeheri et al., 2006).

The selection of the diagnostic tools proposed here should take into account the specificity of education in a given country, including the knowledge of the core curriculum, especially when it comes to examining a child's readiness to undertake school education.

The sociometric method

Pedagogical research is a set of skillfully and purposefully used undertakings aimed at cognition, evaluation and transformation, combined with practical testing of their effectiveness in the field of care, upbringing and educational issues. The social situation in a formal group, such as, for example, school, can be recognized with the use of various methods. However, if – at the same time – we want to get to know the social relations in a group relatively quickly and precisely, the most appropriate way will be to use the socio-metric method, useful in organizing the upbringing and teaching process. The sociometric method can be widely used in pedagogical research, as the undoubted advantage of this method is the ease of each of the sociometric techniques assigned to it. Sociometry in terms of the technique of getting to know a specific reality is the subject of numerous, more or less detailed, stud-ies. Generally speaking, we can say that sociometry deals with the interac-tions between people, occurring in any group. The exact method of making a choice depends on the type of sociometric technique. The type of question asked dictates the appropriate type of sociometric technique.

There are at least several types of sociometric techniques. The best known is the classic sociometric technique developed by Jacob Levy Moreno (Jarosz & Wysocka, 2006, pp. 321–322). Nowadays, sociometry includes several detailed research techniques, which are significantly different from each other in terms of the nature of the obtained detailed data and the research method itself. The proposal for the systematization of sociometric techniques was presented, among others, by Polish methodologist Mieczysław Łobocki (2011), dividing them into a plebiscite of kindness and dislike, the technique of 'Guess who?' and the technique of ranking. The practical use of sociometric techniques (in research) can be found in the works of some British authors, such as, for example, Avramidis et al. (2017, pp. 68–80) or Walker (2009, pp. 339–358).

When conducting sociometric research, it should be remembered that their cognitive value depends not only on correctly formulated sociometric questions and how they are used but also on the use of more than one sociometric technique, because each technique allows us to reveal a slightly different aspect of the problem under study. In addition, it is worth using it simultaneously with other methods of pedagogical research, especially the observation method, the survey method or the dialogue method.

The decision to choose a detailed technique depends mainly on the purpose of the research and the type of detailed data we want to obtain. The instructions for the sociometric test and its detailed course are different, depending on the type of technique used; there are also some differences in relation to the age of the respondents. At the same time, it seems necessary to stress the fact that apart from the advantages and benefits it brings, sociometry is not free from certain limitations.

Each research method is closely related to the research techniques that carry it out. Techniques allow a diagnostician to obtain information, opinions, facts; and are used to achieve specific research goals. The selection of a specific research technique results from the adopted research method and is a way of implementing the method of diagnosis (research) chosen by the diagnostician (researcher), which is the basis for the development of appropriate diagnostic (research) tools.

Diagnostic tools (questionnaires)

Diagnostic (research) tools allow one to collect the data and further implement the selected research technique. They usually take the form of a **sheet of paper – a questionnaire with questions** or research problems, sometimes with proposed answers to these questions, statements, sentences and/or phrases to be completed. Each proprietary research tool is different, because each time it is developed in order to solve a given research problem, using the principles of methodology appropriate for a given scientific field.

The selection of appropriate research (diagnostic) tools requires compliance with the following methodological rules (Guziuk-Tkacz, 2011, pp. 301–302):

* the research process cannot be based on only one research technique;
* we develop research tools after formulating research problems and hypotheses, and after determining the research group and research area;
* we have to properly construct the questionnaire questions (cafeterias);

- we develop research tools accurately and reliably;
- research tools should include a record, that is a register of independent and dependent variables.

It is assumed that a questionnaire is each set of questions, prepared in a specific order and formulated in accordance with the principles of methodological knowledge. In a narrower sense, the questionnaire contains precisely formulated questions, arranged in an appropriate order. It may also have answers (such a form of questionnaire is called 'cafeteria'). The first research step is to include information about who the research tool is intended for and about which research technique it relates to, for example a **survey** questionnaire. Next, the researcher should provide the name of the person conducting the research and the purpose of the research; and state that it is anonymous. The researcher must also include an instruction on how to fill in the questionnaire and give thanks for taking part in the research (Gruszczyński, 1999).

Questionnaire questions should be structured in such a way that their content allows for the achievement of research goals. Each question sentence has a specific response pattern. In general, questionnaire questions are divided into decision-type questions, which begin with *if*, and questions of the complement type, which require a longer introduction and starting with *what*, *which*, *why* and so on. Questionnaire questions may be sentence questions or have a form of expression, but they must always be a task to be solved. Pilch and Bauman (2001, pp. 191–192) rightly observe that, when taking into account the openness of the conducted research, there are direct, indirect and projective questionnaires. The most open-ended direct questions apply when the researcher knows they will receive an honest answer. In turn, in indirect questions, it is required to adopt a specific assumption, which consists in presenting the situation and asking how the respondent will behave. On the other hand, the importance of projection questions is reaching the knowledge of the examined entity. In the research (diagnostic) questionnaire, questions may be closed, open or half open (Guziuk, 2005, pp. 96–97).

The most frequently used research (diagnostic) tools in pedagogical diagnostics are a classical questionnaire and an interview questionnaire, while the observational technique tools include an **observation sheet**, an **observation journal**, and an **observational schedule** (Guziuk, 2005, pp. 118–119).

Each proprietary research tool is different because each time it is developed in order to identify a specific research problem. Proposals of selected tools useful in pedagogical and speech therapy diagnostics along with their application are presented in Chapter 4.

In diagnostic work, it is not always enough to use specific, available ways of learning; quite contrary, it is often necessary to develop new tools appropriate to the goal and the problem under study. Therefore, it is necessary to shape the ability to create research tools and make educators aware of the rules applicable in the preparation of, for example, questionnaires or surveys. As a research area, education covers many complex phenomena, various processes and conditions that determine diagnostic needs. A knowledge of the methods of diagnosis equips educators with knowledge and skills, in this way opening new support possibilities realized in school conditions. A modern teacher who has great professional competences should be prepared to undertake diagnostic activities, not only in terms of teaching, that is being able to assess learners' school achievements, but more and more often to pedagogically recognize various educational situations encountered in everyday work.

If – as Łobocki (2011, p. 304) sees it – the diagnosis is based on *[...] collecting data on the development and physical, mental and social life* of several people who are related to each other by a common subject of research, this research procedure is called *the method of individual cases* (or *Case studies*), that is a study like this concerns the diagnosis of several or a dozen or so cases. On the other hand, a case study, also known as a *clinical method*, consists in a very accurate diagnosis of only one selected case. Nowadays, social sciences emphasize the important role of the case study in research on educational issues.

In pedagogical diagnostics, the method of individual cases and the case study are implemented through the use of many research techniques, which include **interview, observation, conversation**. Both of these methods make it possible to use the results for therapeutic, compensatory, revalidation, educational, caring, intervention and further activities. Their essence is to identify the causes and effects of the problem under study.

Knowledge of research tools combined with the pedagogue's diagnostic skills facilitates early recognition and identification of a student's educational problems, especially when the student's family, peer or school environment have been taken into account. Thus, knowledge of the methods of pedagogical research enables full diagnosis and minimizes the risk of making a diagnostic error.

To ensure the highest quality of (pedagogical) diagnosis in the diagnostic process, Dłużniewska and Szubielska (2017, p. 26) propose a method triangulation, which consists in combining data from the use of both quantitative and qualitative methods. The mixed methods approach (also called the hybrid model) (Hammersley, 1992, pp. 139–175) provides greater opportunities to study educational problems, including problems and/or possible disorders manifested by children, adolescents or students (Almalki, 2016, pp. 288–296). **Triangulation of research enables a richer, more complete and, most importantly, multilateral understanding of the object of interest, because it is associated with presenting it from different points of view, from different perspectives and in a variety of ways** (Kataryńczuk-Mania et al., 2018, pp. 169–170; Palka, 2011, pp. 119–123).

Two methodological approaches are most often used in diagnosis: quantitative (e.g. with the help of tests and/or scales) and qualitative (e.g. in-depth interview, participant observation, analysis of the child's/pupil's products, qualitative text analysis, discussion) (Łobocki, 2011; Panasiuk, 2017, p. 45).

Competences of a diagnostician

Diagnostic competences are one of the important dimensions of the diagnostic process, as they often determine its effectiveness. They are equated with the qualifications of the researcher (or educator) and their skills. In the literature, there is a multiplicity and diversity of definitions and, at the same time, classification of the term 'competences'. Researchers indicate that these are complex dispositions that determine the knowledge, foresight skills, attitudes, motivation, emotions and evaluation of the teacher-diagnostician (Artelt & Rausch, 2014; Dylak, 1995, p. 37; Schrader, 2009). On the other hand, following the remarks offered by Czerepaniak-Walczak (1999, pp. 59–60), it is also the ability and readiness to perform tasks at a certain level; developed skills necessary to deal with problems; ability to specific task areas shaped in the process of human learning, along with the adaptive and transgressive potential of the researched subject (Męczkowska, 2003). It can be said that competences are a kind of triad describing the identity of an individual, constituting the formal structure of a possible contact with the world. It is thus a harmonious composition of knowledge, efficiency, understanding and desire, which enables a person to relate to reality and, subsequently, to relate to another person (Czerepaniak-Walczak, 1999).

The key competences of a teacher-diagnostician are interpretative, communication and methodological competences (Ferenz & Kozioł, 2002; Korczyński, 2005; Kwiatkowski & Walczak, 2017; Wysocka, 2013); obviously, apart from the competences related to their pedagogical education, which are necessary here.

Interpretative competences include, first of all, the researcher's ability to relate to the world, that is the ability to interpret events, facts and situations relevant to the assessment of the functioning of the examined object (or subject). These competences have been classified into the group of practical and moral competences, which include, among others, moral competences (understood as the ability to moral reflection) and communication competences (Kwaśnica, 2003, pp. 298–303).

The group of communication competences includes a whole range of skills related to verbal and nonverbal communication of a diagnostician with the examined object (or subject) and more. Here, one can underline, among others, one's empathetic response, openness to new experiences, concreteness, matter-of-factness, focus on 'here and now', the ability to assess the accuracy and effectiveness of a communicating diagnostician, or the ability to establish and maintain contact with a student along with the ability to properly receive and interpret educational messages. Wysocka (2013, pp. 260–261) remarks that such an attitude improves correctness, readability and ethicality of one's own linguistic behavior: the ability to shape the linguistic sensitivity of pupils, revealing the value of cultural heritage and the function of language as a tool of thinking and communication, understanding the dialogical nature of the teacher-student relationship and the ability to properly formulate educational messages.

Methodological competences include, first of all, the methodological awareness of the researcher, the skills of conceptualizing the diagnostic problem along with methodological knowledge, knowledge of the goal, object of diagnosis, the ability to select appropriate methods, techniques, and research tools included (Wysocka, 2013, p. 262). Many researchers (for example, Helmke et al., 2004; Ophuysen, 2006) emphasize that knowledge about the methods of collecting information about the student, knowledge of psychological criteria of test quality along with knowledge about judgments are important in this group of competences. In other words, what evidently matters is scientific knowledge, along with the ability to translate it into practical (research, diagnostic) activity.

When analyzing competences in the context of psychological and pedagogical assistance at school, a teacher-diagnostician should have skills related to the integration of general knowledge, substantive knowledge from a given scientific discipline, general didactics and detailed methodology with psychological and pedagogical knowledge. The use of this knowledge in practice is associated with the teacher's key diagnostic skills, which include, among others, the ability to conduct pedagogical observation; the ability to use diagnostic tools; the ability to interpret the obtained results and draw conclusions on this basis for further work with the student; and also the ability to discuss the results of the diagnosis with specialists, other teachers, parents and the student (Dorozhovets & Hladush, 2021, pp. 63–73; Klimek, 2016, pp. 167–177; Klug et al., 2013, pp. 38–46).

In addition to the aforementioned competences and skills, the teacher-diagnostician should also have the so-called additional competences, which include, among others, health competences; ecological, therapeutic and cultural competences; action-involving competences (of both conceptual and implementation nature), which include a group of competences that guarantee effective action in a given area (e.g. didactic, educational, organizational competences etc.) at every stage; planning, implementation and evaluation competences; and, also, transgressive competences, associated with crossing limits and creating new qualities in terms of self-creation, innovation and pedagogical creativity along with emancipation (understood as remaining in relation to a wider sociocultural environment) (Pankowska, 2016, pp. 187–206).

The diagnostic competences of teachers should be perceived as being both the foundation and experience in teaching; these can refer to, for example, teachers' ability to analyze and identify errors in students' work, predict these errors and estimate the level of difficulty in performing tasks (Liu, Jacobson, Bharaj, 2020, p. 1892–1896), errors related to pronunciation included.

Referring to the preceding considerations, it should be stated that professional diagnosis requires from the researcher both the skills and competences necessary to perform the profession of a teacher and educator, along with other (advanced) pedagogical competences, that are necessary to know and understand the phenomena and problems occurring in a given individual, child or student.

The diagnostic competences of a teacher-diagnostician-researcher are expressed in the ability to self-realization, the ability to act in a strictly defined area. In the diagnostic process, they should constantly develop and improve, in this way becoming structurally enlarged, enriching themselves and at the same time increasing the efficiency of pedagogical activities.

The course of the diagnostic process

The literature on the subject contains many examples of models showing how the diagnosis process should proceed. One such **model** worthy of attention is the **GAP** (Guidelines for Assessment Process) model developed by a team of international experts appointed by the European Society for Psychological Diagnosis (Fernández-Ballesteros et al., 2001). In the presented model, the main attention was paid to the comprehensive procedure of the diagnostician, from the first contact with the child until the conclusive end of the diagnosis. This model combines diagnosis with intervention and includes the following steps: case analysis (in the form of descriptive diagnosis); organizing and reporting the results, technical preparation of the results and communicating to the respondent (unit or the legal guardian of the child); planning an intervention, defining the objectives of the intervention and criteria for assessing its effects; intervention evaluation and deferred follow-up (Fernández-Ballesteros et al., 2001, pp. 187–201). The model of Jacek Paluchowski (2007) is also useful for pedagogical diagnosis; its author distinguishes the following stages in the research process: prediagnostic, where three groups of factors influencing the behavior of the examined person are being defined; diagnostic examination; and finally the phases of description, interpretation and intervention.

As observed by Krasowicz-Kupis et al. (2015, p. 35), the course of the diagnostic process varies depending on the type of diagnosis and where it is being made. One can discriminate the following aims of the complete diagnosis carried out at school among children at the stage of preschool and early school education:

- determining the current level of development in specific spheres (called development areas);
- determining the child's potential;
- identification of possible development deficits;
- recognizing the needs of students.

These goals are most often carried out by the teacher-educator (or the diagnostician) by working with other specialists employed at the school, for example with a pedagogue, a psychologist or a speech therapist, but also with the child's parents.

Diagnosis in pedagogy is a creative process that requires an individual approach to the assessed case; hence, the diagnosis process is conditioned by both the specificity of the subject and the specificity of the examined object.

The subject of diagnostic activities of teachers and educators are (mainly) educational phenomena, in which it is impossible to ignore the role of educational environments in which the student functions (such as family, school and/or peer group). Pedagogical diagnosis should be carried out in a developmental and environmental context. It should be purposeful and lead to the planned action, in this way being able to provide specific results that will become the basis for taking rehabilitation and compensation actions, along with supporting and improving the areas recognized as disturbed (Przybysz-Zaremba, 2018, pp. 96–109).

An exemplary model of pedagogical diagnosis conducted by teachers

Following is an example of a set of diagnostic activities performed by a teacher (specialist) in a class (Figure 1.2).

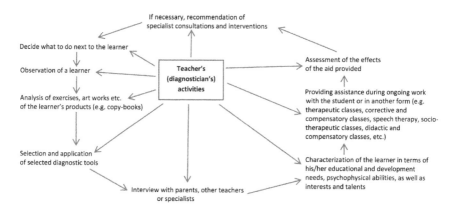

Figure 1.2 A model of the diagnostic procedures of a teacher (specialist) in a class

Source: Authors' own elaboration based on a literature review and practical experience.

An exemplary model of specialist (interdisciplinary) diagnosis

In the case of a specialist diagnosis (e.g. psychological, speech therapy or other), which is often interdisciplinary in nature, the examination is carried out in a psychological and pedagogical clinic by a team of specialists cooperating with each other, for example a psychologist, pedagogue, speech therapist; in some cases (e.g. in respect of neurodevelopmental disorders) the participation of doctors is also necessary.

In the course of the diagnostic process carried out by a team of specialists in a psychological and pedagogical counseling center, one can distinguish six stages, in which the actions (tasks) to be undertaken are specified in detail. Krasowicz-Kupis et al. (2015, p. 35) recognize the following stages:

Stage One: Recognition of the problem

- establishment of the circumstances, conditions, context in which the problem appears; in the case of a child, the analysis covers the problems reported by the parent, but also by the teacher;
- formulation of the purpose of the diagnosis (problem definition) – at this stage, the diagnostician must answer such questions as *Why is s/he conducting the test? What kinds of decisions will be made based on the results of the diagnosis? What kinds of diagnosis will s/he conduct (nosological/ differential or functional)?*

Stage Two: Planning of the diagnosis

- choice of theoretical orientation; within which theory are we looking for explanations of the child's behavior? (this is important due to the different conceptual apparatus that the diagnostician will use – for example, the same problem with the child's behavior will be differently explained and described from a psychoanalytic perspective, and differently in terms of cognitive behavioral psychology);
- formulation of diagnostic questions and hypotheses; what questions is the diagnostician looking for answers to? What hypotheses explaining the problem of a given child are asked by?;
- selection and operationalization of indicators; what information on the subject are necessary to have to answer diagnostic questions? How can they be obtained (what tests or tools should be used)?;
- selection of appropriate diagnostic tools, which should take into account the purpose of diagnosis and the psychometric properties of the tests.

Stage Three: The diagnostic examination

- obtaining diagnostic data should be done in various ways. A diagnostician-examiner may use a psychological conversation or an interview; analyze the documentation concerning the examined person (medical records, opinions from the school, etc.); conduct tests; carry on an observation. The diagnostic test – when applied – is conducted over a longer period of time (there should be at least a few meetings with the diagnosed child (learner)). As observed by Krasowicz-Kupis et al. (2015, pp. 36–37) the key at this stage is to demonstrate methodological competences.

Stage Four: Elaboration of the results of a diagnosis

- analysis of the results of individual tests in accordance with the guidelines contained in test manuals (or specialist handbooks);
- integration of the data obtained from various sources – the diagnostician describes and interprets the obtained data; searches for relationships between the behavior of the respondent in the situation of the test and outside this situation; makes a forecast and creates an intervention plan;
- preparation of feedback (e.g. in the form of a research report (written or oral). According to the Code of Ethics and Profession, the psychologist (or other specialist conducting the diagnosis) is obliged to provide feedback to the examined person, and in the case of a child, the parents or legal guardians Krasowicz-Kupis et al. (2015, pp. 36–37); the clinic has to issue a written opinion at the parent's written request.

Stage Five: Planning and implementation of interventions

- referring to the results of the diagnosis, the specialist (psychologist, therapist, speech therapist, etc.) determines what activities are necessary for the child (learner) and plans them. Krasowicz-Kupis et al. (2015, pp. 36–37) offer the following examples: didactic and compensatory classes, specialist classes (e.g. corrective and compensatory classes, speech therapy, socio-therapy, other therapeutic activities, e.g. psychological therapy), therapeutic classes for a child to attend; classes developing talents; activities related to with the choice of profession and course of study; workshops and training, advice and consultations; supporting parents and teachers and developing their upbringing skills (in the form of advice, consultations, workshops and training).

Stage Six: Assessment of the effects of the intervention and follow-up examination

- each diagnosis should be based on as much information as possible from various sources, that is not only from various diagnostic tools used in the study but also from various specialist people cooperating with a given child. Sillamy (1996) also stresses the fact that it should take into account the influence of many different factors and refer to the history of the respondent along with his/her relationship with the environment.

Following the taxonomy prepared by Guziuk-Tkacz (2011, p. 18) a professional pedagogical diagnosis should be (a) accurate (i.e. useful to achieve a specific goal), (b) in-depth (i.e. precise, insightful, thorough); (c) reliable;

(d) objective (i.e. impartial); (e) comprehensive (diagnostic tests should be as multifaceted and detailed as possible); and (f) impartial (i.e. requiring the use of many different methods, techniques and tools). The point of reference in any pedagogical (school-based) diagnosis is the child learner. Even the most careful research procedure is not free from mistakes or lapses; therefore, special attention should be paid to the preparation of research methods, techniques and tools, and their practical application. The diagnostic process, as a kind of examination, requires careful preparation on the part of each of the people performing the function of a diagnostician – the examiner, teacher, educator and speech therapist, along with other specialists involved.

Summing up, it should be stated that what is absolutely necessary in the diagnostic procedure is to creatively adapt the methods and techniques of cognition to the specificity of the diagnostic situation, and to conceptualize the problem of diagnosis individually. Therefore, one should know how to create new procedures, methods, techniques and tools of a diagnosis, along with constantly monitoring the usefulness of the designed diagnostic strategy, its accuracy and reliability. Finally, it is also necessary to creatively interpret the obtained data according to the cognition scheme created individually for the problem under consideration. The diagnostician's competences are of key importance in this case.

Problems in the process of pedagogical diagnosis and the role of a diagnostician

Pedagogical diagnostics is becoming more and more popular in pedagogical sciences, both in theoretical and practical areas. Recognizing, assessing, examining, looking for causes or dependencies remain some of the definitions concerning the basic nature of this concept. General knowledge about diagnostics, the diagnostic process or the diagnosis itself are elements of a wider problem that are gaining more and more importance in educational practice. Educational reality brings a great demand for the activities that offer various forms of support and/or help based on different cooperation processes with either people or institutions educating children and youth. Pedagogical diagnostics covers a lot more issues related to the functioning of a child as a learner; as a dynamically developing field of pedagogical sciences, it defines new areas of activity, emphasizing the importance of early diagnosis carried out in natural conditions with the help of natural ways of getting to know a person used by people who have constant contact with the learners. Contemporary education is expected to help learners in difficult situations, conditioned by environmental factors and individual developmental characteristics. As observed by Skałbania (2011), systemic changes have contributed to the modification of the aid process along with the tasks of the helper. The educational perspective is significantly expanding, including new spheres of influence of the educator, assigning her/him a new place in the school reality.

The issue of the effectiveness of pedagogical activities is closely related to diagnostics, understood as the initial stage in undertaking activities of a didactic, educational or caring nature. The system of pedagogical interactions should be preceded by a diagnosis, and any such diagnoses should be continuous, systematic and/or intentional. They should also strive for a comprehensive, complete, professional diagnostic description of the problem of an individual or a group.

Pedagogical diagnostics is currently a key process in the education of every child (regardless of the country or education conducted in it), as it relates to the knowledge of its psychophysical development, various disorder of behavioral, mental, or speech type and/or speech impediments, along with many other areas related to social functioning. As indicated in this chapter, pedagogical diagnostics is a complex process, including content, methods, tools, competences and the ethical attitude of a diagnostician (or a teacher-diagnostician). Ethical issues in the context of pedagogical diagnostics concern many issues, but the main principle that should be respected is the old Latin principle *primum non nocere* (which means 'first: do not harm') (cf. Mazurkiewicz, 1993, p. 67). The most common ethical errors committed by the researcher (diagnostician) include incomplete and/or false data of the individual subject to the diagnosis process; erroneous (or too arbitrary) interpretation of the content that is covered by professional secrecy; collecting excess information and data about the examined person (which may lead to stressful conditions and fatigue of the person under examination); being responsible for the creation of situations in which the object under examination experiences a sense of threat, anxiety and/or fear because of not understanding the purpose and meaning of the research; the examined learner may feel compelled to speak on a specific topic that is unpleasant for him, which he does not want to talk about – this may lead to harmful moral and health effects; finally, succumbing to the suggestions of past assessments in the evaluation of the current state and labeling of the examined entity (Jarosz & Wysocka, 2006, pp. 43–46, 90; Skałbania, 2011, p. 61).

Problems resulting from pedagogical diagnosis are related primarily to the process of diagnosis itself, which – as indicated – is complex, interdisciplinary, holistic, decision-making, infinite (Wysocka, 2013, p. 85). The complexity of the phenomena being the subject of pedagogical diagnosis makes it necessary for the diagnostician to adopt holistic actions aimed at recognizing a given state of affairs. In practical activities, such a teacher-specialist-diagnostician ought to overcome many different problems that she/he encounters during the process of pedagogical diagnosis. One of the key problems in the process of pedagogical diagnosis (and oncoming revalidation) is the methodology of the diagnostic process, which – in the examination of an individual case (individual revalidation included) – should include:

- conscious formulation of the purpose of the diagnosis and the adopted model;
- planning the course of the child's characteristics (her/his psychophysical development, social functioning, behavior), her/his family and school environment;
- in a situation where other specialists are also involved in the diagnostic process, the division of diagnostic tasks (or activities) between all specialists should be carefully considered, taking into account their capabilities (i.e. competences, skills, knowledge, etc.), infrastructural and/ or technical conditions in which the process of diagnosis takes place, the possibility of selecting and applying examination methods and tools in multi-aspect diagnosis;
- precise specification of methodological terminology and linguistic communication, respecting the specificity of recommendations;
- preparation of various forms of documenting and transferring diagnostic information for interested persons, such as parents, an educator, a psychologist and/or other specialists (Oleńska-Pawlak, 2006).

When diagnosing disorders in the behavior of a child (a learner), the pedagogue-specialist-diagnostician should be aware that they cannot be categorized in a straightforward way (i.e. only qualitative assessment could be enough), but it is also necessary to assess the level of disorders (or the so-called quantitative assessment); the scope of dysfunction as well as the assessment of their dominant forms (Wysocka, 2013, p. 86). Thus, as the method of assessing information becomes an important problem, so the qualitative assessment alone is insufficient here (i.e. a quantitative assessment is also required).

Due to the nature of the pedagogical diagnosis process, the researcher-diagnostician will face various problems that may result from (a) the continuity of the diagnosis (closed vs open diagnosis); (b) the theoretical-methodological nature of the diagnostic-intervention process and (c) the methods of obtaining data (information) from various sources. They may also be related to the analysis of problem phenomena, the area of the diagnosis (its multifaceted and interdisciplinary nature), the examiner's conduct (e.g. her/his attitude toward the diagnosed subject, her/his social and theoretical attitude – the examiner may have gaps in theoretical knowledge (and/ or shortages in selection skills); obtained information, proper understanding of the content of messages communicated to it by the respondent; deficiencies related to self-knowledge) (Brzeziński & Kowalik, 1998, pp. 206–211; Korczak, 1998, p. 354; Wysocka, 2016, pp. 22–27). A detailed list of problems in pedagogical diagnosis, taking into account their categories, is presented in Figure 1.3.

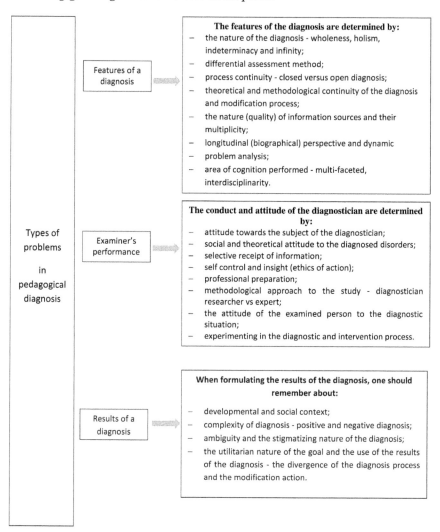

Figure 1.3 Basic categories of problems in the process of pedagogical diagnosis

Source: Authors' elaboration based on Wysocka (2013, p. 84).

References

Almalki, S. (2016). Integrating quantitative and quantitative data in mixed methods research-challenges and benefits. *Journal of Education and Learning, 5*(3), 288–296. https://doi.org/10.5539/jel.v5n3p288 file:///C:/Users/user/Downloads/61406-217344-1-SM.pdf.

Apanowicz, J. (2000). *Metodologiczne elementy procesu poznania naukowego w teorii organizacji i zarządzania* [Methodological elements of the process of scientific cognition in the theory of organization and management] (pp. 140–141). Diocese Publishing House IV Pelplin Bernardinum.

Apanowicz, J. (2002). *Metodologia ogólna* [General methodology]. Diocese Publishing House IV Pelplin Bernardinum.

Apanowicz, J. (2005). *Metodologiczne uwarunkowania pracy naukowej* [Methodological conditions of research] (p. 42). Difin.

Artelt, C., & Rausch, T. (2014). Accuracy of teacher judgments. In S. Krolak-Schwerdt, S. Glock, & M. Böhmer (Eds.), *Teachers' professional development. The future of education research*. Sense Publishers.

Avramidis, E., Strogilos, V., Aroni, K., & Kantaraki, C. T. (2017). Using sociometric techniques to assess the social impacts of inclusion: Some methodological considerations. *Educational Research Review, 20*(2), 68–80. https://doi.org/10.1016/j.edurev.2016.11.004.

Bogdanowicz, M., & Kalka, D. (2011). *Skala Ryzyka Dysleksji dla dzieci wstępujących do szkoły SRD6* [Dyslexia risk scale for children entering the SRD6]. https://pracowniatestow.pl/pl/p/Skala-Ryzyka-Dysleksji-dla-dzieci-wstepujacych-do-szkoly-SRD6/77.

Brzeziński, J., & Kowalik, S. (1998). Modelujący wyniki badania psychologicznego (diagnostycznego) wpływ osoby badanej (pacjenta) i badacza (klinicysty) [The result modeling influence of a psychological (diagnostic) issues of an examined person and his/her clinical examiner]. In H. Sęk (Ed.), *Społeczna psychologia kliniczna* [Social clinical psychology] (pp. 269–302). PWN.

Chojak, M. (2021). *Nauczycielska diagnoza pedagogiczna w przedszkolu i w szkole* [Teachers pedagogical diagnosis in kindergarten and at school]. Difin. https://bonito.pl/produkt/nauczycielska-diagnoza-pedagogiczna-w-przedszkolu-i-w-szkole?gclid=CjwKCAjwwoWBhAMEiwAV4dybds5lDWkbc0bi0Un2axOD4IQozdwfk9e4Su66sMRwic-5Y06wPGXwBoCOooQAvD_BwE.

Czerepaniak-Walczak, M. (1990). Kompetencja: Słowo kluczowe czy "wytrych" w edukacji? [Competence – a keyword or a passkey in education]. *Neodidagmata, 20*(4), 59–60.

Dłużniewska, A., & Szubielska, M. (2017). Diagnoza – Definicja, klasyfikacje, modele, narzędzia [Diagnosis – definitions, classifications, models and tools]. In K. Krakowiak (Ed.), *Diagnoza specjalnych potrzeb rozwojowych i edukacyjnych dzieci i młodzieży. Standardy, wytyczne oraz wskazówki do przygotowywania i adaptacji narzędzi diagnostycznych dla dzieci i młodzieży z wybranymi specjalnymi potrzebami rozwojowymi i edukacyjnymi* [Diagnosis of special developmental and educational needs of children and adolescents. Standards, guidelines and guidelines for the preparation and adaptation of diagnostic tools for children and adolescents with selected special development and educational needs] (pp. 20–44). Center of Development of Education.

Domagała-Zyśk, E., Knopik, T., & Oszwa, U. (2017). *Diagnoza funkcjonalna rozwoju społeczno-emocjonalnego uczniów w wieku 9–13 lat* [Development of instruments for conducting psychological and pedagogical diagnosis of children aged 9–13] (pp. 58–59). Lechia Consulting Sp. z o.o.

Dorozhovets, O., & Hladush, V. (2021). Diagnostic competence of the special education teacher in Slovakia. *InterConf, 63*–73. https://doi.org/10.51582/interconf.7-8.06.2021.007.

Dylak, S. (1995). *Wizualizacja w kształceniu nauczycieli* [Visualisation in teacher education] (p. 37). UAM Scientific Publishers.

Elbeheri, G., Everatt, J., Reid, G., & Mannai, H. (2006). Assessment of dyslexia in Arabic. *Journal of Research in Special Educational Needs, 6*(3), 143–152. https://doi.org/10.1111/j.1471-3802.2006.00072.x.

European Commission. (2010). *Structures of education and training systems in Europe* (2009/10 ed.). Finnish National Board of Education. http://daneshnamehicsa.ir/userfiles/file/Resources/18-3)%20Europa/Finland_EN.pdf.

Eurostat. (2013). *Smarter, greener, more inclusive? Indicators to support the Europe 2020 strategy.* Publications Office of the European Union. http://ec.europa.eu/eurostat.

Eurydice Unit. (2003). *Structure of education, vocational training and adult education systems in Europe.* Germany 2002/2003. Eurydice Unit.

Eurydice Unit. (2008). *Structure of education, vocational training and adult education systems in Europe.* Poland 2008. Eurydice Unit.

Ferenz, K., & Kozioł, E. (Eds.). (2002). *Kompetencje nauczyciela wychowawcy* [Competences of a teacher-educator]. Publishing House of the University of Zielona Góra.

Fernández-Ballesteros, R., De Bruyn, E. E., Godoy, A., Hornke, L. F., Ter Laak, J., Vizcarro, C., Westhoff, K., Westmeyer, H., & Zaccagnini, J. L. (2001). Guidelines for the assessment process (GAP): A proposal for discussion. *European Journal of Psychological Assessment, 17*(3), 187–200. https://doi.org/10.1027//1015-5759.17.3.187.

Frydrychowicz, A., Koźniewska, E., Matuszewski, A., & Zwierzyńska, E. (2006). *Skala gotowości szkolnej, centrum metodyczne pomocy psychologiczno-pedagogicznej* [School readiness scale, methodological center for psychological and pedagogical aid]. http://bc.ore.edu.pl/Content/172/Skala+Gotowo%C5%9Bci+Szkolnej+(SGS)_podr%C4%99cznik.pdf.

García Medina, M. S., & García Caicedo, J. M. (2021). Pedagogical diagnosis following a proposed framework for the implementation of educational robotics. *IEEE Revista Iberoamericana de Tecnologias del Aprendizaje, 16*(3), 248–257. https://doi.org/10.1109/RITA.2021.3122895.

Góralski, A. (1987). *Metody opisu i wnioskowania statystycznego w psychologii i pedagogice* [Methods of description and statistical inference in psychology and pedagogy] (pp. 7–19). PWN.

Gruszczyński, L. A. (1999). *Kwestionariusze w socjologii. Budowa narzędzi surveyowych* [Questionnaires in sociology. Building survey tools]. Publishing House of the Silesian University.

Guziuk, M. (2005). *Podstawy metodologiczne prac promocyjnych. Nauki społeczno-pedagogiczne* [Methodological foundations of promotional works. Socio-pedagogical sciences] (pp. 96–97). Foundation of Educational Studies Research.

Guziuk-Tkacz, M. (2011). *Badania diagnostyczne w pedagogice i psychopedagogice* [Diagnostic research in pedagogy and psychical pedagogy]. Żak Academic Press.

Hammersley, M. (1992). *What's wrong with ethnography? Methodological explorations* (pp. 139–175). Routledge.

Helmke, A., Hosenfeld, I., & Schrader, F. W. (2004). Vergleichsarbeiten als instrument zur verbesserung der diagnosekompetenz von lehrkräften [Comparative tests as an instrument for the improvement of teachers' diagnostic competence]. In R. Arnold, & C. Griese (Eds.), *Schulmanagement und schulentwicklung* [School management and school development] (pp. 119–144). Schneider, Hohengehren.

Hess, R. J., & Hahn, R. T. (1974). Predicting school failures and the scale of Hess school readiness. *Psychology in Schools, 11*(2), 134–136. https://doi.org/10.1002/1520-6807(197404)11:2<134::AID-PITS2310110204>3.0.CO;2-Z.

Jäger, R. S. (2007). *Beobachten, bewerten, fördern. Lehrbuch für die Aus-, Fort- und Weiterbildung* [Observing, assessing, fostering. Textbook for education and further education]. Empirische Pädagogik.

Jarosz, E. (2003). Diagnoza [Diagnosis]. In T. Pilch (Ed.), *Encyklopedia pedagogiczna XXI wieku* (*Vol. century1*, pp. 674–6767). PWN.

Jarosz, E., & Wysocka, E. (2006). *Diagnoza psychopedagogiczna. Podstawowe problemy i rozwiązania* [Psycho-pedagogical diagnoses. Basic problems and solutions] (pp. 43–46). Żak Academic Press. 90.

Kataryńczuk-Mania, L., Kołodziejski, M., & Kisiel, M. (2018). *Orientacje w metodologii badań edukacyjno-muzycznych* [Orientations in the methodology of educational and musical research] (pp. 169–170). Publishing House of the University of Zielona Góra.

Kawula, S. (2003). Diagnostyka pedagogiczna środowiska [Pedagogical diagnostics of the environment]. In T. Pilch (Ed.), *Encyklopedia pedagogiczna XXI wieku* [Pedagogical encyclopedia of the 21st century] (*Vol. 1*, pp. 664–674). Żak Academic Press.

Kazubowska, U. (2020). Holistyczna diagnoza rodziny jako najważniejszego środowiska wychowawczego w perspektywie familiologii [Holistic diagnosis of the family as the most important educational environment from the perspective of familiology]. In E. Stokowska-Zagdan, M. Przybysz-Zaremba, & J. Stepaniuk (Eds.), *Wybrane obszary diagnozy, profilaktyki, terapii w teorii i praktyce pedagogicznej* [Selected areas of diagnosis, prevention, therapy in pedagogical theory and practice] (pp. 51–68). Difin.

Klimek, L. (2016). Kompetencje diagnostyczne nauczyciela w kontekście pomocy psychologiczno-pedagogicznej w szkole [Diagnostic competences of a teacher in the light of psycho-pedagogical help in school]. *Lubelski Rocznik Pedagogiczny, XXXV*(1), 167–177. https://journals.umcs.pl/lrp/article/view/3879/3451.

Klug, J., Bruder, S., Kelava, A., Spiel, C., & Schmitz, B. (2013). Diagnostic competence of teachers: A process model that accounts for diagnosing learning behavior tested by means of a case scenario. *Teaching and Teacher Education, 30*, 38–46. https://doi.org/10.1016/j.tate.2012.10.004.

Korczak, J. (1998). *Szkoła życia. Obrazki szpitalne. Artykuły pedagogiczne i medyczne (1900–1912)* [School of life. Hospital pictures. Pedagogical and medical papers (1900–1912)]. Latona Publishers.

Korczyński, S. (2005). Kompetencje zawodowe nauczyciela [Professional competences of a teacher]. In R. Gmoch, & A. Krasnodębska (Eds.), *Kompetencje zawodowe nauczycieli i jakość kształcenia w dobie przemian edukacyjnych* [Professional competences of teachers and the quality of education in the times of educational changes]. Opole University Publishing House.

Krasowicz-Kupis, G., Wiejak, K., & Gruszczyńska, K. (2015). *Katalog metod diagnozy rozwoju poznawczego dziecka na etapie edukacji przedszkolnej I wczesnoszkolnej, tom I – narzędzia dostępne w poradniach psychologiczno-pedagogicznych I szkołach* [Catalog of methods for the diagnosis of a child's cognitive development at the stage of pre-school and early childhood education] (*Vol. I*). Publishing House of the Instytut Badań Edukacyjnych.

Kwaśnica, R. (2003). Wprowadzenie do myślenia o nauczycielu [Introduction to teacher dillemas]. In Z. Kwieciński, & B. Śliwerski (Eds.), *Pedagogika* (*Vol. II*, pp. 298–303). PWN.

Kwiatkowski, S. T., & Walczak, D. (Eds.). (2017). *Kompetencje interpersonalne w pracy współczesnego nauczyciela* [Interpersonal competences in the work of a modern teacher]. Akademia Pedagogiki Specjalnej Publishers.

Lepalczyk, J., & Badura, A. (Eds). (1987). *Elementy diagnostyki pedagogicznej* [Elements of pedagogical diagnostics] (p. 45). PWN.

Liu, J., Jacobson, E., & Bharaj, P. K. (2020, December). *Examining in-service teacher's diagnostic competence. Conference paper.* pp. 1892–1896. https://doi.org/10.51272/pmena.42.2020-309.

Łobocki, M. (2010). *Metody i techniki badań pedagogicznych* [Methods and techniques of pedagogical research]. Impuls Publishing House.

Łobocki, M. (2011). *Metody i techniki badań pedagogicznych* [Methods and techniques of pedagogical research]. Impuls Publishing House.

Majzub, R. M., & Rashid, A. A. (2012). School readiness among preschool children. *Procedia – Social and Behavioral Sciences*, *46*, 3524–3529. https://doi.org/10.1016/j.sbspro.2012.06.098.

Marzec-Holka, K. (1990). *Wybrane zagadnienia diagnostyki pedagogicznej* [Selected topics in pedagogical diagnostics]. WSP Publishers.

Mazurkiewicz, E. (1993). Diagnostyka w pedagogice społecznej [Diagnostics in social pedagogy]. In T. Pilch, & I. Lepalczyk (Eds.), *Pedagogika społeczna. Człowiek w zmieniającym się świecie* [Social pedagogy. Man in the changing world] (pp. 49–68). University Publishing House.

Męczkowska, A. (2003). Kompetencja [The notion of a competence]. In T. Pilch (Ed.), *Encyklopedia pedagogiczna XXI wieku* [Pedagogical encyclopedia of the 21st century] (*Vol. II*). Żak Academic Press.

Montgomery, D. (2017). Identification and remediation of year zero dyslexia, a new opportunity? *SfL*, *32*(1), 60–84. https://doi.org/10.1111/1467-9604.12150.

Mykyteichuk, K., Tymchuk, L., & Zvozdetska, V. (2021). Pedagogical diagnostics at the stage of preparing a child for school in Poland. In O. Clipa (Ed.), *Lumen proceedings* (*Vol. 16*, pp. 285–304). ATEE 2020 – Winter Conference. Teacher Education for Promoting Well-Being in School. Suceava, 2020. Lumen Publishing House. https://doi.org/10.18662/lumproc/atee2020/19.

Niemierko, B. (1993). Diagnostyka dydaktyczno-wychowawcza [Didactic and educational diagnostics]. In W. Pomykało (Ed.), *Encyklopedia Pedagogiczna* [Pedagogical encyclopedia] (pp. 96–99). Innowacja Foundation Publishers.

Niemierko, B. (2009). *Diagnostyka edukacyjna* [Educational diagnostics] (pp. 30–40). PWN.

Oleńska-Pawlak, T. (2006). Podstawy procesu diagnozowania dziecka o specjalnych potrzebach edukacyjnych [Basics of the process of diagnosing a SEN child]. In M. Klaczak, & P. Majewicz (Eds.), *Diagnoza i rewalidacja indywidualna dziecka ze specjalnymi potrzebami edukacyjnymi* [Individual diagnosis and revalidation of a child with special educational needs] (pp. 7–15). Pedagogical Academy Scientific Publishers.

Ophuysen, S. V. (2006). Vergleich diagnostischer Entscheidungen von Novizen und Experten am Beispiel der Schullaufbahnempfehlung [Comparison of diagnostic decisions of novices and experts at the example of school career recommendation]. *Zeitschrift Für Entwicklungspsychologie Und Pädagogische Psychologie*, *38*, 154–161.

Palka, S. (2011). Triangulacja w badaniach procesu dydaktyczno-wychowawczego [Triangulation in research on the didactic and educational process]. *Przegląd Pedagogiczny*, (1), 119–123.

Paluchowski, W. J. (2007). *Diagnoza psychologiczna. Proces – narzędzia – standardy* [Psychological diagnosis. Process – Tools – Standards]. Academic and Professional Publishers.

Panasiuk, J. (2017). Etapy diagnozy dziecka ze specjalnymi potrzebami rozwojowymi i edukacyjnymi [Stages of diagnosis of a child with special developmental and educational needs]. In K. Krakowiak (Ed.), *Diagnoza specjalnych potrzeb rozwojowych i edukacyjnych dzieci i młodzieży. Standardy, wytyczne oraz wskazówki do przygotowywania i adaptacji narzędzi diagnostycznych dla dzieci i młodzieży z wybranymi specjalnymi potrzebami rozwojowymi i edukacyjnymi* [Diagnosis of special developmental and educational needs of children and adolescents. Standards, guidelines and guidelines for the preparation and adaptation of diagnostic tools for children and adolescents with selected special development and educational needs] (p. 45). Center of the Development of Education Press.

Pankowska, D. (2016). Kompetencje nauczycielskie – Próba syntezy (projekt autorski) [Teaching competences – an attempt at synthesis (author's project)]. *Lubelski Rocznik Pedagogiczny, XXXV*(3), 187–209.

Pilch, T. (2001). *Zasady badań pedagogicznych. Strategie ilościowe i jakościowe* [Pedagogical research principles. Qualitative and quantitative strategies]. Żak Academic Press.

Pilch, T., & Bauman, T. (2001). *Zasady badań pedagogicznych. Strategie ilościowe i jakościowe* [Principles of pedagogical research. Quantitative and qualitative strategies] (pp. 191–192). Żak Academic Press.

Podgórecki, A. (1962). *Charakterystyka nauk praktycznych* [Characteristics of practical sciences]. PWN.

Przybysz-Zaremba, M. (2013). Być nauczycielem dzieci z zespołem nadpobudliwości psychoruchowej. Kilka uwag na temat metod pracy nauczycieli z uczniami klas początkowych [To be a teacher of children with attention deficit hyperactivity disorder. A few remarks on the methods of teachers work with first-grade students]. In B. Ostrowska, & P. Prüfer (Eds.), *Edukacja i niepełnosprawność w wyobraźni socjopedagogicznej* [Education and disability in socio-pedagogical dimensions] (pp. 63–76). Scientific Publishers of the Państwowa Wyższa Szkoła Zawodowa im. Jakuba z Paradyża in Gorzów Wielkopolski.

Przybysz-Zaremba, M. (2018). Dymorficzny wymiar diagnozy dziecka z niepełno-sprawnością intelektualną w stopniu lekkim – Studium przypadku [The dimorphic dimension of the diagnosis of a child with mild intellectual disability – a case study]. *Społeczeństwo i Rodzina, 56*(3), 96–109.

Przybysz-Zaremba, M. (2020). Diagnoza pedagogiczna – Studium jednego przypadku. W kierunku "autentycznej" pomocy i wsparcia [Pedagogical diagnosis – one case study. Towards "authentic" help and support]. In M. Przybysz-Zaremba, J. Stepaniuk, & A. Szczygieł (Eds.), *Szkoła – nauczyciel – uczeń w przestrzeni edukacyjnej* [School – teacher in the educational space] (pp. 52–65). Difin.

Przybysz-Zaremba, M., & Gołębieska, K. (2020). Uczeń o specjalnych potrzebach edukacyjnych w szkole – pomoc i wsparcie psychologiczno – pedagogiczne. Propozycje praktycznych rozwiązań [On School Activities of a SEN Student; Forms of Psychological and Pedagogical Help and Support. Proposals for Practical Solutions]. In A. Niekrewicz, J. Gebreselassie, & D. Skrocka (Eds.), *Wielowymiarowość zdrowia i choroby* [Multidimensionality of health and disease] (pp. 95–111). Scientific Publishers of the Akademia im. Jakuba z Paradyża in Gorzów Wielkopolski.

Pytka, L. (2005). *Pedagogika resocjalizacyjna* [Resocialization pedagogy]. APS Publishers.

Richmond, M. E. (1917). *Social diagnosis*. Russell Sage Foundation.

Salomon, A. (1926). Sociale diagnose. *Die Wohlfartspflege in Einzeldarstellungen* (*Vol. 3*). Carl Heymann Verlag.

Schrader, F. W. (2009). Anmerkungen zum Themenschwerpunkt Diagnostische Kompetenz von Lehrkräften [The diagnostic competency of teachers]. *Zeitschrift Für Pädagogische Psychologie, 23*(34), 237–245.

Sillamy, N. (1996). *Słownik psychologii* [A dictionary of psychology]. Książnica Publishers.

Skałbania, B. (2011). *Diagnostyka pedagogiczna. Wybrane obszary badawcze i rozwiązania praktyczne* [Pedagogical diagnostics. Selected areas and practical solutions] (pp. 49–52). Impuls Publishing House.

Skarbek, W. W. (2013). *Wybrane zagadnienia metodologii nauk społecznych* [Selected issues of the methodology of social sicences]. Scientific Pubishers in Piotrków Trybunalski.

Sochacka, I. (2014). Wywiad z rodzicami jako element diagnozy logopedycznej dzieci w wieku przedszkolnym [Interview with parents as an element of speech therapy diagnosis of preschool children]. *Edukacja Elementarna w Teorii i Praktyce* [Elementary Education in Theory and Practice], *3*(33), 175–190.

Thal, D., Jackson-Maldonado, D., & Acosta, D. (2000). Validity of a parent-report measure of vocabulary and grammar for Spanish-speaking toddlers. *Journal of Speech, Language, and Hearing Research, 43*(5), 1087–1100.

Turner, S. M., DeMers, S. T., Fox, H. R., & Reed, G. M. (2001). APA's guidelines for test user qualifications. *American Psychologist, 56*(12), 1099–1113. https://doi.org/10.1037/0003-066X.56.12.1099.

Walker, S. (2009). Sociometric stability and the behavioral correlates of peer acceptance in early childhood. *The Journal of Genetic Psychology, 170*(4), 339–358. https://doi.org/10.1080/00221320903218364.

Węglińska, M. (2010). *Jak pisać pracę magisterską? Poradnik dla studentów* [How to write a master thesis? A handbook for students] (pp. 51–68). Impuls Publishing House.

Wysocka, E. (2013). *Diagnostyka pedagogiczna. Nowe obszary i rozwiązania* [Pedagogical diagnostics. New areas and solutions]. Impuls Publishing House.

Wysocka, E. (2016). Diagnoza pozytywna w działalności pedagoga resocjalizacyjnego – założenia teoretyczne i metodologiczne identyfikacji zaburzeń w przystosowaniu [Positive diagnosis in the activity of a social rehabilitation pedagogue – theoretical and methodological assumptions of the identification of disorders in adaptation]. *Lubelski Rocznik Pedagogiczny* [Lublin Pedagogical Yearbook], *35*(2), 195–222. https://doi.org/10.17951/lrp.2016.35.2.195.

Ziemski, S. (1973). *Problemy dobrej diagnozy* [Problems of good diagnosis] (pp. 17–19). Wiedza Powszechna Press.

2 Introduction to the theoretical and methodological foundations of speech therapy

Speech therapy diagnosis and speech therapy procedures

Development of speech therapy as a scientific discipline in Poland – selected aspects of its history, theory and practice

Speech therapy – gr. *logos* 'word', 'speech'; *paideia* 'upbringing' – is a science dealing with the development and shaping of speech along with the improvement and correction of its various irregularities. Although the term 'speech therapy' itself began to function in Polish scientific literature in 1960, Maria Łączkowska used this term in the meaning of 'the therapy of speech' much earlier, that is, in 1976 in the periodical *Nowiny Lekarskie (Doctor News)* (Kaczmarek, 1991, p. 5). Pre-war lexicons did not include this expression in their contents, although the following definitions can be found in the lexicon compiled by Lama (1931, pp. 1198–1199):

- *logopathia* – speech deviation;
- *logoneurosis* – speech disorders related to inorganic nervous changes;
- *logomania* – morbid speech words.

The term 'speech therapy' as part of special education, dealing with the research and treatment of speech impediments, appeared only in Witold Doroszewski's *Dictionary of the Polish Language*, issued in 1969.

The beginnings of Polish speech therapy are related to the activity of Jan Łukasz Siestrzyński (1784–1824) – a doctor, teacher and lithographer. His work at the Institute of the Deaf in Warsaw, and his visits to institutions for the deaf in Linz, Fryzynga, near Munich, Saxony, Prussia, Prague and Leipzig, contributed to the decision to teach speech to the deaf. Doctor Siestrzyński was in favor of the so-called *Leipzig method*, proposed by Samuel Heinicki; the method itself consisted in speaking out loud, supported by gestures and images. In the work entitled *The Theory and Mechanism of Speech*, completed in 1820, though never published, Siestrzyński presented the most important concepts and views on teaching speech to deaf people. While discussing his achievements, Kaczmarek (1969, pp. 142–145) observes the following issues to be found there:

DOI: 10.4324/9781003354758-3

- indication of the need for early speech formation (4–5 years of age);
- creation of a separate system of hand-oral signs imitating the shape of the location of speech organs appropriate to the pronunciation of individual sounds;
- an attempt to distinguish the five stages of hearing loss (together with further promotion of the use of hearing residues during therapy);
- preparation of the selected pronunciation exercises to consolidate the sounds, along with didactic games ('checkers', 'soldiers', 'cards', 'shepherds'), used to facilitate the acquisition of reading and writing skills;
- drawing attention to the importance of observing facial movements (lower jaw, larynx, cheek muscles and/or neck) in perceiving speech with insufficient auditory residues;
- an attempt to determine the mechanism of the occurrence of voice impediments (nasal, muffled voice, muted, etc.), as well to work out possible ways to eliminate them;
- emphasis on the importance of making use of tactile or vibration phenomena in teaching the deaf.

Jan Łukasz Siestrzyński classified the sounds taking into account two criteria: (a) acoustic (voice and exhalation) and (b) the place of sound articulation. This researcher also described the way of articulating individual sounds. Due to the pitch of the tone, he distinguished soft consonants from their hard counterparts, developed tables of consonant connections in the onset and on-voice of words both in Polish and in German; he also took up the topic of similarity of sounds in terms of voicing.

Another person who undoubtedly contributed to the development of the Polish speech therapy was Władysław Ołtuszewski (1855–1922) – a doctor and phoniatrist. In 1880, in a building at 8 Długa Street in Warsaw, he founded the Health Center, where he dealt with the removal of speech disorders, as well as treated different nervous and mental diseases. After 12 years of successful functioning, the Health Center opened the Speech Deviation Treatment Facility, specializing in stuttering therapy. With time, it took the name Warsaw Institute for Speech Deviations and Noso-Gullet Suffering for the Permanent and Incoming Sick. Together with his wife, Zofia, Ołtuszewski worked in this center until 1922, combining medical practice with scientific activity. He was mainly interested in speech physiopathology and mental underdevelopment of children. He presented his research and observations in such magazines as *Medicine, The Doctor Review, The Medical Gazzette, Health, The Głos Mistrzycielski* and *The Pedagogical Review*; he also gave numerous speeches during meetings of the Medical Society or the Hygiene Society of Warsaw. He believed that the science of speech organization was composed of physiology and pathology of speech, as well as the research on the stages of speech formation in children. According to W. Ołtuszewski, there are motor centers in the brain that are responsible for articulation, writing and the accumulation of visual-auditory and associative memory, thanks to which the memory of words is formed. Speech is therefore a cerebral, coordinated function of the organs: breathing, voice, articulation. He noticed a correlation between speech disorders and the functioning of the hearing organ, the structure of articulators, mental and neurological state, and environmental, educational and general development problems. He created 'hygiene rules' for speech development, addressed to parents or teachers, at the same time emphasizing the need to stimulate both the sensory organs and motor skills. In the process of acquiring speaking skills, he emphasized the special role of the teacher, the peer environment and the closest environment of the learner. In his opinion, the pedagogue is the master of the content and form of speech, as well as the main associate of the doctor – the phoniatrist. Specialist treatment of speech disorders was divided into general (pharmacological agents, psychotherapy, motor improvement) and local, that is planned breathing, phonation and articulation exercises. Kiśniowska (2001, pp. 183–185) remarks that among speech therapy methods, he preferred play or task exercises; during rehabilitation, he emphasized the essence of the patient's awareness and activity, paying attention to the importance of cooperation with the child's parents. W. Ołtuszewski was not only the author of works such as *Sputtering Speech and Writing* (1893), *Hygiene of Speech* (1896) and *Sketches of the Science of Speech and Its Deviations* (1905); Demelowa (1975, p. 113) observes that by creating the foundations of the methodology of correction of speech disorders and speech therapy prophylaxis, Ołtuszewski became a pioneer of speech therapy, of both educational and therapeutic types.

Jan Baudouin de Courtenay (1845–1929) is considered to be the precursor of modern speech therapy (Kaczmarek, 1983, pp. 5–13). This outstanding scientist, lecturer and social activist not only made studies on the history of language, historical grammar with onomastics and dialectology but also created the concept of an Old-Polish dictionary, participating in the creation of the Warsaw Dictionary (etymology of words). However, most importantly, Baudouin de Courtenay undertook research and prepared theoretical foundations in embryology and the pathology of speech. He determined the meaning and also developed such terms as linguistic analogy, phonetic alternation, alternation, progressive palatalization and the phoneme, which he considered to be the basic phonetic unit. He definitely distinguished phonetics, that is the science of sounds, from phonology, dealing with the function of sounds in linguistic communication. By analyzing the processes of language evolution, he initiated the era of structuralism in linguistics. J. Baudouin de Courtenay also distinguished the following speech factors: logical, psychological and physiological. With the publishing of his essay *Einige Beobachtungen an Kindern* (1867–1868), J. Baudouin de Courtenay began speech therapy research on the formation and development of speech. He also made detailed observations of the physical and mental development of his five children. The collected materials were partly used by Maria Chmura-Klekotowa in her selection of essays entitled *Observations over the Language of a Child* (1974).

Huge merits in the diagnosis and treatment of speech and voice diseases and dysfunctions in children and adolescents should be attributed to another outstanding Polish otolaryngologist and phoniatrist – Benedykt Dylewski (1894–1988), known as the founder of the speech therapy system. He was the initiator of speech therapy courses for doctors, teachers and psychologists. He argued that re-education of speech disorders should take the form of an out-patient clinic and should be carried out in special classes or schools intended only for people who speak incorrectly. Therefore, he organized the first classes in Poland for students with speech and voice impediments, believing that the most effective results can only be achieved through long-term and systematic therapy combined with learning to read and write, conducted by teachers. According to the researcher, each educational institution should have a speech therapist, what he referred to as a 'phonologist'. As observed by Styczek (1983, p. 17), Dylewski did not prefer counseling activities, pointing to their negative organizational side; at the same time he was an enthusiast of compulsory speech therapy classes addressed to units with more severe dysfunctions, taking place in the central phonological clinic, which played the role of controlling and coordinating the work of school speech therapists. Based on the analysis of the language skills of the population of Vilnius children, he developed a statistic of speech and speech impediments. Another Polish researcher, Święch (2001, pp. 186–187) mentions one more activity ascribed to Dylewski; he opted for regular hearing tests, based on various speech and facial exercises. He also fought against the imitation of the incorrect pronunciation heard in the closest environment. He is the author of more than 80 papers on throat physiology, inhalation, speech and voice disorders, and clinical otolaryngology. His scientific heritage includes, for example, such titles as *What Should a Doctor Know about the Development of a Child's Speech?* (1930), *Speech Defects and Their Treatment at School* (1936) and *Oxygenation and Its Treatment in the Light of More Recent Research and Observations* (1936).

The dynamic development of speech therapy took place in the 1960s. In 1960, the journal *Speech Therapy; Various Problems of Live Word Culture* appeared, under the scientific editorship of Leon Kaczmarek (1911–1996); the journal soon took on an international scope. By integrating researchers from different parts of the world (e.g. Austria, the Netherlands, Great Britain, the United States of America, France, Argentina, Canada, Belgium) the journal, which mostly dealt with various issues of development and speech disorders, undoubtedly contributed to the growing importance of this field of knowledge. At the basis of Kaczmarek's interests lay the broadly understood issues of the development of a child's speech and the processes aimed at ensuring its proper course. By assigning tasks to speech therapy, he developed the structure of a multilevel speech therapy system. This model assumed the practical use of all aspects of speech: embryological, pathological, social, artistic and also written. The first of them concerned the study of the determinants of speech development, the elaboration of the results and methods of counteracting disorders. The pathological aspect included eliminating any disturbances and speech impediments, also at the level of writing or reading. The social aspect was related to the elimination of the mental and social effects of the impediments or disorders, and the artistic one focused on the culture of a living colloquial, journalistic and artistic word. On his initiative, in 1963, the Polish Speech Therapy Society was established, popularizing achievements in the field of the theory, prevention and pathology of speech. In 1970, the first postgraduate speech therapy study program was established at the Maria Curie-Skłodowska University in Lublin, and, in 1974 – the postgraduate speech therapy study program at the Faculty of Polish Studies at the University of Warsaw. Over time, similar facilities were opened in other Polish towns: Gdańsk, Kraków, Opole, Poznań, Wrocław, Katowice and Bydgoszcz.

The first Polish speech therapy textbook – *The Outline of Speech Therapy* by Irena Styczek – was published in 1970. This publication not only presents the issues of speech and hearing in detail, and emphasizes the need for early re-education of emerging abnormalities, but above all it also discusses the methods enabling the implementation of proper speech therapy techniques in the case of various speech and hearing disorders. The research activity of I. Styczek (1924–1981) focused mainly on the problem of speech pathology and the influence of partial or complete hearing loss on the formation of verbal communication. She also conducted experimental work on Polish dentalized consonants.

The development of speech therapy was influenced by specialists in various scientific disciplines, for example, doctors, educators, linguists, psychologists, neurobiologists and physicists. Since the end of the 1980s, Polish speech therapy has largely benefited from the achievements of Soviet, Czech and East German researchers. Hence, nomenclature, classifications of speech therapy phenomena or theoretical concepts other than those in force in Western countries began to appear (Jastrzębowska, 2003, p. 315). Initially, speech therapy was classified as either a medical discipline and placed in the pedagogical and methodological area of phoniatrics, or recognized as a component of pedagogical sciences, especially special education. Due to the importance of applied phonetics, there were also positions opting for the affiliation of speech therapy to linguistics. According to L. Kaczmarek (1991, p. 5), speech therapy is an *[...] independent, multi-inter-disciplinary discipline*, being a part of the humanistic and biological block. However, the unilateral perception of the subject of language communication disorders was not conducive to an effective therapeutic approach. According to Stanisław Grabias (1997, p. 15), speech therapy is not a simple combination of medical, psychological, pedagogical and linguistic knowledge, but an organized structure that takes into account the results of research in these disciplines. Speech therapy deals with a complex of issues related to linguistic communication, analyzed in various aspects: medical, linguistic, psychological, pedagogical, artistic and – in a broader context – from the pattern, through the norm, to pathology (Skorek, 2000, p. 94).

According to the concept of S. Grabias, when taking up theoretical and practical issues related to speech disorders and prevention, this field must have a coherent system of concepts and methods of describing specific phenomena. Thus, the theory of speech therapy should develop the topics of diagnostics, forecasting and anagnostics. The first one provides empirical descriptions of speech dysfunctions, along with their interpretation, treating disorders from a biological, psychological or social perspective. The process of forecasting leads to the creation of rational therapeutic programs based on research. At the same time, anagnostics tracks knowledge relating to the methods of explaining various manifestations of speech disorders, as well as methods aimed at their removal. The speech therapy practice, however, should build linguistic or communicative competence or improve the implementation of communication acts using appropriate techniques. In this way speech therapy belongs to a broad scientific discipline, referred to as *linguistic communication,* or *metalinguistics,* the object of which is interested in all forms of linguistic behavior (Grabias, 1997, pp. 19–20). Making an attempt to develop this approach, Jastrzębowska (1999, p. 241) proposes the following list:

- a properly running process of acquiring competences and developing linguistic and communicative skills (improving the forms of developing and already formed speech);
- prophylaxis, that is methods of preventing incorrect linguistic behavior;
- origins (etiopathogenesis) and causes (etiology) of deviations from the norm in speech development;
- the mechanism of their formation (pathomechanism);
- their relationship with other developmental disorders (disorders of orientation-cognitive, emotional-motivational and executive processes);
- their influence on the psyche and social functioning;
- correction of speech impediments;
- re-education of speech disorders – in the case of loss of the already acquired communication skills;
- therapy (treatment, removal) of all disturbances and disorders of speech development and speech disorders;
- influencing the patient's psyche in order to enable the patient to function properly in society;
- preventing secondary effects of speech disorders (e.g. emotional and behavioral disorders).

On the interdisciplinary aspects of speech therapy

The placement of a given discipline of knowledge in the circle of other sciences is determined by at least three factors: the subject of research, the selection and advancement of cognitive means and the degree of development of meta-scientific reflection (Grucza, 1983; Siedlaczek-Szwed, 2010). Each science should have a hierarchical structure. The research procedure begins with diagnostic activities that provide empirical phenomena with explanations (in the case of speech therapy, these are various manifestations of speech disorders). A comprehensive description and a thorough explanation of the phenomena (i.e. explication) opens up the forecasting perspective (application), consisting in the creation of effective programs of corrective actions. The applicative area plays an extremely important role in speech therapy, as evidenced by the fact that theorists want to assign it the status of 'applied science' (Grabias, 2002, p. 21; see also Hughes et al., 2004, pp. 205–230). Over the last two decades, in the field of diagnostics, there has been a boom in research on, for example deafness (Rakowska, 1992), disorders caused by brain damage (Herzyk, 1992; see also American Psychiatric Association, 2000; Kent. 2004; World Health Organization, 1992), dyslalia (Kozłowska, 1998) and language behavior in autism or schizophrenia (Gałkowski, 1995). In this period researchers began to consider the process of shaping a child's speech in the communicative and pragmatic aspect, with particular emphasis on the text and linguistic interaction (Bokus, 1991).

Although speech therapy is an independent scientific discipline, taking up extensive issues of linguistic communication, it does not only make use of the achievements of other fields of knowledge but also integrates the results of their research. A Polish researcher, Grażyna Jastrzębowska (2003, pp. 327–328), points to the links between speech therapy and the following sciences:

- pedagogy – methods of dealing with and working with children;
- phoniatrics – physiology and pathology of speech, voice and hearing;
- audiology – diagnosis and treatment of hearing disorders;
- orthodontics – etiology of speech impediments caused by incorrect bite or dentition;
- neurology and physiology – making people aware of the mechanisms governing the process of transmitting and receiving speech, defining the pathogenesis of speech disorders;
- linguistics – information on the structure of the language;
- developmental psychology – psychomotor development of a child, stages of the formation and development of speech;
- clinical psychology – the consequences of speech disorders, the relationship between speech disorders and other developmental disorders;
- psycholinguistics and developmental sociolinguistics – the mechanism of acquiring language skills, the course of the process of shaping and developing speech;
- speech psychology, cybernetics, neurobiology, neuropsychology – the brain's organization of language and its disruptions;
- acoustics and acoustic phonetics – the structure of voice waves and their course: sender-receiver;
- philology – arranging and reading texts;

- stylistics – the linguistic structure of the text;
- palaeography – forms of writing, their history, evolution and distribution in time and space;
- graphology – individual characteristics of handwriting, psychological properties of the writers;
- living word culture – verbal (colloquial, journalistic, artistic etc.) expression.

When considering the problem of the scope and subject of speech therapy research, three applicable concepts should be distinguished (Jastrzębowska, 2003, pp. 321–322):

- medical – where the subject of research embraces disorders, prophylaxis and speech correction;
- pedagogical – where focus is on two areas: the area of interest with the topics of speech development in children with impaired hearing, and the area of content related to communication between the deaf and/or the blind;
- holistic – where the scope of speech therapy concerns all aspects of speech: embryological, pathological, social, artistic.

According to the assumptions of the holistic concept (Kaczmarek, 1982, p. 146), speech therapy, understood as a science that consolidates the results of research in all disciplines dealing with speech issues, includes:

- speech theory;
- speech embryology (speech development in ontogenesis);
- teaching speech to children with various dysfunctions: hearing impairment, intellectual disability, damage to the central nervous system;
- language communication of the deaf and/or the blind;
- auditory and visual perception of verbal utterances along with visual and sensory perception of written utterances;
- articulation, acoustic, auditory and visual phonetics;
- speech pathology – disorders of linguistic communication (verbal, written);
- living word culture.

According to Jastrzębowska (2003, p. 324), the following specialties can be distinguished within speech therapy:

1. theoretical speech therapy;
2. applied speech therapy:

    a   general speech therapy:

    - educational;
    - artistic;

b   special speech therapy:

- corrective;
- surdologopedia.

Speech therapy tasks

Following Jastrzębowska (2003, pp. 325–326), the principal task of theoretical speech therapy is to combine and present the possibilities of practical use of the results of research in various fields of knowledge concerning linguistic communication and its irregularities. This discipline also deals with the determination of methods and tools necessary to diagnose various speech dysfunctions and the creation of preventive or therapeutic programs. At the same time, applied speech therapy is aimed at the following aspects: training competences, linguistic and communication skills, counteracting irregularities in the acquisition of the above-mentioned competences, removing speech disorders and preventing their mental or social effects.

In the opinion presented by Styczek (1983, pp. 13–14), the tasks of general speech therapy boil down to taking care for the proper development of speech (phonetically, grammatically and/or lexically); and to improving the already formed pronunciation. As for special speech therapy, it includes elimination of speech impediments, teaching speech in the case of its absence or loss, elimination of voice disorders and elimination of difficulties in writing and reading.

The tasks of speech therapy, according to Elżbieta Maria Minczakiewicz (1997, pp. 8–9), can be grouped into four basic areas:

1   shaping speech in children from the earliest moments of life, paying attention to its adequate stimulation (speech therapy prophylaxis);
2   correcting speech impediments and disorders (diagnosis);
3   formatting speech in people with hearing impairments;
4   caring for the culture of colloquial, journalistic and artistic words in singing and recitation.

These tasks, distinguished in this way, make it possible to distinguish the following speech therapy specializations (Kaczmarek, 1991):

- educational speech therapy – counteracting speech and voice disorders;
- surdologopedia – shaping speech in the deaf, hard of hearing and deaf-blind;
- corrective speech therapy – removing speech and voice disorders, and problems in reading and writing;
- artistic speech therapy – care for the culture of the living word.

A Polish researcher, Elżbieta M. Minczakiewicz (1997, pp. 10–12), lists down the following speech therapy specialists:

- general speech therapist – a specialist in the diagnosis, prevention and therapy of articulation and phonation disorders caused by damage or dysfunction of peripheral speech organs;
- surdologopedist – a professional in the field of diagnosis and speech therapy for people (children, adolescents, adults) with hearing impairment (deaf, hard of hearing, deaf-blind);
- neurologopedist – a specialist in the diagnosis and speech therapy of people with aphasia, alalia, dysarthria and cerebral palsy;
- balbutologopedist – a specialist in the diagnosis and therapy of people who stutter as well as those who exhibit other speech fluency dysfunctions (rush, bradilla, tachylalia);
- oligophrenologopedist – a professional in the diagnosis and speech therapy of people with intellectual disabilities, Down syndrome, autism, mutism or the mentally ill;
- orthoepic – a specialist interested in the culture of the living word, that is, the technique of speaking, creating and interpreting texts;
- glottodidactician – a specialist in language education, diagnosis, prevention and therapy of children with reading and writing difficulties (dyslexia, dysgraphia, dysorthography).

What are the specialties of speech therapy?

Currently, the following speech therapy specializations are distinguished:

- general speech therapy;
- neurologopedia;
- surdologopedia.

The first of them concerns the knowledge of general speech therapy in the field of prophylaxis, diagnosis and therapy of people with speech disorders resulting from damage, deficit or malfunction of the speech organs. This specialization can be obtained after completing two-year postgraduate studies in speech therapy or five-year full-time pedagogical studies with a specialization in speech therapy. Specialization in neurologopedics, acquired during the second cycle of postgraduate studies, covers knowledge of speech disorders caused by damage to the central and peripheral nervous system, and surdology concerns diagnosis and therapy for the deaf or hard of hearing, as well as deaf-blind or deaf people (Błachnio, 2001, p. 17).

In his book, Kurkowski (2010, pp. 75–76) recognizes the following qualifications of the neurologist:

1 neurological diagnosis of newborns, infants, children, adolescents and adults with damages and/or dysfunctions of the nervous system, as well

as all those patients who suffer from disorders in the development and/or the course of linguistic communication;

2   analyses of specialist research: neurological, psychological, audiological and other, enabling the explanation of the pathomechanism of disorders in the development and/or course of linguistic communication in people with damage, and/or dysfunction of the nervous system;

3   programming of neurologopedic therapy for people with dysfunctions and/or lesions of the nervous system; those patients who suffer from disorders of the development and/or course of language functions; taking into account the results of neurologopedic diagnosis and the results of specialist examinations, by defining the goals, procedures and strategies of therapy;

4   adaptation of methods, forms and means to implementation established as a result of programming therapy of language disorders in people with damage and/or dysfunctions of the nervous system;

5   conduct of neurological therapy in newborns, infants, children, adolescents and adults with damages and/or dysfunctions of the nervous system; those patients who suffer from disorders in the development and/or the course of linguistic communication;

6   control of the results of neurological therapy in people with speech disorders resulting from damage and/or dysfunction of the nervous system, together with modifying the goals, methods and forms of therapy;

7   cooperation with members of the multi-specialist treatment and rehabilitation and certification team;

8   conduct of research works and preparation of scientific publications.

The same researcher (ibid. p. 77) lists down the following areas of professional activity of a surdologist:

1   diagnoses of speech perception, linguistic and communicative competence and articulation;

2   development of surdology therapy programs;

3   conducting classes developing the ability to understand and create verbal statements, that is acquiring linguistic competences as well as communicative competences in people with various hearing disorders;

4   conducting classes in the field of acquiring reading and writing skills in children with various hearing disorders;

5   conducting classes that develop psychomotor and cognitive functions;

6   introduction of elements of various supporting and alternative methods (e.g. phonogestos, total communication, sign language);

7   cooperation with members of the multi-specialist treatment and rehabilitation, and certification team;

8   conducting research works and preparing topical scientific publications.

How is the Polish speech therapy system organized?

Making an attempt to describe the speech therapy system that functions in Poland, Grażyna Jastrzębowska, (2003, pp. 303–304) recognizes the activity of two counseling centers – psychological and pedagogical – which supervise the overall speech therapy work in kindergartens and schools, providing diagnostic, therapeutic or instructional assistance to children with speech impediments or their parents. These institutions are managed by the provincial educational authorities, supervised by the Ministry of National Education. In large urban agglomerations there are also phoniatric clinics supervised by the Ministry of Health. Graduates of postgraduate studies in speech therapy are also employed by some hospitals, specialist centers or special institutions for children with intellectual disabilities, deaf, apathy, etc. Speech therapy care is organized within two ministries:

- Ministry of Health – taking care of phoniatric clinics, specialist offices in mental health and general clinics, rehabilitation centers and hospitals;
- Ministry of National Education – responsible for the functioning of psychological and pedagogical counseling centers; speech therapy offices in mainstream schools and kindergartens; speech therapy offices in special schools for mildly mentally impaired children; kindergartens and schools for moderately and severely mentally impaired children (see also Minczakiewicz, 1998).

The substantive and formal shape of today's speech therapy in Poland is undoubtedly also influenced by the activities of various institutions or societies, such as the Polish Speech Therapy Society; the Speech Therapy Section of the Language Culture Society; the Polish Audiophonology Committee; the Polish Neuropsychological Society; the Scientific Society of Hearing, Voice and Language Communication Disorders; the Polish Foundation of Speech Disorders; the Polish Phonetic Society; or the Polish Neurolinguistic Society.

The scope of interest in speech therapy among other sciences

Education in the EU countries differs in the structure of the curriculum, as well as in granting authorization to practice the profession of speech therapy. Some countries are in the process of creating new curricula (e.g. Iceland or Cyprus), or extending modifications to existing ones (e.g. Hungary). Several EU countries do not have any speech therapy curricula developed, and they train their speech therapists in other EU countries (e.g. Luxembourg or Liechtenstein). These countries are considering setting up educational programs in the future. In most countries, the model based on full-time speech therapy studies, implemented in the Bologna system, prevails.

The model of education and gaining competences by speech therapists is different in the world, but their analyses prove the correctness of the idea to establish stationary speech therapy studies, observed in Poland, because only such solutions can bring future speech therapists closer to the global requirements.

The system of providing speech therapy services is similarly diverse. In most countries, it is divided into hospitals, educational establishments, social welfare and counseling centers, and private practice. There are countries with an extreme medical model of speech therapy, such as Italy, Great Britain or Ireland; there are also countries with a mixed model of educational and medical employment, such as the USA, Denmark and Spain. Still others have a medical-private model, such as Germany, or a private-medical model, such as France. An interesting example is Greece, where the educational-private model dominates. A review of the issues related to education and the labor market of speech therapists in the world proves that there is no one model solution. The various solutions adopted in individual countries are respected and recognized by the international community of speech therapists (provided, however, that basic standards of competences resulting from education are met). A separate issue is the implementation of speech therapy in developing countries.

Speech therapy is a science that is interested in all issues related to linguistic communication, which are analyzed in various perspectives: medical, linguistic, psychological, pedagogical and artistic (i.e. from the point of view of various disciplines). It follows that it is interested not only in deviations from the norm but also in the norm and all that can be defined above it (i.e. developing linguistic and communicative skills, striving for excellence in this area and finding ways to prevent possible irregularities). Thus, it is interested in various aspects of linguistic communication, not only communication disorders. Such an approach helps to understand the essence and basis of all pathological linguistic behaviors, their etiology, pathogenesis, pathomechanism and factors influencing their development and recovery. It enables them to be classified and distinguished, but also to conduct different forms of speech therapy. Currently, there are three concepts defining the scope and subject of speech therapy research, because representatives of various sciences participated in the creation of this discipline. Different theoretical approaches resulted in the fact that the subject of speech therapy research is defined differently.

The basic concepts defining the area of activity of speech therapy, both in theory and in practice, include:

- medical (or paramedical) concepts – where the scope of the subject of speech therapy research is limited to disorders, prophylaxis and speech correction;
- pedagogical concepts – where this area expands to include problems of speech development and/or different communication issues;

- holistic concepts – which consist in treating speech therapy as an independent science that deals with all aspects of speech (embryological,
pathological, social and artistic).

The process of mastering language and communication skills is complex,
multidimensional and long term. Its determinants are mostly biological in
nature; they are related to the social context and, above all, interactions with
adult language users (at the early stages of ontogenesis) and with their peers
(at later stages). Mastering the individual basic linguistic and communicative
competences is similar for all children; regardless of the type of language,
each child is capable of using it in a more or less correct way.

Development of linguistic communication and educational environments

Speech plays an extremely important role in human life. It is an asset in
establishing social contacts; it allows for the possibility of precise communication; it is a tool for acquiring information; it also allows for the expression of individual opinions, feelings or preferences. Beyond all that, it is
a testament to intellect and culture. However, the processes of education
of communication skills do not take place without contact with the social
environment. To an equal extent, the course of these processes depends on
biological and social factors.

The communicative function of speech is the engine of the entire verbal development of a child. Whether or not the communication function
appears at the right time depends on how quickly the child masters the
highest levels of intellectual and social development (Siedlaczek-Szwed,
2003, p. 121). Speech cannot be equated solely with human communicative
behavior or with only the biologically perceived process of speaking. It is an
entity composed of linguistic and communicative competences on the one
hand and the process of implementing these competences on the other. This
concept should be equated with linguistic communication. Thus, following
Kaczmarek (2001, pp. 19–24), there are three basic codes in speech: linguistic, paralinguistic and nonlinguistic. In the linguistic code, the social aspect
seems to be the most important, although the individual characteristics of
the speaker and the listener also have an impact on the communication
process. Cultural factors are important as well; they not only determine the
appropriate selection of vocabulary but also correlate with the syntax and
style of an utterance.

According to one of the seminal Russian researchers and philosophers,
Lev Vygotsky (1978, in: Pollard, 2000, p. 113), *[t]he acquisition of language
can provide a paradigm for the entire problem of the relation between learning and
development. Language arises initially as a means of communication between the
child and the people in his environment.* When learning how to live and how to
function in society, children have to learn how to communicate, in other

words, how to ask, answer and comment on different issues they should get in touch with in their life. In communicating with people, the following two levels of information transfer could be discovered – the language-based (i.e. verbal) channel and the nonverbal communication channel. The act of speaking results in mastering two basic skills: understanding the meaning of words (and their grammatical systems) and pronouncing sounds with a specific meaning. According to Słodownik-Rycaj (2000, pp. 76–78), full communication not only requires one to choose the right content but also to know how to convey it both on the segmental and suprasegmental levels. Over time, children shape the language in both planes. They use prosodic features not only for a better understanding but also to improve their own statements.

According to modern linguistic interpretations (Gazzaniga et al., 2002; Grabias, 2002), within speech it is possible to distinguish the sphere of common behaviors that unites all members of a social group from the sphere of individual behaviors that belongs to its individual members. The sphere of collective behavior is determined by linguistic competence (i.e. the knowledge that allows one to build grammatically correct sentences) and communicative competence (i.e. the knowledge that allows one to create meaningful statements). The sphere of individual behavior reveals itself as specific for each group member, conditioned by the mental and physical abilities of the speakers, the implementation of sentences and statements. The formation and development of speech are closely related to social development. Frequent verbal contacts of the child with the environment accelerate this development, perfecting the pronunciation, enriching the vocabulary, teaching the correct application of grammar rules, proper use of the melody, accent and rhythm, all of which are the components that determine the correct image of speech. At the same time, in the case of environmental neglect, that is lack of role models, there is a delay in the development of speech or its various disorders.

Speech can therefore be considered as a means of socialization and interpersonal communication, that is as a complex and specifically organized form of conscious activity in which two entities – transmitting and receiving statements – participate.

Recent years have been dominated by significant progress in many fields of science. There are also new, more mature linguistic concepts, for example in the field of linguistic and communicative competence, which puts a new light on the broadly understood issue of linguistic skills. Linguistic competence should be defined as one's ability to form and understand sentences in a given language; communicative competence is considered as one's ability to make use of language in respect of a listener as well as the current social conditions that require this form of interlingual communication. Another name for communicative (pragmatic) competence is social intelligence (or intra-interpersonal intelligence); the expressions are commonly connected with the so-called theory of mind (TM), described as *[...]*

a theory that generally allows for ascribing various mental states to oneself as well as others (Premack & Woodruff, 1978, p. 515). In other words, the theory claims that mentally able people can imagine themselves as functioning in the 'other's shoes' and, subsequently, behave accordingly (cf. Pinker, 2002). A good example used to test one's TM is a False Conviction Test, which is generally applied to diagnose autism. Social life requires its participants to know the communication system that the group has constructed over the centuries and passed on to its members, thus ordering the constant interactions between them. The most important role in these relations should be assigned to language. It is formed spontaneously, unconsciously and without excessive effort in the first years of a child's life.

At the same time, along with the increasing participation of the individual in social life, interactive skills are formed and developed. These skills allow a person to exist in a social group, understand the relationships between participants in social life and effectively implement their own intentions. Communication competence is a prerequisite for the development of interactive skills. A linguistic text, with its entire context, is called a discourse. Participation in the discourse seems effective if the members of the communication act are able to properly read and interpret everything that is contained in and around the text. Therefore, discourse is a complex communicative phenomenon, which consists of a text and extralinguistic elements necessary to understand this text (Ożdżyński & Surowaniec, 2000, p. 33). However, each text, regardless of its value, represents the highest degree of linguistic complexity, so using the text, both from the sender's and the recipient's side, gives us the most information about the competence of a language user.

What is communication competence?

Communication is one of the most important categories of human functioning, being both a manifestation and a condition of social life. The very term communication means mutual exchange of opinions, transmitting thoughts, giving messages (Tokarski, 1980, p. 374). According to Philip George Zimbardo (1999, pp. 169–170), communication is the process by which an individual receives and transmits information. The information can be facts, thoughts or feelings delivered to the recipient in a variety of ways, such as by speech, gestures, pictorial symbols and/or handwriting symbols.

Linguistic competence is the ability to use a given language freely, the ability to communicate with it and express your thoughts with it. The most important, however, is communicative competence, that is the ability to use language as a communication tool, to use it for the intended purpose, to adapt linguistic means to the current situation within the speech act. The level of linguistic competence varies among language users. It also depends on a person's education, individual predispositions and individual attitude toward the language, and on the state of health (Łuczyński, 2005, pp. 38–40).

Thus, linguistic communication is conditioned by three types of competences: linguistic competences, communicative competences and cultural competences. Certain biological skills and mental communication activities determine the acquisition and development of the above-mentioned types of competences and the methods of their use (Jastrzębowska, 2003, pp. 335–337). Biological skills, taking the form of perceptual and realization processes, shape the human mind and affect the quality of its functioning in the environment. Following Grabias (2012a, 2012b, pp. 52–53), mental communication activities take the form of performance skills. On the other hand, the system of perceptual and realized biological skills just mentioned includes efficient physical, phonetic, phonemic and prosodic hearing; mobile brain; efficient memory; properly functioning peripheral nervous system; and the muscular and skeletal systems of speech organs. As for mental performance skills, they embrace systemic skills (the ability to construct grammatically correct sentences) and communication skills (the ability to use language in various situations of social life), both of which are ways of using the above-mentioned competences (linguistic, communicative, cultural) previously developed in the mind of an individual. Language and communication competences and skills remain the most important area of research and practical activities in speech therapy. According to S. Grabias (2010/2011, pp. 20–22), building cognitive (cultural), linguistic and communicative competence seems to be a key task in the following disorders:

- deafness and/or hearing loss – lack of developed competences due to improperly functioning physical hearing;
- alalia and/or dyslalia – uneducated competences due to improperly functioning phonemic hearing, where alalia refers to all types of competences, and dyslalia is a disruption of the implementation of an incomplete phonological structure;
- oligophasia – lack of educated competences associated with intellectual disability;
- autism – undeveloped competences due to brain dysfunction;
- childhood epilepsy – brain dysfunction causing incomplete development of competences or their degradation.

The necessity to improve the activities of speaking with the possessed competences is created by:

- dysglosia – incorrect implementation of phonemes resulting from anomalies in the structure of speech organs (e.g. cleft palate and upper lip, malocclusion, shortened sublingual frenulum, removal of the larynx);
- stuttering and rattling – disfluency in talking about various etiologies of an organic nature reinforced by logophobia;
- dysarthria – disturbed articulation clarity in the realization of phonemes and consonant groups, distorted prosody due to cerebral palsy.

The preceding disorders result in incomplete or even substitute use of acquired competences.

Stabilizing the breakdown and restoring the functions of speaking and mind functioning relate to:

- aphasia – disintegration of linguistic competence, disturbance of communicative competence, implementation difficulties caused by mechanical damage to the left hemisphere of the brain;
- pragnosia – the breakdown of semantic competence related to damage to the right hemisphere of the brain;
- schizophasia – specific narrative, shaky coherence of dialogue statements as a result of schizophrenia;
- dementia – disappearance of narrative, low dialogue skills, breakdown of linguistic social skills, inability to interpret events due to the death of neurons and synaptic connections.

A human being, endowed with specific biological abilities, acquires the given competences only in contact with the social group in which the person lives and grows. Therefore, it is difficult to limit language and linguistic communication to the sum of their determinants, as they constitute their accumulation (Grabias, 2000, vol. 28, p. 32; see also Chiat, 2000).

The role of basic educational environments in the development of speech

The function of family

The basic environment that shapes thinking and speech is the family, which is the social and educational foundation of a young person (Siedlaczek-Szwed & Jałowiecka-Frania, 2016, pp. 119–125; Żebrowska, 1979; see also Siedlaczek-Szwed & Przybysz-Zaremba, 2018, pp. 811–817). The role of this context seems to be particularly important in one's individual development in early childhood, but it also applies to developmental changes and transformations in later periods. The essence of the influence of the family context on the development of an individual should be reduced to the statement that a person is able to learn from people with whom the person has a social and emotional bond. The family can therefore be treated as an area of activity that results in various experiences. These experiences, in turn, constitute a rich material for development processes. Thus, the development of a child's speech occurs spontaneously in contact with various everyday situations. Parents, taking actions supporting the formation of the speech of their children, should express themselves correctly. Linguistic patterns are especially important here, along with the use of a developed code, which determines how quickly the semantic field will be activated. Therefore, from early childhood, it is necessary to present the child with the right speech patterns, so the ability to critically look at one's own articulation appears to be a necessity every parent should never forget about. It is then easier to see how much can be done to improve or modify it. From their birth, children should learn how to use the language of their parents and relatives; they, however, should not be required to use the language of the adults, as such behavior hinders learning to speak. Parents should listen to what the children say to them, never forgetting about an old truth: the more eagerly children are listened to – the more they are willing to talk. Having fun when playing with the language together remains a very important element of the atmosphere children can find (and experience) at home. While implementing the principles of language education at home, children play with words with pleasure, rhyming, twisting and rearranging the words, trying to find out how far the freedom of using the language reaches and where the necessity to adjust themselves to the existing grammatical rules begins. Equally important issues of parental stimulation of speech development in a young person include emotional factors and attractive events that enrich and dynamize the speech. Close attention should be paid not only to the level of language development but also to how it is used in various situations. The role of parents in shaping speech should not be limited only to developing a communicative attitude. Being with children and satisfying their basic needs enables them to develop properly. Providing stimuli that stimulate general development also promotes the development of speech. In the process of acquiring language skills, apart from the appropriate patterns and stimuli to motivate to speak, one should also remember about encouraging the child to speak and ask questions, to answer questions, to listen attentively and to maintain the statement. Such actions aimed at awakening interest in the language in children are important, as they tend to prepare an individual for further school work. If we hear words that are misspelled, we should repeat them aloud in the correct form. One should not force children to repeat the same word many times; one should remember that the position of a child in the family as well as the role and model of communication characteristic of a given family are important in the development of speech. The occurrence of various forms of communication in the family influences the later functioning of a human being. The restricted code, expressed in the use and/or a specific selection of vocabulary, indicates little chance of acquiring the developed code (Bernstein, 1971). Therefore, not only correct articulation should be at the center of parents' attention but also other components of the statement, including the one related to understanding. A statement is both a way of realizing sounds and prosodic features, as well as linguistic content and form. Children gradually achieve an ability to communicate as they improve their linguistic systemic, linguistic, social, situational and pragmatic skills (Vygotski, 1978). It should be emphasized, however, that although speech is formed individually by a child, the role of parents in this respect is huge. Family communication is managed by parents who are responsible for its quality. They can, more or less consciously, enrich the development of speech by providing linguistic patterns and creating appropriate conditions. Sometimes they take actions spontaneously, and their effectiveness is determined by the interest shown to the child or concern for their needs. Effective communication of an individual with the environment determines their development and improvement of many cognitive and social functions, also satisfying emotional needs. Knowledge of speech mastery allows for giving tips, advice and recommendations to parents; obviously when taking into account the fact that the development of speech begins at the moment of the child's birth and continues all the time afterwards. Although disharmonies between functions are often observed, the efficiency of the activities mentioned earlier depends on the maturity and readiness of the child's nervous system. It should also be remembered that although the process of speech development, genetically determined and based on the individual predispositions of the organism, takes place in certain stages and covers several years, it is possible only in contact with the family and social environment. The claim that the language of adults is a role model for a child does not raise any doubts today, what can be translated into an assumption is that the importance of proper language development carried out in a warm and caring family environment cannot be underestimated. All disturbances on this level cause difficulties, both in the cognitive sphere, as language is a tool of cognition, and in the communicative sphere, because linguistic communication is the main means of general acts of communication carried out by people. Along with cognitive development, the length and complexity of linguistic messages also increases (Bernstein, 1971).

Remember that the first years of a child's life, when the child is completely dependent on adults, determine what their linguistic functioning will look like in the future, when they will have to take responsibility for improving their own language and make a choice in terms of communication strategies. The experiences at home will then become decisive, as the role of the family also consists in transmitting culture and its educational influences (Vygotsky, 1962).

The influence of peers

Peer groups that an individual is in contact with from earliest childhood constitute an extremely important element of the educational environment, influencing social intercourse, and thus shaping the personality of their members (Skorny, 1992, p. 46). Between the ages of 3 and 6, there is a gradual increase in linguistic and communicative skills, and in the cognitive complexity of statements (Szpotowicz & Szulc-Kurpaska, 2013). Children begin to use grammar rules, apply various language functions to convey specific information (naming, differentiating), transform the expressions just met (categorizing, inferring) and make attempts to communicate with the environment (matching the message to the recipient). However, in terms of linguistic and communicative skills, there is a significant differentiation, as some skills are fully acquired (e.g. imitating grammatical structures), while others are mastered at the initial stage (e.g. the process of adjective gradation). Coherence of action, dynamics, proposing a personal solution strategy, inclusion of unreal elements and interest in the task develop significantly, but the ability to use multiple materials, transform the meanings of objects or rename them does not increase (Vygotski, 1978). There is a specific interaction between linguistic and communicative skills, and cognitive functions. Improving management functions facilitates the processes of planning, organizing and strategic action also in the verbal area, while the development of language, especially the development of regulatory function, is conducive to cognitive development, especially categorization, inference and operation of abstract concepts. Language and communication skills are related to predicting mental states of other people; understanding false beliefs correlates with communication skills related to naming people in social relationships, coding and recoding the intended intention. As observed by Kielar-Turska (2012, pp. 85–86), understanding the mind is therefore closely related to the understanding of social situations, while gaining a higher level of cognitive complexity of statements enables more effective use of individual cognitive resources (see also Zull, 2006). The kindergarten, although it does not provide such ideal conditions for taking care of a child's pronunciation as a properly functioning family, has enormous advantages. First, it is a purposeful action program, creating intended situations that enable children to listen to correct and varied speech, ask questions, answer them, and even eliminate mistakes or impediments (Demel, 1998, p. 18; Szpotowicz & Szulc-Kurpaska, 2013). The kindergarten that is sensitive to the pupils takes into account their various experiences gained mainly in the family environment. The quality, type and richness of these experiences imply the cognitive, social and emotional functioning of an individual as a preschooler. The more often the children participated in positive interactions in their environment, observed respect for the norms of kindness, and the evaluation of others in terms of trust, acceptance and respect, the more willingly they would replicate these experiences in social contacts established in the institution (Michalak & Misiorna, 2006, p. 5). At preschool age, a young person acquires numerous skills of considerable importance for the learning process, acquiring a number of social and personal competences. The list of social competences designed by Anna Izabela Brzezińska (2005, p. 320) includes (a) the ability to express oneself in a large and small group; (b) listening to others and being heard; (c) undertaking joint tasks in various conditions; (d) establishing and maintaining contacts with new people; (e) making first friendships; and (f) noticing the needs of peers and adults. As part of personal competences, on the other hand, she also distinguishes increasing the sense of competence, self-confidence and self-worth; recognizing and expressing needs; noticing the similarities of one's own and other people's problems; and an increase in the sense of agency in solving problems. Therefore, as Brzezińska (2000, pp. 231–232) observes, during this period, the individual has to face such life tasks as:

- achieving physiological stability;
- constructing simple concepts relating to social and physical reality;
- learning to build emotional relationships with parents, siblings and others;
- shaping the ability to distinguish between good and evil and the beginnings of conscience;
- acquiring skills essential in games and activities;
- forming an attitude toward oneself as an evolving organism;
- learning to live with peers.

The aforementioned tasks, taking into account all areas of preschool activity, are also associated with the acquisition of cognitive, social, physical and emotional competences, which are the basis of a child's readiness to fulfill school duties. Intellectual maturity for school learning, however, determines the appropriate level of speech development (Brzezińska, 1987, p. 27), which can characterized by:

- a vocabulary that is diversified in terms of content and form;
- the presence of neologisms;
- learning elementary grammatical forms: conjugation, declension, adjectives, adverbs, pronouns;
- acquisition of the basic rules of syntax (with possible agrammatisms and syntax errors);
- operating in short sentences while simultaneously understanding various sentence structures in the speech of others;
- more varied speech development in girls than in boys;
- presence of situational speech, visible symptoms of social speech – questions, assessments, requests.

Therefore, when completing preschool education, a child covered by the support of speech development should (the core curriculum issued by the Ministry of National Education, 2009, pp. 18–19):

- address the interlocutor directly, try to speak correctly in terms of articulation, grammar, inflection and syntax;
- speak fluently, not too loudly, adjusting the tone of the voice to the situation;
- listen carefully, ask about incomprehensible facts and make longer statements about important matters;
- understand another person's needs and decisions in an understandable way.

A child's language skills remain one of the key elements in achieving educational success. Effective use of speech is also a condition for active and creative participation in the life of adult society (Vygotski, 1978).

A new model of upbringing has been developed in recent years; in it, teachers play a significant role in this model, alongside the children's parents.

School as an educational environment undoubtedly influences shaping the personality of an individual. According to Sowińska (2004, pp. 414–415), the school beginning period is connected with the need to overcome numerous barriers and changes of experience. The researcher provides the following list:

- expanding the social environment, both peer and adult, requiring control of more social space;
- a system of control resulting from personal relations with an adult in favor of institutional control related to rules, traditions, duties, which may cause a discrepancy between the expectations of the environment and individual needs;
- dominant activity: from play to learning already understood as an obligation;
- transition from ideational to intentional learning;
- the nature of institutional roles;
- gaining independence – for example traveling to school, managing finances;
- position of the child in relation to the parents – parents have to submit to the needs resulting from the role of the student, ceasing to be the only authority;
- peer contacts – relationships based on the performance of entrusted tasks force constant comparison and competition.

When a child attends an educational institution, the position in the class becomes extremely important for them, because the process of socialization takes place through the participation of the pupil in social life (Łobocki, 2006, p. 324). By establishing interpersonal relationships, the student assimilates the norms of functioning in society adopts the prevailing system of values and social roles played by individual members of the group. In late childhood, the importance and attractiveness of contacts with peers increases. Social contacts inside and outside the classroom become one of the most important topics of children's conversations and statements. Communication skills are further developed at school. The whole process consists in extending the scope of the roles of the sender and recipient of a message with sensitivity to messages addressed to the entire student team. Entering a peer group is one of the basic developmental tasks of late childhood, but it is also a social need of the children themselves. For the individual, peers become models of patterns of thinking, perception, evaluation and ways of communicating; that is why a positive assessment from colleagues is so important for a young person, which is also influenced by the correctness of expression and the form of communicating with the environment.

The development of a child's speech also involves the gradation of differentiation of linguistic means. Naturalness should be a feature of the teacher's language, which helps to develop spontaneity in speaking, in expressing feelings, thoughts, ideas and attitudes in the student. Correct pronunciation is a *conditio sine qua non* for anyone who intends to teach others. Correct, clear articulation is the basic requirement for language teachers. We must remember that a child in the resonance phase (this is what specialists call the period from birth to adolescence) takes over the phonetic features of the environment. The teacher's own phonetic balance will help her (or him) become aware of, for example, retardation elements appearing in a continuous utterance, disrupting its fluency. Auditory perception of phonetic phenomena, and their proper implementation, are extremely important in the process of communication. The teacher's diagnosis should be based on the auditory method. Parents sometimes do not know that their child speaks badly, and even if they perceive it incorrectly, they are helpless and do not know where to seek help. They must therefore receive appropriate guidance from teachers. Eye contact is also very important in the area of linguistic support. During didactic activities, the teacher should look at the listener as much as possible, because it stimulates the concentration of students, who then listen more carefully, observe the face, lips and tongue. A good teacher does not use words and forms that emphasize her (or his) domination. A teacher selects linguistic means in such a way as to maintain a dialogical relationship even when the partner is a small child. The role of the teacher is to support the pupils in their development, making them aware of their own capacity for creative expression by, for example, providing, analyzing and interpreting stimuli that come from the environment or selecting appropriate language games and games that stimulate or compensate for individual communication deficiencies. It is the teacher's duty to pay close attention to the child's linguistic competence in understanding and speaking, especially in the period leading up to the transition to new, difficult skills, for example reading and writing.

The student, according to the concept of humanistic pedagogy, is a central part of the teaching process around which all school activities are organized (Bernacka, 2001; see also Cornelius-White & Harbaugh, 2010). The tasks of the educational institution focus mainly on supporting the comprehensive development of the pupils, while the teacher, thanks to the triggering of specific behaviors, shapes their personality, along with the image in terms of linguistic, communication, cultural, moral and emotional competence (Burszta, 1985; McCombs, 2013). This is why Machowska-Gąsior (2010) draws a conclusion that one of the obligations the student must do is – in addition to taking part in the appropriate educational atmosphere – to meet a reflective master – a teacher equipped with a number of professional skills.

Mastering the systemic language skills at the phonological, morphological, syntactic, situational, social and pragmatic levels is a condition for understanding other people and being understood. The ability to use a language fluently is the foundation of school and later professional success, as the type of the language code largely determines the life possibilities of a person (Bernstein, 2000).

Speech therapy diagnosis

The methodology of speech therapy diagnosis should be understood as a set of specific principles and methods of diagnostic procedure, the purpose of which is to confirm or exclude the existence of speech therapy phenomena. Symptoms are determined from observation and interview data, language trials and tests. Depending on the results of supplementary psychological, orthodontic, phoniatric and audiological pedagogical tests, both a qualitative and a quantitative assessment of linguistic behavior is performed.

The term *diagnosis* (Greek: *diágnōsis* – recognition) is present in many scientific disciplines, but representatives of particular fields of knowledge understand and define this term differently (Parol, 1989). In Polish literature, Zbigniew Tarkowski (1993, p. 229) offers the following definition of speech therapy diagnosis: this is a recognition of the current state of affairs and its development trends based on the knowledge of human general regularities. Therefore, speech therapy diagnosis is a set of specific rules and research methods aimed at assessing the development of speech in a specific individual, along with determining the disturbances appearing during the communication process (Iskra & Szuchnik, 2005, pp. 271–302; see also Siedlaczek-Szwed, 2007, pp. 31–37).

Jacek Jarosław Błeszyński (2013, pp. 31–39), when postulating a departure from negative analysis in favor of a holistic and interdisciplinary diagnosis focused on the overall functioning of the examined person, lists the following diagnostic goals:

*   classification goals – classifying a phenomenon or state of affairs to a specific species or type;
*   typological goals – assigning an identified state of affairs to a given species or type;
*   genetic goals – examining the relation of the diagnosed phenomenon to one or several types, determining common features, assessing their intensity, indicating the specificity of the state of affairs;
*   prognostic-causal goals – searching for explanations, causal conditions of the perceived symptoms, determining the significance of pathological symptoms for a specific system, the degree of their harmfulness and the purposefulness of the phenomenon under consideration;
*   prognostic goals – presentation of the development of the phenomenon expected in the near future.

At the same time, following the observations of Jastrzębowska and Pelc-Pękala (2003, p. 403), speech therapy diagnosis (in the case of speech disorders) is primarily aimed at indicating/specifying:

- incorrectly articulated sounds and the way they are pronounced;
- reasons for incorrect implementation of sounds;
- the impact of disorders on the course of the interpersonal communication process;
- effects of incorrect articulation;
- primary and secondary symptoms of a speech impediment – type of speech disorder and its influence on the child's functioning in various areas.

S. Grabias (2012a, 2012b, p. 61) analyzes the model of diagnostic activities; in his opinion it should include the following two elements:

1 description – registration and description of states along with linguistic behavior of an individual and, primarily, testing of the interactive skills: motor skills, pronunciation, language, conceptual structures, implementation of the dialogue and realization of narrative statements.
2 interpretation – explanation of the observed states and behaviors based on general knowledge about a person, specialist knowledge (e.g. medical, psychological, pedagogical) and information obtained from the caregivers of the learner in respect to analysis of the results of specialized research, family history, differential diagnosis and case recognition.

The scheme for the diagnosis of phonological and articulation disorders was elaborated by Jastrzębowska and Pelc-Pękala (2003, pp. 404–405) and Czaplewska (2015, pp. 99–110). According to the researchers, it should take the following shape:

1 problem definition, that is, preliminary research, which includes:

- interview with particular emphasis on the child's psychomotor development, speech development, frequency and type of illnesses and the way of feeding in infancy;
- indicative speech research on the ability to establish verbal and non-verbal contact, formulating and expressing one's own thoughts, vocabulary, grammatical correctness of created messages, phonetic aspect of speech;
- observation – conducted during an indicative speech test;

2 selection of appropriate methods and tools of diagnosis for in-depth problem analysis;
3 effective application of diagnostic procedures adjusted to the age, psychophysical state of the examined person and the type of disorder;

4 systematic data collection aimed at supplementing the information with the opinions of other specialists (e.g. orthodontist, ENT specialist, phoniatrist, psychologist, neurologist);
5 information integration, reasoning and analysis;
6 processing the results of diagnosis and making the diagnosis;
7 formulating remedial recommendations;
8 providing the respondent with understandable and useful feedback.

Scheme of speech therapy diagnosis

In line with the current scientific cognition procedure, each diagnostic activity requires the completion of certain agreed stages (Table 2.1), which include:

1 posing the problem;
2 making a hypothesis;
3 verification of the hypothesis.

The proposed scheme is universal and can be used in the diagnosis of all speech disorders, which will be modified depending on the type of disorder.

At the first stage, the speech therapist collects information that is necessary to enable him/her to make a preliminary diagnosis in order to determine what the patient's problem is; the therapist conducts preliminary tests, which include interview, observation, indicative speech test and supplementary examinations. The interview is used to gather information on age; education; environment in which the patient lives; his/her interests, achievements, general course of development, including his/her speech; and presumed causes of the disorder or irregularities. The observation concerns general reactions and behavior of the respondent, with particular emphasis on the patient's verbal behavior. The indicative speech test is carried out during the conversation with the patient, where particular attention is paid to their verbal and nonverbal behavior and the attitude of these behaviors

Table 2.1 Scheme of speech therapy diagnosis

Definition of the problem	Formulating hypotheses	Verification of hypotheses
Initial examination	Basic research	Acceptance/rejection of hypotheses
• interview • observation • indicative speech test	• comprehension test • speaking test • reading and writing research	
Complementary examination	Specialized tests	

Source: Authors' own elaboration (based on the idea of Jastrzębowska & Pelc-Pękala, 2003).

toward each other. It is important to initially recognize the level of speech understanding, as not only the quantity but also the quality of speech is to be assessed. In addition, it should be initially assessed whether the examined person understands the commands and questions; is able to answer them; conducts a dialogue; and can tell stories. Additionally, attention is paid to whether verbal behavior and its level comply with the age norm.

Complementary tests, which should follow initial examination, may include the following forms of assessment, depending on the type of presumed dysfunction:

- examination of the condition and efficiency of the articulation apparatus;
- examination of respiratory functions;
- indicative hearing test;
- phonemic hearing test;
- auditory memory test;
- examination of the swallowing function;
- speech kinesthesia examination;
- praxia and gnosia testing;
- voice emission testing;
- testing fluency of speech and speech prosody (rhythm, melody, accent);
- indicative study of lateralization.

The aim of the second stage of speech therapy diagnosis is to accurately determine abnormalities in linguistic behavior that disturb or disrupt the communication process. The basic examination includes the general assessment of the patient's language skills, the assessment of the patient's reading and writing skills included, all of them to be carried out with the use of available tests or questionnaires. From the point of view of speech therapy, the most important thing is the assessment of systemic language proficiency and this is done by examining speech, both the patient's manner of speaking and his/her understanding. The study of speech involves the study of speaking in terms of phonetic, lexical, grammatical and expressive aspect. In addition, the study of speech understanding concerns the level of single words and focuses upon studying the understanding of activities, names of objects, phenomena and so on; the words describing spatial and temporal relations; and the patient's ability to understand grammatical (or syntactic) structures.

In addition, the assessment of linguistic situational skills will allow a speech therapist to determine whether the patient can adapt his/her statement in respect to the recipient, and/or to the communicative situation. Another form of assessment is the assessment of the patient's linguistic social efficiency necessary to determine whether the patient can adjust the statement to the social rank of the addressee, and thus to the communicative situation. Finally, the assessment of pragmatic linguistic skills is carried out; it determines whether the patient is able to achieve the initially intended goal of the statement.

On the basis of the data obtained from both the observation and the interview, followed by the results of the indicative speech test and those of supplementary and basic tests, the hypothesis about the type and cause of the disorder is formulated. In order to obtain more complete data, the patient can be referred for specialist examinations to a doctor, psychologist, educator or other specialists.

At the third stage, that is, the verification of hypotheses, the therapy program is established. It should be emphasized that the processes of diagnosis and speech therapy complement each other, because during the therapy, the accuracy of the previously made diagnosis has to be verified.

Phases of speech therapy

According to Rodak (2002, p. 11), the long process of effective diagnostic procedure begins in the moment of establishing an individual program of speech therapy that relates to a given patient. Speech disorder therapy is a complex of activities aimed at eliminating articulation abnormalities and reducing the effects of dysfunction in both adults and children. Its aim is to increase the intelligibility of statements (with substitutions), verbal aesthetics in the auditory and visual sphere (with deformations), but also to remove any defective elements that draw the attention of the audience (Sołtys-Chmielowicz, 2008, p. 77). Thus, the program of the therapeutic procedure, which can be modified during any of its consecutive phases (Grabias, 2010/2011, p. 32; see also Aram & Nation, 1980, pp. 159–170), includes areas such as:

I Therapy program framework:

1 Aims of speech therapy.
2 Strategies and methods of proceeding.
3 Organization of the procedure.

II Therapeutic management:

1 Organization of therapy stages and their evaluation; selection of resources and assistance.
2 Record keeping.
3 Verification of diagnostic hypotheses.
4 Modification of the program.

Anna Sołtys-Chmielowicz (2002, pp. 70–73; see also Matuga, 2004, pp. 267–281; Smidts et al., 2004, pp. 385–401; Stackhouse, 2006, pp. 15–35; Walker, 2009, pp. 339–358) distinguishes three stages of corrective work in the case of dyslalia:

1 preparatory stage – exercises to improve phonemic hearing and motor skills of speech organs;
2 the stage of developing the sound using various methods;

3 the recording stage, that is using the correct sounding sound in various situational contexts.

Another Polish researcher, Józef Surowaniec (1993, p. 101), suggests the activation of the following stages:

- a preparatory stage that assumes establishing contact with the patient and encouraging him to actively participate in the therapy;
- the stage of shaping the skills and habits of correctly pronouncing the phone calls previously carried out incorrectly;
- the stage of developing skills and habits of correct verbalization in every communication situation and place.

Within the correction of articulation disorders, Grażyna Jastrzębowska and Olga Pelc-Pękala (2003, pp. 410–412) propose the following stages:

1 the preparatory stage – a set of activities preceding the proper speech therapy work, which includes exercises to improve the articulation, respiratory, rhythmic and auditory organs;
2 the stage of proper speech therapy work – inducing the correct articulation of a disturbed phone in isolation;
3 the stage of recording the evoked sound, stabilizing it in controlled speech – consolidating the sound in isolation, syllables, words in all possible positions (onset, mid-voice, end-voice) and phonetic neighborhoods, two-word expressions, sentences, short texts;
4 the stage of automation of the evoked sound, its implementation in spontaneous speech – detachment from the awareness of the fact of pronunciation by consolidating kinesthetic-motor patterns and auditory self-control.

The individual therapeutic stages determining the order of the speech therapy procedure are illustrated by the lalometer scale by Elżbieta Sachajska (1992, pp. 47–49):

1 *I know how to pronounce the sound.*
2 *I can pronounce a sound.*
3 *I can pronounce a sound in syllables.*
4 *I can pronounce a sound at the beginning of a word next to a vowel.*
5 *I can pronounce a middle word next to a vowel.*
6 *I can pronounce a word ending next to a vowel.*
7 *I can pronounce a sound in a word in a consonantal group.*
8 *I can pronounce a sound in two words.*
9 *I can pronounce a sound in a sentence.*
10 *I can pronounce a sound while reading.*
11 *I can pronounce a sound while speaking from memory.*

12 *I can pronounce a sound while telling a text.*
13 *I can pronounce a sound when naming pictures.*
14 *I can pronounce a sound while differentiating sounds.*
15 *I can pronounce a sound while speaking freely in the speech therapy post.*
16 *I can pronounce a sound while speaking freely at home.*
17 *I can pronounce a sound while speaking freely at school.*
18 *I can always pronounce a sound when speaking freely.*

When planning and conducting speech therapy, it is necessary to make use of general didactic rules, such as (Demel, 1987, pp. 67–68):

- The principle of regularity – an established sequence of actions when teaching individual sounds; each practiced sound is subject to a certain scheme, that is the preparation of articulation organs; calling a sound in isolation; pronouncing it in a syllable; connecting with a vowel at the beginning, in the middle and at the end of a word; then with a consonant and so on. Only after mastering this sound, is it possible to move to the next sound.
- The principle of gradation of difficulty – starting corrective work with things that are easiest for a given individual and moving to more and more difficult elements.
- The principle of preservation – repeating the acquired skills until they become a habit.
- The principle of individualization – individual approach to each person regarding both the therapy program and the form of conducting classes.
- The principle of active and conscious participation – interest and mobilization of the patient to make an effort to eliminate the defect; developing a sense of the need for classes and active participation in them.

During articulation exercises, according to Grażyna Gunia (2011, pp. 81–82), the following rules apply:

1 Beginning with the sounds in the child's speech according to the natural stages of automation. The starting point for various degrees of opening of the speech organs are compact sounds (compact–compact-slit–slit).
2 The principle of phonetic oppositions, for example:

   - voiceless – voiced: /p/-/b/, /t/-/d/, /s/-/z/;
   - oral – nasal: /b/-/m/, /d/-/n/;
   - place of articulation, for example, bilabial – dental: /b/-/d/;
   - hard – soft: /p/-/p'/;
   - degree of closeness of speech organs: compact – slit.

3 The principle of shaping the three elementary systems of tongue mass: flat tongue, high tongue, high tongue in the front, middle and back parts, and the arrangement of the lips: rounded or flattened lips.

4 The principle of integrative and smooth functioning of the breathing, phonation and articulation apparatus, aimed at developing self-control of the movements of the speech organs during the production of phonic substance.

5 The principle of using knowledge in the field of articulation, acoustic, auditory and visual phonetics in exercises.

6 Selection of linguistic material with a preference for simple vocabulary, free from distortions or no sounds, adjusted to the patient's age and his/ her abilities. When recording articulation, the sound must appear in pronunciation, but not in writing.

The responsibilities any speech therapy requires from the person conducting the classes can be verbalized as follows: (a) providing the child with a sense of security, psychological comfort and trust in the speech therapist – giving attention, positive evaluation, focusing on what is good in the child; (b) marking the development, changes that have taken place, and not the lack of specific skills; (c) selecting working methods in terms of preferences and level of development; (d) shaping positive motivation to learn, self-confidence and the ability to overcome difficulties – gentle persuasion, approval, stimulating reinforcement, equivalent; (e) revealing pedagogical optimism – faith in the child's abilities, noticing the smallest successes; and, finally, (f) close cooperation with parents and teachers – involving them in the therapeutic process.

References

American Psychiatric Association. (2000). *Diagnostic and statistical manual of mental disorders*. APA.

Aram, D., & Nation, J. E. (1980). Preschool language disorders and subsequent language and academic difficulties. *Journal of Communication Disorders, 13*, 159–170.

Bernacka, D. (2001). *Od słowa do działania* [From word to action] (p. 11). Żak Academic Press.

Bernstein, B. (1971). Class, codes and control. *Theoretical studies towards a sociology of language (Vol. 1)*. Routledge and K. Paul.

Bernstein, B. (2000). *Pedagogy, symbolic control and identity: Theory, research, critique*. Rowman and Littlefield Publishers Inc.

Błachnio, K. (2001). *Vademecum logopedyczne. Dla studentów pedagogiki* [Speech therapy handbook. For students of pedagogy]. The UAM Press.

Błeszyński, J. J. (2013). Podejście pozytywne w diagnozie logopedycznej. Problem metatezy. In J. J. Błeszyński (Ed.), *Medycyna w logopedii. Terapia. Wspomaganie. Wsparcie. Trzy drogi – jeden cel* [Medicine in speech therapy. Therapy. Assistance. Support. Three ways – one goal] (pp. 31–39). Harmonia Universalis Publishing House.

Bokus, B. (1991). *Tworzenie opowiadań przez dzieci. O linii i polu narracji* [Creating stories by children. About the line and field of narration]. Energeia Publishing House.

Brzezińska, A. (1987). *Gotowość dziecka w wieku przedszkolnym do czytania i pisania* [Preschool child's readiness to read and write] (p. 27). The UAM Scientific Press.

Brzezińska, A. (2000). *Społeczna psychologia rozwoju* [Social psychology of development] (pp. 231–232). Scholar Scientific Press.

Brzezińska, A. I. (2005). *Psychologiczne portrety człowieka. Praktyczna psychologia rozwojowa* [Psychological portraits of a man. Practical developmental psychology] (p. 320). Gdańsk Psychological Press.

Burszta, W. (1985). Lingwistyka a etnologia [Linguistics and etnology]. In K. Zamiar (Ed.), *O kulturze i jej badaniu. Studia z filozofii kultury* [About culture and its research. Studies in the philosophy of culture] (p. 89). PWN.

Chiat, S. (2000). *Understanding children with language problems*. Cambridge Unviersity Press.

Cornelius-White, J., & Harbaugh, A. (2010). *Learner centered instruction*. Sage.

Czaplewska, E. (2015). Diagnoza zaburzeń rozwoju artykulacji [Diagnosis of articulation development disorders]. In E. Czaplewska, & S. Milewski (Eds.), *Diagnoza logopedyczna. Podręcznik akademicki* [Speech therapy diagnosis. Academic textbook] (pp. 99–110). Gdańsk Psychological Press.

Demel, G. (1987). *Elementy logopedii* [Elements of speech therapy] (pp. 67–68). School and Pedagogical Press.

Demel, G. (1998). *Minimum logopedyczne nauczyciela przedszkola Wydanie V* [Speech therapy minimum for a kindergarten teacher] (5th ed., p. 18). School and Pedagogical Press.

Demelowa, G. (1975). Źródła do biografii i bibliografii prac [Sources for the biography and bibliography of works]. *Logopedia* [Speech Therapy], *12*, 113.

Gałkowski, T. (1995). *Dziecko autystyczne w środowisku rodzinnym i szkolnym* [An autistic child in a family and school environment]. School and Pedagogical Press.

Gazzaniga, M., Ivry, R. B., & Mangum, G. R. (2002). *Cognitive neuroscience. The biology of the mind*. W. W. Norton & Co.

Grabias, S. (1997). Mowa i jej zaburzenia [Speech and its disorders]. *Audiofonologia* [Audiophonology], *10*, 2–30.

Grabias, S. (2000). Mowa i jej zaburzenia [Speech and its disorders]. *Logopedia* [Speech Therapy], *28*, 32.

Grabias, S. (2002). Perspektywy opisu zaburzeń mowy [Prospects for the description of speech disorders]. In S. Grabias (Ed.), *Zaburzenia mowy* [Speech disorders] (pp. 15–21). Maria Curie-Skłodowska Publishing House.

Grabias, S. (2010/2011). Logopedia – nauka o biologicznych uwarunkowaniach języka i zachowaniach językowych [Speech therapy – the study of biological determinants of language and linguistic behavior]. *Logopedia* [Speech Therapy], *39/40*, 20–22.

Grabias, S. (2012a). O ostrość refleksji naukowej. Przedmiot logopedii i procedury logopedycznego postępowania [On the sharpness of scientific reflection. The subject of speech therapy and speech therapy procedures]. In S. Milewski, & K. Kaczorowska-Bray (Eds.), *Logopedia. Wybrane aspekty historii, teorii i praktyki* [Speech therapy. Selected aspects of history, theory and practice] (p. 61). Harmonia Universalis.

Grabias, S. (2012b). Teoria zaburzeń mowy. Perspektywy badań, typologie zaburzeń, procedury postępowania logopedycznego [The theory of speech disorders. Research perspectives, typologies of disorders, speech therapy procedures]. In S. Grabias, & M. Kurkowski (Eds.), *Logopedia. Teoria zaburzeń mowy* [Speech therapy. The theory of speech disorders] (pp. 52–53). Uniwersity Maria Curie-Skłodowska Publishing House.

Grucza, F. (1983). *Zagadnienia metalingwistyki. Lingwistyka – jej przedmiot, lingwistyka stosowana* [Metalinguistics. Linguistics – its subject, applied linguistics]. PWN.

Gunia, G. (2011). Dyslalia. *Wprowadzenie do logopedii* [Introduction to speech therapy] (pp. 1–82). Impuls Publishing House.

Herzyk, A. (1992). *Afazja i mutyzm dziecięcy. Wybrane zagadnienia diagnozy i terapii* [Aphasia and childhood mutism. Selected issues of diagnosis and therapy]. Publishing House of the Polish Foundation of Speech Disorders.

Hughes, C., Graham, A., & Grayson, A. (2004). Executive functions in childhood: Development and disorder. In J. Oates, & A. Grayson (Eds.), *Cognitive and language development in children* (pp. 205–230). Oxford University Press.

Iskra, L., & Szuchnik, J. (2005). Diagnoza logopedyczna [Speech therapy diagnosis]. In T. Gałkowski, E. Szeląg, & G. Jastrzębowska (Eds.), *Podstawy neurologopedii. Podręcznik akademicki* [Fundamentals of neurologopedics. Academic textbook] (pp. 271–302). Opole University Press.

Jastrzębowska, G. (1999). Przedmiot, zakres zainteresowań i miejsce logopedii wśród innych nauk [Subject, scope of interests and place of speech therapy among other sciences]. In T. Gałkowski, & G. Jastrzębowska (Eds.), *Logopedia. Pytania i odpowiedzi. Podręcznik akademicki* [Speech therapy. Questions and answers. Academic textbook] (p. 241). Opole University Press.

Jastrzębowska, G. (2003). Przedmiot, zakres zainteresowań i miejsce logopedii wśród innych nauk [Subject, scope of interests and place of speech therapy among other sciences]. In T. Gałkowski, & G. Jastrzębowska (Eds.), *Logopedia. Pytania i odpowiedzi. Podręcznik akademicki: Interdyscyplinarne podstawy logopedii. Wydanie II ed. zmienione i poszerzone* [Speech therapy. Questions and answers. Academic textbook: Interdisciplinary fundamentals of speech therapy. 2nd edition changed and extended] (*Vol. 1*, p. 315). Opole University Press.

Jastrzębowska, G., & Pelc-Pękala, O. (2003). Diagnoza i terapia zaburzeń artykulacji (dyslalii). Logopedia. Pytania i odpowiedzi. Podręcznik akademicki: Zaburzenia komunikacji językowej u dzieci i osób dorosłych [Diagnosis and therapy of articulation disorders (dyslalia). Speech therapy. Questions and answers. Academic textbook: Language communication disorders in children and adults]. In T. Gałkowski, & G. Jastrzębowska (Eds.), *Interdyscyplinarne podstawy logopedii, Wydanie II zmienione i poszerzone* (*Vol. 2*, pp. 410–412). Opole University Press.

Kaczmarek, B. (1969). Jan Siestrzyński. *Logopedia* [Speech Therapy], *8*(9), 142–145.

Kaczmarek, B. (2001). Pozajęzykowe aspekty porozumiewania się [Non-linguistic aspects of communication]. In E. M. Minczakiewicz (Ed.), *Komunikacja – mowa – język w diagnozie i terapii zaburzeń rozwoju u dzieci i młodzieży niepełnosprawnej* [Communication – speech – language in the diagnosis and therapy of developmental disorders in children and adolescents with disabilities] (pp. 19–24). WSP Scientific Publishers.

Kaczmarek, L. (1982). O polskiej logopedii [On Polish speech therapy]. In J. Rieger, & M. Szymczak (Eds.), *Materiały konferencji naukowej Warszawa, 25 października 1978. Język polski i językoznawstwo polskie w sześćdziesięcioleciu niepodległości (1918–1978)* [Materials of the scientific conference Warsaw, October 25, 1978. Polish language and Polish linguistics in the 60th anniversary of independence (1918–1978)] (p. 146). National Institute Ossolińskich – Publishing House of the Polish Academy of Sciences.

Kaczmarek, L. (1983). Jan Baudouin de Courtenay – Prekursor polskiej logopedii [Jan Baudouin de Courtenay – Precursor of Polish speech therapy]. *Logopedia* [Speech Therapy], *14*(15), 5–13.

Kaczmarek, L. (1991). *Model opieki logopedycznej w Polsce (Projekt)* [Model of speech therapy care in Poland (project)] (p. 5). Gdańsk Association of Speech Therapists.

Kent, R. D. (Ed.). (2004). *The MIT encyclopedia of communication disorders*. Cambridge University Press.

Kielar-Turska, M. (2012). Sprawności językowe i komunikacyjne a inne funkcje psychiczne, Logopedia. Wybrane aspekty historii, teorii i praktyki [Language and communication skills and other mental functions, speech therapy. Selected aspects of history, theory and practice]. In S. Milewski, & K. Kaczorowska-Bray (Eds.), *Seria: Logopedia XXI wieku* [Series: 21st century speech therapy] (pp. 85–86). Harmonia Universalis Press.

Kiśniowska, M. (2001). Wkład Władysława Ołtuszewskiego w rozwój polskiej logopedii [Władysław Ołtuszewski's contribution to the development of Polish speech therapy]. In E. M. Minczakiewicz (Ed.), *Komunikacja – mowa – język w diagnozie i terapii zaburzeń rozwoju u dzieci i młodzieży niepełnosprawnej* [Communication – speech – language in the diagnosis and therapy of developmental disorders in children and adolescents with disabilities] (pp. 183–185). Scientific Publisher of the Pedagogical University in Cracow.

Kozłowska, K. (1998). *Wady wymowy możemy usunąć (Poradnik logopedyczny)* [We can remove speech impediments (Speech therapy guide)]. ZNP Pedagogical Publishers.

Kurkowski, Z. M. (2010). Specjalizacje logopedyczne [Speech therapy specializations]. *Biuletyn Logopedyczny* [Speech Therapy Bulletin], *1*(24), 77.

Lama, S. (Ed.). (1931). *Leksykon ilustrowany* [Illustrated lexicon] (pp. 1198–1199). The Trzaska, Ewert and Michalski Bookstores.

Łobocki, M. (2006). *Teoria wychowania w zarysie Wydanie III* [An outline of the theory of education] (3rd ed., p. 324). Impuls Publishing House.

Łuczyński, E. (2005). Mowa a język. Podstawy językowe neurologopedii [Speech and language. Linguistic basics of neurologopedics]. In T. Gałkowski, E. Szeląg, & G. Jastrzębowska (Eds.), *Podstawy neurologopedii. Podręcznik akademicki* [Basics of neurologopedics. Academic textbook] (pp. 38–40). Opole University Publishing House.

Matuga, J. M. (2004). Situated creative activity: The drawings and private speech of young children. *Creativity Research Journal, 16*(2–3), 267–281.

McCombs, B. L. (2013). The learner-centered model: From the vision to the future. In J. H. D. Cornelius-White, R. Motschnig-Pitrik, & M. Lux (Eds.), *Interdisciplinary applications of the person-centered approach* (pp. 83–113). Springer Science + Business Media. https://doi.org/10.1007/978-1-4614-7144-8_9.

MEN (Ministry of National Education). (2009). Podstawa programowa z komentarzami [Core curriculum with comments]. *Edukacja przedszkolna i wczesnoszkolna* [Pre-school and early school education] (*Vol. 1*, pp. 18–19). Ministry of National Education Press.

Michalak, R., & Misiorna, E. (2006). Gotowość, dojrzałość szkolna dziecka a dojrzałość instytucjonalna [Readiness, child's school maturity and institutional maturity]. In R. Michalak, & E. Misiorna (Eds.), *Konteksty gotowości szkolnej* [Contexts of school readiness] (p. 5). Methodological Center for Psychological and Pedagogical Assistance.

Minczakiewicz, E. M. (1997). *Mowa – Rozwój – Zaburzenia – Terapia* [Speech – Development – Disorders – Therapy] (pp. 10–12). WSP Scientific Press.

Minczakiewicz, E. M. (1998). *Początki i rozwój polskiej logopedii* [The beginnings and development of Polish speech therapy]. Educational Publishing House.

Ożdżyński, J., & Surowaniec, J. (2000). *Teoria i praktyka terminologii logopedycznej* (p. 33). Pedagogical Academy Scientific Press.

Parol, U. (1989). *Dziecko z niedokształceniem mowy. Diagnoza – analiza – terapia* [A child with speech impairment. Diagnosis – analysis – therapy]. School and Pedagogical Publishers.

Pinker, S. (2002). *The blank slate: The modern denial of human nature.* Viking.

Pollard, A. (2000). *Readings for reflective teaching.* Continuum.

Premack, D., & Woodruff, G. (1978). Does the chimpanzee have a theory of mind? *Behavioral and Brain Sciences*, 1(4), 515–526. https://doi.org/10.1017/S0140525X00076512.

Rakowska, A. (1992). *Rozwój systemu gramatycznego u dzieci głuchych* [Development of the grammatical system in deaf children]. WSP Scientific Press.

Rodak, H. (2002). *Terapia dziecka z wadą wymowy* [Therapy of a child with a speech impediment] (p. 11). Warsaw University Press.

Sachajska, E. (1992). *Uczymy poprawnej wymowy, Wydanie IV zmienione* [We teach correct pronunciation, 4th edition amended] (pp. 47–49). School and Pedagogical Publishers.

Siedlaczek- Szwed, A. (2003). Rola nauczyciela w procesie komunikowania [The role of the teacher in the process of communication]. In W. Szlufik, U. Ordon, A. Siedlaczek-Szwed, & E. Skoczylas-Krotla (Eds.), *Edukacja w jednoczącej się Europie. Wybrane aspekty* [Education in uniting Europe. Selected aspects] (p. 121). WSP Press.

Siedlaczek-Szwed, A. (2007). Speech defects in children with cleft palate in terms of ICD-10 classification. In A. Siedlaczek-Szwed (Ed.), *Pedagogika specjalna – wybrane problemy edukacyjno-wychowawcze* [Special education – selected educational problems] (pp. 31–37). Publishing House Stanislaw Podobiński Academy of Jan Długosz in Częstochowa.

Siedlaczek-Szwed, A. (2010). The importance of logopedic diagnosis in the formation and development of speaking. In A. Nelesovska (Ed.), *Primarni a preprimarni pedagogika v teorii, praxi a vyzkumu* [Primary and pre-primary pedagogy in theory, practice and research] (pp. 280–286). ALTYN Press.

Siedlaczek-Szwed, A., & Jałowiecka-Frania, A. (2016). The importance of family in children's speech development. In A. Žilova, A. Novotna, & M. V. Joseph (Eds.), *Research reflections on the current problems in society in the context of social work III* (pp. 119–125). International Scientific Board of Catholic Researchers and Teachers in Ireland.

Siedlaczek-Szwed, A., & Przybysz-Zaremba, M. (2018). Speech disorder among people with neurological diseases based on surveys conducted in Alzheimer's support center in association with Yava club Czestochowa. In Education and Educational Research, Science & Society Issue 3,4. Albena-Bulgaria. pp. 811–817.

Skorek, E. M. (2000). *Z logopedią na ty. Podręczny słownik logopedyczny* [Speech therapy and you. A handy speech therapy dictionary] (p. 94). Impuls Publishing House.

Skorny, Z. (1992). *Psychologia wychowawcza dla nauczycieli, Wydanie II* [Educational psychology for teachers] (2nd ed., p. 46). School and Pedagogical Publishing House.

Słodownik-Rycaj, E. (2000). *O mowie dziecka, czyli jak zapobiegać powstawaniu nieprawidłowości w jej rozwoju* [On a child's speech, or how to prevent abnormalities in its development] (pp. 76–78). Żak Academic Press.

Smidts, D. P., Jacobs, R., & Anderson, V. (2004). The object classification task for children (OCTC): A measure of concept generation and mental flexibility in early childhood. *Developmental Neuropsychology*, 26, 385–401.

Sołtys-Chmielowicz, A. (2002). Wady wymowy i ich korygowanie [Speech defects and their correction]. *Logopedia* [Speech Therapy], 31, 70–73.

Sołtys-Chmielowicz, A. (2008). *Zaburzenia artykulacji. Teoria i praktyka* [Articulation disorders. Theory and practice] (p. 77). Impuls Publishing House.

Sowińska, H. (2004). Próg szkolny w świetle współczesnej psychologii rozwoju [The school threshold in the light of contemporary development psychology]. In W. Ambrozik, & K. Przyszczypkowski (Eds.), *Uniwersytet. Społeczeństwo. Edukacja. Materiały konferencji naukowej z okazji X-lecia Wydziału Studiów Edukacyjnych Uniwersytetu im. Adama Mickiewicza, Poznań 13 – 14 października 2003 roku* [University.

Society. Education. Materials of the scientific conference on the occasion of the 10th anniversary of the Faculty of Educational Studies at the University of Adama Mickiewicza, Poznań, October 13–14, 2003] (pp. 414–415). UAM Scientific Press.

Stackhouse, J. (2006). Speech and spelling difficulties what to look for. In M. J. Snowing, & J. Stackhouse (Eds.), *Dyslexia, speech and language. A practitioner's handbook* (2nd ed., pp. 15–35). Wiley.

Styczek, I. (1983). *Logopedia, Wydanie IV* [Speech therapy] (4th ed., p. 17). PWN.

Surowaniec, J. (1993). Metodyka postępowania logopedycznego w przypadku dyslalii [Methodology of speech therapy in the case of dyslalia]. In T. Gałkowski, Z. Tarkowski, & T. Zaleski (Eds.), *Diagnoza i terapia zaburzeń mowy* [Diagnosis and therapy of speech disorders] (p. 101). Polish Educational Press.

Święch, E. (2001). Benedykt Dylewski jako twórca systemu opieki logopedycznej [Benedykt Dylewski as the creator of the speech therapy system]. In E. M. Minczakiewicz (Ed.), *Komunikacja – mowa – język w diagnozie i terapii zaburzeń rozwoju u dzieci i młodzieży niepełnosprawnej* [Communication – speech – language in the diagnosis and therapy of developmental disorders in children and adolescents with disabilities] (pp. 186–187). Cracow Pedagogical University Press.

Szpotowicz, M., & Szulc-Kurpaska, M. (2013). *Teaching English to young learners.* PWN.

Tarkowski, Z. (1993). Ocena rozwoju mowy dziecka [Assessment of the child's speech development]. In T. Gałkowski, Z. Tarkowski, & T. Zaleski (Eds.), *Diagnoza i terapia zaburzeń mowy* [Diagnosis and therapy of speech disorders] (p. 229). Maria Curie-Skłodowska Publishing House.

Tokarski, J. (Ed.). (1980). *Słownik wyrazów obcych* [Dictionary of foreign words] (p. 374). PWN.

Vygotsky, L. S. (1962). *Thought and language.* MIT Press. (Original work published in 1934.)

Vygotski, L. S. (1978). *Mind in society: The development of higher psychological processes* (14th ed.). Harvard University Press.

Walker, S. (2009). Sociometric stability and the behavioral correlates of peer acceptance in early childhood. *The Journal of Genetic Psychology, 170*(4), 339–358.

World Health Organization. (1992). *The classification of mental and behavioural disorders.* Clinical Description and Diagnostic Guidelines.

Żebrowska, M. (Ed.). (1979). *Psychologia rozwojowa dzieci I młodzieży, Wydanie IX* [Developmental psychology of children and adolescents] (9th ed.). PWN.

Zimbardo, P. G. (1999). *Psychologia i życie* [Psychology and life] (E. Czerniawska, Radzicki, J.,Łuczyński, J. Kowalczewska, J., Suchecki, J, Jaworska, A.. , trans, pp. 169–170). PWN.

Zull, J. (2006). *The art of changing the brain: Enriching the practice of teaching by exploring the practice of learning.* Stylus.

3 Pedagogical and speech therapy diagnosis

Exploration of selected cases

Pedagogical diagnosis – case studies

The chapter presents case studies of children diagnosed in terms of pedagogy. Case 1 (David) concerns the diagnosis of a boy in terms of his readiness to start primary school education (in terms of the first stage of education), and Case 2 (Kamil) concerns the diagnosis of a child with concentration disorders and a tendency to aggressive behavior. Both cases contain in-depth diagnostic material that covers the examined children, and also generally refers to their families; this additional material allows for a deeper understanding of the causes of the problem (i.e. the disorder) under study. The presented diagnostic material was collected with the use of several methods and tools and then subjected to a detailed analysis. The complete material presented here also contains a summary, conclusions and practical tips addressed to parents and teachers, which, put into practice, make it possible to minimize the children's disorders. This material is an excellent example for debuting teachers of early childhood education (or diagnosticians) from various countries, along with practitioners and students of pedagogy who intend to work with children in the future.

The diagnostic material refers to the core curriculum that is in force in Polish preschool (and/or school) institutions that prepare children for various school hardships and obligations under the so-called 'zero-class' preparation (i.e. various kindergarten-placed one-year-long activities before they begin their school education). It was collected with the consent of all parents of the surveyed children and the teachers interviewed. All personal data has been changed to prevent the identification of those involved in the investigated cases. People participating in the study voluntarily consented to participate in the diagnosis and ensured that they would not claim any rights to the published material.

Case 1 (David) – diagnosis of a child's readiness to start primary school education

A boy named David comes from a twin pregnancy. The diagnosis was made at the turn of October-November 2021, when David was age 6 years and 3 months. The following methods and tools were used: (a) interview with

DOI: 10.4324/9781003354758-4

the child's parents; (b) observation sheet of a 6-year-old child (Kwaśniewska & Żaba-Żabińska, 2015); (c) a diagnosis questionnaire and (d) a work card (Tomczak & Ziętara, 2009).

The interview with the boy's parents was conducted using a questionnaire consisting of 34 questions, designed by us before the beginning of the diagnosis. The questions concerned the boy's skills and competences in the areas of shoelace tying, the development of fine motor skills (plasticine figures molding, drawing straight lines, using scissors, arranging blocks and creating buildings from them, writing and proper use of a writing tool, etc.) and gross motor skills (jumping on one leg, on both legs, etc.) along with intellectual and social development.

The observation sheet for the developmental traits of a 6-year-old child included physical, mental and socio-emotional development (Kwaśniewska & Żaba-Żabińska, 2015).

The diagnosis questionnaire included boy characteristics, communication area, phonemic hearing development, reading, writing, motor sphere, visual perception, orientation and thought processes (Tomczak & Ziętara, 2009).

The study of the physical sphere included four tasks related to checking the developmental level of fine and gross motor skills and determining lateralization. The study of the mental sphere included 34 tasks, and that of the socio-moral sphere – 12 tasks (Kwaśniewska & Żaba-Żabińska, 2015).

General characteristics of the boy and his family

The boy comes from a complete family, of the type classified as an average family (cf. the family classification developed by Kawula, 2005). The family consists of mom, dad and three children: a girl (9 years old), David (6 years and 3 months) and his twin brother Piotr. Their father has a secondary education and works as a policeman. Their mother is currently a second-year student of full-time pedagogical studies at one of the public universities in Poland. She does not work professionally; she deals with raising children and running the house. There is good understanding between the parents, but the decisive person seems to be the mother; she makes all the decisions related to the rearing of children, their education and even the housing conditions of the family. In the school environment, the boy's mother is perceived as a conflict person; she often complains to the school headmaster and reports her dissatisfaction to the teacher for various reasons, often trivial. The family's living conditions are very good.

David comes from a twin pregnancy which was in danger. He and his brother were born in the 28th week of pregnancy, each receiving seven points on the Apgar scale. After his birth, David stayed in the hospital for almost three months. He underwent sepsis, second-degree strokes and first- and second-degree retinopathy. During the first year of his life, he was under the supervision of ophthalmology, audiology, neonatal pathology, neurology, cardiology and urology clinics. Due to the increased muscle tension, he was rehabilitated for a year. Up to about 4 years of age he suffered from auditory and tactile hypersensitivity. In his early childhood, David had pneumonia, bronchitis and pharyngitis. During the course of the study, the boy attended the 'zero' grade of a primary school located near his residence. David is a cheerful boy, friendly toward newly met people. In the classroom, he willingly responds to the questions asked; he enjoys it when he manages to give the correct answer or when he is praised by the teacher. The boy willingly carries out the teacher's instructions and understands them, but the time taken to execute the tasks is much longer than that of his peers. David willingly participates in games and physical exercises. He is a cheerful and at the same time 'energetic' child. He adheres to the standards set by the group. When expected, he waits for his turn without any problems. He cares about cleanliness around him.

Diagnosis of school readiness – analysis of the material

The interview with the boy's parents shows that the child is physically fit; the only difficulty in this respect is skipping rope (the child is unable to perform this activity). The boy is very good at art and manual work. He likes to cut out with scissors and/or mold figures with plasticine. He has a good spatial orientation. He likes games such as 'find ten differences in the picture' and 'arrange puzzles'. With help, David is solving a puzzle consisting of 120 pieces. There is no problem in dealing with peers; he takes care of order in his environment. He obeys his parents, but when they direct more than one command, he only obeys the command he hears first. He is able to button the buttons, but he cannot tie the laces. David does not pronounce all sounds correctly, but he has no problem expressing himself in full sentences and building a sentence correctly.

David's observation sheet of developmental traits shows that he achieved a high level in terms of his physical development. And, in terms of mental (intellectual) development, most of the indicated features are at a high level. At the average level, the following features were noted: the correct articulation of sounds, phonemic hearing, recognition and naming of letters and the reproduction of an indicated pattern. His ability to read words, however, is at a low level. In terms of socio-emotional development, all of the indicated features have reached a high level; however, in terms of:

> communication, the boy was found to have speech impediments in the following areas: faulty articulation of sounds: /ʃ/, /ž/, /tʃ/, /d͡ʒ/, /r/, /ɕ/, /t͡ɕ/, /ź/; otherwise the stylistic and grammatical forms are correct; the vocabulary is at an average level, within the age norm. In order to minimize the indicated defect, the boy attends speech therapy classes.
> phonemic hearing, the boy repeats all vowels and consonants except the following: /r/, /rz/, /dʃ/, /ʃ/, /tʃ/. He repeats incorrectly x/x/, /bʃ/, /fʃ/, which results from a speech impediment diagnosed by a speech therapist.

The boy correctly repeats words related to oppositional sounds. He repeats simple words (except for sounds related to a speech impediment). He correctly repeats words that make no sense. He differentiates between the sounds in the initials, but does not distinguish between the sounds in the middle and in the final position.

reading, the boy knows the basic handwritten and printed letters; he, however, has a problem with letters such as: /p/, /g/, /h/, /ł/, /r/, /w/, /y/, /ą/, /ę/, /ć/, /ń/, /ś/, /ź/, /cz/, /sz/, /dz/, /dż/, /dź/, /ó/, /ż/, /rz/, /ch/. David can spell a word or a simple sentence indicated by the teacher, but he has problems with synthesizing them.

writing, the boy tries to write on his own. He holds the writing tool properly. He tries to reproduce the letters according to the pattern, but he does not always manage to do so.

the motor sphere, the boy's movements are smooth, quick and energetic. As for his dexterity, David draws a picture taking into account the details. He can present a human figure with great accuracy. He cuts straight-line pieces fairly accurately but has difficulty when cutting round-shaped pieces. He sticks the right elements in the right places, but he does that in an uneven, a bit sloppy manner. He can't tie shoelaces. He carelessly draws along the trail. In terms of lateralization, he is right-side dominant and the dominant ones are: eye, hand and right leg.

visual perception, the boy is accurate in perceiving differences and looking for similarities; he differentiates and names basic geometric figures; he also knows all the basic colors but mostly associates them with a known object.

orientation, the boy knows and names all parts of the body correctly; he also correctly identifies directions and names spatial relations; he understands the concepts of position and direction (*further, closer, up, down, right*, etc.); he understands the concepts of relations (*less, greater, equal; shorter, longer,* etc.); he knows the automated sequences (he knows the days of the week and lists them one by one, similar to the seasons, but has problems with naming, listing and associating the names of the months).

thought processes, the boy arranges a picture story correctly, talking about the details presented in the pictures and showing the correct way of thinking. He likes to tell fairy tales and create his own ending. He names sets correctly; he does it quickly and efficiently. He combines individual elements into sets, which he also classifies correctly.

The analysis of the observation sheet to assess school readiness (Kwaśniewska & Żaba-Żabińska, 2015) shows that as far as each of the three developmental spheres is concerned (physical, mental and socio-emotional), David is classified in the area indicating a high level of school readiness (120 points). (Score ranges for each readiness level are high level: 144–109 points; average level: 108–73 points; low level: below 73 points.) For physical development he scored 19 points (for this sphere of development the point range is 22–17 points); for mental development, 71 points (for this sphere of development the point range is 90–68 points); and for socio-emotional development, 30 points (for this sphere of development, the point range is 32–24 points).

Summary, conclusions and tips

David is a physically fit, energetic boy who likes to play and run. He is willing to take actions, even those whose effects are recognized as not always correct. He has a high level of physical development, he has difficulties in tearing paper, he is not good at skipping rope and is unable to lace his shoes. In terms of mental development, David reached a high level, but some areas (features) still require improvement, help and support.

David distorts the shapes of letters and geometric figures; he confuses letters; he also has problem with syntheses of read words and simple statements.

David is completely unsuccessful in voting words; he does not make words from letters; he also does not make sentences out of words; he does not read; he does not follow simple commands given in a modern foreign language; he does not execute commands when more than one is given; he cannot name the capital of Poland; he does not know the names of the months.

In terms of socio-emotional development, David has reached a high level of readiness, but nevertheless he shows anxiety and withdrawal, especially in situations where he has problems.

The presented pedagogical diagnosis shows that the boy is ready to start school education, but for it (to proceed without major problems) David's parents, in cooperation with specialists, should begin speech therapy now. Tips and recommendations for parents follow. It seems the parents should:

- continue speech therapy in a specialist office and perform exercises indicated by a specialist at home;
- read a lot and talk to the child so that his vocabulary is constantly enriched;
- undertake fun and exercises related to reading and writing, with the analysis and synthesis of words, nursery rhymes and chants, which will help one remember the names of the months and events that take place in each month;
- undertake exercises consisting in tearing out paper, cutting out shapes of geometric figures;
- undertake exercises and movement games with the use of a skipping rope;
- practice lacing shoes, for example creating a 'dummy' shoe from a cardboard box with a threaded shoelace and hanging it on the wall so that David can come up and tie the shoe at any time;
- take actions related to overcoming David's shyness; build in him a sense of self-confidence and by everyday contact with each other, joint

conversations and games, supplement and enrich general knowledge about the surrounding world;

- be in direct contact with teachers and other specialists working with the child.

Case 2 (Kamil) – pedagogical diagnosis of a child with concentration disorders and a tendency to aggressive behavior

The diagnosed child, a boy named Kamil, is a first-grade primary school learner. The diagnosis was made at the turn of November and December 2021. The following methods and tools were used: observation sheet; interview with the boy's mother; interview with the boy's teacher; conversation with the boy; worksheets (Tomczak & Ziętara, 2009) and analysis of documentation from a psychological and pedagogical counseling center (the opinion given to the boy at the request of the parent was analyzed).

General characteristics of the boy and his family

Kamil was born as the third child in the family (he still has a sister and a brother). At the time of the diagnosis, Kamil was a first-grade student in primary school. The family consists of five people: mother, stepfather and three children. The mother has a basic education and has never worked professionally – she deals with raising children and running the house. The family lives in a single-family house in the countryside.

Kamil is a cheerful, independent and active, but undisciplined, boy. He is willing to take action, but rarely completes it. His attention is short-lived. He easily establishes contacts with the environment and willingly collaborates in a group. Although Kamil is interested in football, he spends most of his free time watching fairy tales on TV and – what his mother particularly dislikes – playing computer games. Both of these last two activities take him more than four hours a day. Besides that, Kamil also has unlimited access to the internet on a mobile phone. Kamil eats regular meals (breakfast, lunch, dinner), but they are not always wholesome. Sweet products dominate, such as chocolate bars, crisps, and for breakfast or dinner he drinks cocoa or sweet drinks. Kamil often suffers from pneumonia. The boy has no responsibilities at home. The people in the family who devote the most time to Kamil are his grandmother and his cousin; they help him with his homework and often do his homework for him.

Kamil's attitude to school and education

Kamil does not show much interest in learning – as he does not like going to school, sitting at a desk and writing, he is often reprimanded by the teacher. But he shows great interest in different forms of fun and art activities that take place during the lessons.

Kamil willingly cooperates with the group, but his goal is to dominate it. He hardly accepts the fact that – when in school – he should submit himself to the established rules and norms.

The teacher's opinion shows that Kamil is very easily distracted during the lessons ('even several times in one lesson'). Distracting stimuli are *noises coming from behind a window, corridor or behind a wall, a flying insect, a chair being rattled by another child, an object that falls off a bench, etc.* (teacher's statement).

Kamil gets tired sitting at the bench – he is waiting impatiently for a break, during which, as his teacher relates – *he runs, screams, jumps, and sometimes plays with his friends, but only with the chosen ones.* When he fails, he rebels; he is aggressive, and has no control over his emotions and behavior. On the other hand, when he experiences success, he [...] *draws attention to himself, is happy, communicates to everyone about his success* (teacher's statement).

Kamil's behavior disorders are mostly revealed in relations with his peers, especially in situations where he experiences opposition from them. Then conflicts are resolved with the use of force; he kicks, punches, clenches his jaw, tugs and spits. Similar behaviors also occur during lessons, especially when the boy can no longer remain attentive. He rocks a lot in the chair, walks under the desk, hits the desk with his fists and makes strange noises, for example *buuuuuuuuu* or *meeeeeeee*, and so on; he also exclaims single difficult-to-follow words, rolls on the floor, runs around the classroom, shakes his head strongly, kicks the furniture or – what has been noticed by one of the authors of the book – *makes bubbles out of his saliva.*

Pedagogical diagnosis

A questionnaire with worksheets (Tomczak & Ziętara, 2009) was used in Kamil's pedagogical diagnosis. The following areas were analyzed: communication, phonemic hearing, the skills of reading and writing (separately), Kamil's motor sphere, visual perception, orientation and his thought processes.

Communication: the boy's speech is spontaneous. The statements are simple; the stylistic and grammatical forms are incorrect. The vocabulary is poor and the thought resource is chaotic, with numerous off-topic interjections. The boy also communicates with the environment by means of gestures and facial expressions. The boy's speech is characterized by faulty articulation of sounds, lisp and rotacism (there is an incorrect pronunciation of the /r/ sound). The boy understands simple questions and commands.

Phonemic hearing:

- repeating vowels: /a/, /e/, /i/, /o/, /u/, /y/ – Kamil pronounces individual vowels correctly, but he cannot repeat the whole sequence;
- repeating diphthongs: /ao/, /ou/, /ui/, /io/, /ue/ – Kamil pronounces single sequences correctly but cannot repeat three sequences in a row, for example /ae/-/io/-/ou/ and/or triphthongs /aou/-/ioe/;

- repeating consonants: Kamil pronounces the sounds /m/, /d/, /n/ correctly, but he has problems with the pronunciation of the sound /r/. When pronouncing the plosives /p/ and /b/, he cannot hear the difference. There is a lisp when pronouncing the cluster /psh/. The boy pronounces the /ml/ sound clusters correctly;
- repeating and differentiating oppositional sounds: Kamil repeats correctly *a pill – a hill, a rat – red, three – a tree.* During pronunciation, the differences in the following words are invisible: *sitting – setting.* In the words *pin – bin –* the sound /p/ is pronounced like /b/;
- repeating simple words: Kamil pronounces the following words correctly: *cat, forest, pencil, friend, Monday,* but he reveals difficulties in speaking words in which the consonant /r/ appears, for example *a radiator;*
- repeating nonsense words: *mod, kemod* – pronounces the sound /d/ like /t/; the words *narab,* or *retumok* – are pronounced incorrectly;
- listening to different sounds: Kamil correctly differentiated between the following pairs of words: *cat – car, roll – room, peel – bit, shop – shot, concert – cancer.*

Auditory analysis and synthesis:

1   word analysis of the sentence:

- *Tom eats ice cream* – correct word analysis;
- *Betty has a new bike* – Kamil combines the word *has* and the phrase *a new bike*; there is a lisp;
- *On the desk there is a lamp and a glass of milk* – in the word *there* Kamil does not say the sounds correctly, and in the phrase *of milk* the correct pronunciation cannot be heard.

2   syllable analysis of the word:

- *seal, domino, lamp* – correct syllable analysis;
- the boy pronounces the word *chess* as /tchi:z/;
- in the word *tomatoes* the consonant /m/ is said as /v/;
- deep lisp is visible in the word *hypermarket.*

3   voice analysis of the word:

- in the word *rose* – Kamil did not say the diphthong /ou/ correctly;
- in the word *soap*, he left the end of the word unsaid, saying /sou/;
- the word *notebook* was said as /nobuk/.

4   highlighting sounds in words:

- in the initials of the words *shoe, milk* – he distinguished the sounds correctly; the word *artist* was said as /a:tizt/;
- in the finals of the words *wasp, night, summer* – he cannot distinguish the sounds;

- in the middles of the words *night, Eve* – he could not indicate the sounds.

5   aural identification of the sound in words:

- in the word *picture* – instead of /p/, Kamil said /b/; he correctly identified the sounds of the words *mom, pop*.

Reading: Kamil knows basic printed and handwritten letters, although he had problems pointing to the printed letter /I/. He also had problems naming the printed letter /y/. He can form a simple sentence out of a mess and read it. He is also eager to start working with the text, but while reading it, he produces a number of uncontrolled arm and leg mimic movements. He quickly shows signs of fatigue; he complains, sighs, yawns, stretches.

Kamil recognizes the letters, reads the first letters and syllables, and votes them aloud. But he has problems with their synthesis (connection), for example, he interpreted the word *juice* as *joy*, the word *poppy* as *poppies*, the word *source* as *saucer*, the word *fox* as *box* or *foxes*, and the word *fate* as *rate*.

Kamil understands simple commands and short texts. While reading, he skips the letters and guesses the end of the word. The text read by him is often incomprehensible to the listener due to speech impediments.

Writing: Kamil correctly writes down handwritten letters in his notebook. He starts his work willingly. The writing tool is held in the left hand, but the orientation (fingers, wrist, arm) is incorrect. While writing, he takes the wrong posture: he twists his head, props himself up, lies down on the bench, and there are also many assisting movements of the whole body. He shows signs of fatigue, such as complaining, sighing, stretching, yawning. When writing, he dictates himself in an undertone. He often requires the repetition of a dictated text.

The pace of writing is normal, but Kamil slows down when the task is carried out for a long time. The graphic form of the letter is mixed, the slope is variable, the letters are wide, angular. The boy adheres to writing in ruled lines, but the aesthetics of the handwriting is not the best – there are corrections, the writing is not very careful and he is chaotic in running the notebook.

Motor sphere: Kamil is an energetic boy; his movements are efficient, but his small motor skills are not properly developed. Kamil holds a crayon correctly, but his written works are unsightly and carelessly done. He colors willingly, with interest, relatively accurately, and tries not to go beyond the contours. Unfortunately, he does not pay attention to the storage of his works. They are sloppy, creased and the corners are bent.

Kamil has problems with cutting, especially when it comes to small and complicated elements. It is also difficult for Kamil to stick small elements. He is great at drawing along lines; he adheres to the lines and he is eager to do this kind of work.

Visual perception: his visual perception is developed properly. Plasticine products are colorful, multicolored, well planned. Compared to the works made by other children, his works are distinguished by precision and ingenuity. In terms of naming and distinguishing between geometric figures, Kamil knows only some of them, such as *a circle* and *a rectangle*. However, he has trouble distinguishing between *a square* and *a triangle*. He distinguishes colors and indicates differences between pictures, and also quickly and efficiently finds similarities in pictures. He remembers a lot of details and easily replaces the elements in the picture.

Orientation: Kamil knows the basic parts of the body, such as *head, arms, legs, abdomen, eye, nose, ear, fingers*. The problem arises when he has to differentiate between *a foot* and *a heel*. The boy correctly sets directions when asked questions about the pictures in question. He understands position and direction concepts such as *What's next?, Closer?, Up?, Bottom?, Right, Left, Above, On, Below, In front of, Behind*. He also understands relationship concepts, for example *Who is the tallest? Who is the lowest? Where is the most ice cream? Where is the least ice cream? Which balloon is the biggest? Which balloon is the smallest?*

He can easily indicate relations in a drawing. Kamil knows the names of individual days, but is unable to list them chronologically. He has problems with the names of the months – he lists the first three months, that is *January, February* and *March*, and then adds the names of weekdays, such as *Sunday* or *Thursday*. He knows the seasons and can list them in the correct order.

Thought processes: cause–effect thinking was diagnosed on the basis of picture stories. The assigned tasks were carried out in groups. When working in a group, Kamil showed no difficulties with the exercises the group was requested to do. Problems occurred when the task was performed individually. As for the concepts of generalization and collection, Kamil had no problems. He named the individual collections correctly.

Diagnosis of the boy's individual developmental and educational needs, and his psychophysical abilities

The diagnosis of the child's (a) individual developmental and educational needs along with his (b) psychophysical abilities and (c) the description of the mechanisms explaining the child's functioning in relation to a specific problem was carried out on the basis of the analysis of the opinion issued by a psychological and pedagogical counseling center.

Kamil has been under the care of the clinic since 2014. He was diagnosed for the purpose of postponing compulsory education. In 2017, he was diagnosed again at the mother's request due to educational and behavioral difficulties. He was then consulted by an expert.

The boy's psychological diagnosis shows that the overall cognitive performance is below average and shows features of dissonance. The boy's strength has been found to be the ability to analyze visually perceived material. Kamil lacks general information about the world, but he is familiar with the expected norms and forms of social behavior. His logical and abstract thinking function at an average level. As for his arithmetic reasoning, along with the ability to define concepts and perceptiveness, both his arithmetic reasoning and the ability to define are developed at a low level. Kamil has great difficulties in building a definition of concepts and phenomena. The functioning of eye-hand coordination and the ability to learn on nonverbal material are clearly reduced. In the course of perceptual-motor functions, there are disturbances in both auditory and visual perception. Left homogeneous lateralization was established.

In turn, the partial pedagogical diagnosis shows that Kamil knows the primary and derivative colors, and geometric figures. He recognizes and names objects from the closest social and natural environment. He knows the seasons and their characteristic features. He cannot list the days of the week in sequence. He notices cause and effect threads and arranges picture stories correctly. He is able to count to 13, but does not recognize digits correctly. Low graphomotor efficiency was found.

In contact with peers and adults, Kamil is nice and very open. He works at a fast pace, being sketchy and with little insight. He requires constant confirmation of the performed tasks. There are visible great difficulties with maintaining attention on the task at hand. He also betrays problems with motivation to mental effort. There is visible excessive mobility and infantility of the reaction.

Based on the psychological and pedagogical diagnosis, it is concluded that Kamil's educational difficulties and his problems with concentration and memory may result from a reduced level of cognitive development and certain perceptual disturbances. Educational problems also include the boy's functioning, unfixed educational material and variable (often drastically reduced) motivation to learn. It is recommended to adjust the educational requirements to Kamil's cognitive and perceptive abilities and to cover him with didactic-compensatory and corrective-compensatory classes at the school.

Practical tips for working with Kamil, aimed at teachers

- adapting educational requirements to the abilities and needs of the learner through the use of appropriate principles, methods, forms and didactic means;
- individualization of the educational process by, among others: assistance in selecting the most important content to be mastered; providing support in the logical ordering of facts, frequent recall and consolidation of educational content; directing Kamil's attention; preventing periods of distraction; performing tasks with the help of the teacher; using clearly formulated questions and instructions;
- well-designed and reasonable work to improve Kamil's auditory perception;
- psychological and pedagogical assistance at school (corrective and compensatory classes to improve deficit functions, didactic and compensatory classes aimed at recalling and consolidating educational material);

- appreciating the boy's commitment to the mastery of the educational material;
- consistent adherence to school rules and regulations;
- rewarding the boy for appropriate behavior and reactions;
- frequent contacts with the boy's parents to exchange information about his current progress and to provide guidance for working with the boy at home.

Practical tips for working with Kamil, aimed at his parents

- frequent contact with the boy's teacher to monitor his educational process;
- systematic help in mastering the current material;
- stimulating the boy's potential by means of stimulating cognitive curiosity, developing interests, providing educational materials, and so on;
- conducting exercises to improve memory and concentration;
- in the case of persistent problems, periodic meetings with a psychologist at the clinic are recommended.

Summary, conclusions, recommendations and suggestions
for exercises to improve disturbed areas

Kamil is a cheerful and very brave, but not fully disciplined, child. He is characterized by hyperactivity and a short attention span. He willingly cooperates with the group, but has problems adjusting to the rules prevailing in the team. He willingly performs assigned tasks, but rarely completes them. Recommendations: consistency in observing the rules and norms prevailing at school and in other places of common coexistence; shaping discipline and applying an appropriate upbringing system, for example by rewarding and punishing. It is also recommended to apply appropriate exercises in the field of coping with emotions (suggestions for exercises and games are provided in Chapter 5). The method of conducting classes is also important. It should be varied and reduce the child's distraction. Help from a teaching assistant (or support teacher) is desirable.

The analysis of the diagnostic material concerning phonemic hearing shows that the boy knows vowels and consonants and pronounces them correctly when they are expected to be produced separately. However, he has a problem with longer sequences. He does not pronounce the /r/ sounds; he does not distinguish the sounds in the voice middles and finals. He cannot indicate the sounds in the second, third and fourth place in the spoken word. Recommendations: participation in corrective and compensatory classes are recommended to improve Kamil's disturbed functions. It is also recommended that parents cooperate with the school to prepare them for working with and supporting Kamil in his disturbed areas of functioning.

Kamil knows written letters, reads them aloud, can spell a read word and a simple sentence. He reads the first letters and guesses the end of a word/sentence. Kamil does not understand what has been read. Recommendations: the teaching content and the method of conducting classes should be adapted to the needs and abilities of the child. Kamil should participate in extracurricular activities and systematically carry out exercises improving learning to read both at school and at home. (Suggestions for exercises are found in Chapter 5.)

Kamil writes with his left hand, observing the spelling in the ruled lines. The graphic form of the letters is mixed; the writing is legible but not very careful. The way the notebook is kept is careless. Recommendations: Kamil's participation in exercises to develop the quality and aesthetics of the hand-writing (see Chapter 5 for exercise suggestions) is necessary. Exercises should be carried out both at school and at home.

Kamil's movements are agile but not always coordinated. Manual dexterity in the scope of the low motor activity is within the normal range. Recommendations: exercises to improve fine motor skills (suggestions for exercises can be found in Chapter 5).

Although there are frequent inclusions that testify to mental chaos, the boy's speech is spontaneous, and he formulates simple sentences. There appears faulty articulation of sounds, lisp and rotacism. Recommendations: it is advisable to work with a speech therapist and systematically use the exercises recommended by the therapist (suggestions for exercises can be found in Chapter 5). On the part of parents, it is necessary to support the child in the implementation of these exercises and in the logical ordering of facts, selecting the most important content.

The development of visual perception is normal. Kamil's plasticine creations are accurate and colorful. He knows the basic geometric shapes but has trouble distinguishing between a triangle and a square. He does great at arranging pictures from parts, remembering, distinguishing colors, noticing differences and finding similarities. Recommendations: it is advisable to stimulate the boy's curiosity of the world, develop his interests, enrich his knowledge, for example through the use of various and complex teaching aids.

Spatial orientation is developed correctly. Kamil has problems listing the names of the months; he is unable to name the days of the week one by one. Recommendations: the use of didactic exercises improving and consolidating the educational content is advised.

Kamil's thought processes are characterized by a reduced level of cognitive development. Recommendations: covering the boy with didactic and compensatory classes aimed at systematizing and consolidating the material processed. It is also necessary to keep frequent contact between Kamil's parents and his teacher, who should help them collect the necessary information about their child and show the right way to further educational work.

Summing up the material from Kamil's pedagogical diagnosis, it should be pointed out that the proposed help and support should have a holistic dimension. The proposed steps and/or activities should relate to the work and development of all areas of the child, with particular emphasis on improving the areas with detected disorders. In this case, the systematic cooperation of Kamil's parents with the school, especially the teachers conducting the classes the boy attends, and the support of appropriate specialists are extremely important.

Diagnoses in speech therapy – exploration of selected cases

The process of speech therapy diagnosis may a take longer period of time, if the speech therapist wants to support her/his opinion with the opinions of other specialists – an orthodontist, an ENT specialist, a phoniatrist, a psychologist or a neurologist – to confirm or rule out the malfunction of, for example, physiological hearing, the presence of some defects of anatomical articulators or organic disorders causing difficulties related to praxia and pandering. There are many methods and techniques of speech therapy diagnostics:

- methods of observation (e.g. observation sheet);
- exploratory methods (e.g. questionnaire, interview);
- diagnostic examination (e.g. articulation examination);
- test methods (e.g. lateralization test);
- case studies;
- analysis of the results of activities (e.g. school results);
- instrumental methods (e.g. articulation).

At this stage, the speech therapist integrates all the collected information, analyzes it and draws conclusions, which allows the therapist to determine the causes of the disorder and make a diagnosis, and then to decide on the type of speech therapy. The diagnostic procedure presented in Chapter 2 should help speech therapists make an accurate diagnosis.

For many authors, the varieties of speech therapy terminology (phoniatric, pedagogical, psychological, etc.) are used to denote the same concepts; for example, movement aphasia, motor aphasia, Broc's aphasia, central motor aphasia, cortical motor aphasia, kinetic motor aphasia, expressive aphasia and so on refer to the same disorder.

Case 3 (Izabela) – child with motor dysphasia

Izabela, aged 4 years and 1 month, comes from a Polish family permanently living in England. Physically, the patient is developed properly; she began to stutter in the third month of her life and babble three months later (in the sixth month). Her first words appeared around the first year of life. The child hears (indicative hearing test). She makes quick contact with a speech therapist and is focused. She is willing to perform the tasks requested of her.

Izabela's orientation-cognitive skills were assessed on the basis of the perception of cause-and-effect relationships. Izabela actually arranges a multi-element picture story. She requires help in starting her story; she uses simple sentences or sentence equivalents.

In spontaneous speech, sentences with an incorrect grammatical and stylistic structure and word distortions appear; sometimes she uses words in English (they reflect the meaning of Polish equivalents of terms). The analysis of the collected diagnostic material revealed common interferences (the penetration of structures of one language into another), which cause the formation of new, partially erroneous linguistic structures at the level of vocabulary (atypical juxtaposition of words) and at the level of sentence structure and pronunciation (incorrect accent). In certain situations, there are difficulties in receiving the message. Izabela understands and uses both singular and plural.

Izabela has no phonemic hearing impairment. She also correctly distinguishes the sounds made by percussion instruments, but has difficulties in the field of auditory memory. She does not tap out the proposed auditory sequences correctly and does not remember the correct order of pronounced words. She understands the instructions addressed to her. Sometimes, however, she requires additional repetitions.

When it comes to the phonetic and phonological system, there are substitutions, deformations, elisions and simplification of difficult consonant groups. The pre-lingual-gingival sounds /ʃ/, /ž/, /tʃ/, /dʃ/ are replaced with the sounds /s/, /z/, /c/, /dz/, which undergo deformation (interdental realization) as a result of reduced muscle tone of the lips and cheeks. The sound /r/ is replaced with the sound /l/, and the sound /v/ with the diphthong sound /uo/. Izabela bites and chews correctly.

Izabela understands and uses many terms, but her passive and active vocabulary is lower in relation to the age norm. If she does not know a word, she describes it, for example, *This is for combing.* [*brush*]; *This is for pouring.* [*jar*]. However, upon hearing a new auditory pattern, she repeats a concept that she does not know. She mainly uses nouns and verbs in her statements. The use of adjectives, pronouns, and numerals is rare.

Izabela has a reduced efficiency of the articulation organs. The sublingual frenulum was undercut twice. Crossed laterality (left ear, left eye – right leg, right hand) was also found during examination.

The rate of language acquisition is evidently slower, which may be influenced by left-ear auditory perception disorders in the area of direct auditory memory, in addition to bilingualism.

Speech therapy is recommended to stimulate and observe the further development of Izabela's speech, to shape and stimulate all language subsystems (phonetic-phonological, syntactic-morphological, semantic-lexical, sentence-semantic); if necessary, additional specialist examinations (hearing examination, psychological tests) to verify the initial speech therapy diagnosis could be carried out.

Case 4 (Mark) – a child with motor aphasia

Motor aphasia is diagnosed based on the qualitative techniques of speech therapy and the AFA scale in the patient (Mark, a boy).

Despite long-term therapy, Mark's verbal expression is very slow, while maintaining an understanding of simple messages and commands. The greatest difficulties relate to the processes of naming and repeating. An inability to integrate individual speech elements significantly hampers progress in acquiring language competences. The patient presents a very limited range of correct articulation of sounds, syllables and words. In communicating with the environment, he uses mainly nonverbal means of expression (gestures and facial expressions), and creates proper names to describe various objects. When making attempts to produce messages, Mark does not perform pronunciation autocorrection; he also does not look for the correct wording. The word-conceptual store requires development. The speech apparatus is built properly, but it is advisable to improve it.

In view of such complex difficulties in the development of verbal communication, it is advisable to cover the boy with individual speech therapy aimed at:

- introduction of additional alternative communication as a means of supporting the development of active speech, for example, Makaton;
- improvement of speech organs;
- processes aimed at exercising attention and auditory memory;
- evoking missing articulations and fixing them in isolation, syllables and simple words;
- developing the resource of passive and active vocabulary;
- adapting the exercise material to the child's abilities and making it more attractive by using games and activities;
- providing support in communication with the environment;
- development of the child's cognitive functions, that is memory and thinking;
- numerous activities aimed at the development of enforceable self-motivation to express himself by asking questions and making other attempts related to the use of language in a situational context;
- encouragement to participate in social contacts and in the life of the peer group.

Case 5 (Sara) – child with motor aphasia

Based on the qualitative techniques of speech therapy and the AFA scale, motor aphasia has been diagnosed in the patient (Sara, a girl).

In terms of active speech, Sara makes a lot of linguistic mistakes, which is manifested by the distortion of the word structure by phonetic and verbal paraphrases. She can correctly describe a picture story. She also demonstrates good skill in updating the right concepts; she defines well the relationships between the elements of the picture; she understands the content of short stories correctly, however, only in relation to the illustrated situation. The greatest difficulty is in repeating and writing names with a complex phonetic structure, which results in numerous errors in writing the expressions she hears, or remembers. Despite long-term speech therapy, the pace of language skills acquisition remains slow. Sara's speech development is still adversely affected by impaired articulation kinesthesia and poor auditory memory. The cause of these disorders is the insufficient development of neurological processes and brain structures that condition the correct mastery of speech, including the ability to write and understand the read text.

It is recommended to continue speech therapy in order to develop language skills, which should have a positive effect on the ability to establish and maintain social contacts. Particular attention should be paid to:

- motivating people to express themselves (not forcing) by asking questions;
- increase in oral response time;
- taking into account problems with pronunciation and articulation while speaking;
- support in the editing of oral and written statements;
- helping to read and understand the commands and instructions given during the lessons;
- practicing impaired articulation kinesthesia;
- developing passive and active vocabulary;
- conducting exercises in the field of word analysis and synthesis;
- practicing the correct spelling of words;
- practicing concentration of attention and auditory memory;
- developing cognitive functions, that is memory, thinking, consolidation of acquired knowledge;
- encouraging the development of proper social contacts and participation in interactions by engaging to work in small teams;
- development of individual interests by supporting passions and hobbies;
- limitation of the presented language forms along with the amount of material, adaptation of the tests to the girl's abilities.

Explanations, tips and suggestions

In the Polish literature dealing with speech therapy, there is a variety of taxonomies of speech disorders of the central origin in children and adults, which are the result of brain damage. According to the International Classification of Diseases and Health Problems (ICD-10, commissioned by WHO), it is assumed that aphasia/dysphasia is a specific disorder of speech and language development, which consists in complete or partial loss of the ability to speak and understand verbal statements. In the case of children with developmental aphasia, specialists from Great Britain and the United States use the term SLI (Specific Language Impairment) to emphasize specific disorders in the development of the language system with a difficult to determine etiology, duration of the pathogenic factor and the type of damage of a structural or functional nature (Paluch et al., 2003).

Contemporary studies (Herzyk, 2000) on the definition of developmental aphasia/dysphasia take into account the multidimensionality of the issues of diagnosis and therapy, observing that:

- it is a specific speech development disorder that is not a secondary conse-quence of cognitive impairment due to specific brain dysfunctions;
- this disorder is the result of a cerebral pathology arising as a congenital, perinatal or acquired defect in the first weeks of life;
- the child's speech has never developed in accordance with the natural periods of the formation of the language system.

There are two groups of disorders: (1) expressive–receptive, where the main symptoms are difficulties in shaping speech, and (2) receptive–expressive, where speech understanding disorders are dominant.

In clinical practice, the study of narrative, also known as narrative dis-course, mostly uses storytelling methods based on situational drawings and picture stories. Another form of storytelling applied in practice is the one in which the patient reproduces the text, determines the main character, iden-tifies the main thought of the fairy tale and constructs a moral. Typically, the act of naming is tested by giving the patient the name of the designate. The most frequently used categories of designates include objects, activ-ities, body parts and colors. The activity of repetition is diagnosed with the use of verbal material, with the following criteria taken into account: (a) length (from a sound to a few-sentence text); (b) articulation complexity (from syllable to words); (c) frequency of use; (d) meaningfulness; (e) the period of acquisition in individual development, and so on; (f) the patient's numerical sequence, alphabet, names of days of the week and months; and/ or (g) reciting poems. The research on the understanding of heard speech shows the greatest variety of methods, among which the following two can be mentioned: (a) indicating referents of the name and (b) carrying out commands of different length, grammatical and conceptual complexity, involving the processes of categorization and inference to a different extent. The set of methods for diagnosing the skill of reading usually includes rec-ognizing letters of various font sizes, matching captions to drawings and carrying out written orders. Likewise, the evaluation of the skill of writing can be applied to copying letters, words and sentences; signing; writing down personal data; signing drawings; and describing situational drawings and picture stories.

The direction of cognitive neuropsychology as the basis for the therapy of patients with aphasia takes complex models of individual speech activities and models of mental representation of the language system, developed on the basis of research on healthy people. As a rule, brain damage causes disruption or elimination of a given element in the model, while maintaining the others within the norm. The complexity of the models developed by the representatives of cognitive neuropsychology explains the preference for the case study method aimed at a precise diagnosis of linguistic functions and other cognitive processes (attention, memory, thinking) involved in communication. Depending on the pathomechanism of language disorders, appropriate methods are proposed, such as, for example, relearning or regaining access to preserved representations of linguistic information.

This brief description of the selected directions of therapy does not exhaust the wealth of theoretical propositions and ideas for their implementation that appear along with the development of neuropsychology.

Case 6 (Leo) – child with Asperger's syndrome

Speech therapy examination reveals speech impediment, impaired articulation kinesthesia and impaired communication skills.

Leo incorrectly differentiates the dental sounds. He is unable to start and maintain conversations on his own. The only form of dialogue he continues is the imposed one. He does not always answer the questions posed. A high emotional lability is observed in the child; he quickly gets dispersed (then he screams and/or cries). Due to the recognition (speech impediment, impaired articulation kinesthesia and impaired communication skills), speech therapy is recommended at school and systematic work at home.

It is hoped that as a result of close application of the following recommendations, the boy has a chance to improve his articulation and – ultimately – improve his communication with the environment:

- practicing the articulation skills by perfecting the differentiation of the dental sounds in everyday speech;
- developing the ability to use speech in order to establish and maintain appropriate interpersonal contacts.

Explanations, tips and suggestions

In numerous descriptions of the forms of behavior along with the definitions characterizing the autistic spectrum of disorders, much attention is paid to difficulties in the communication process. These difficulties are a very common set of symptoms, and, above all, they are of a specific nature, requiring a thorough assessment, in which both the neuronal conditions and the environmental influences should be taken into account. The specificity of these problems concerns both those people with autism who function at a higher cognitive and social level and who are assessed by some researchers as people suffering from Asperger's syndrome, and those representing a lower level of adaptation and intellectual efficiency.

Due to its complexity, assessing the communication ability of children suffering from the autism spectrum that, subsequently, influences their proper development, requires a particularly insightful approach. Following Gałkowski (2005, pp. 736–749), the most serious deficiency characterizing the communication process of children with autism spectrum disorders is the lack of pragmatic aspects that appear in the form and content of the messages communicated by them. This type of deficit results from the overlapping of cognitive dysfunctions, such as, for example, difficulties in creating mental representations. It is about a tendency, quite common in a healthy child, to imitate games, in which there occurs a process of playing specific roles, that is using symbolism. These deficiencies are the basis of difficulties in building the so-called meta-representations, consisting in creating and using ideas that help other people experience some emotional states and display certain mental states.

Both people with autism and those with Asperger's syndrome, apart from disorders in social relations and specific interests and behaviors, present deficits and deviations from the norm in the sphere of speech and communication. Linguistic behavior paves the way for proper social and cognitive development. The interaction of people with Asperger's syndrome depends on the level of severity of the disorder's symptoms. It is widely recognized that people with Asperger's syndrome do not show delays in acquiring speech, and their speech development can be defined as normal. Asperger's syndrome is more and more often treated as a characteristic way of cognitive functioning, a different cognitive style. It also manifests itself in the linguistic layer, at all levels of the language. In the development of people with Asperger's syndrome, the ability to acquire linguistic competence is indeed observed, the deficit of which distinguishes this disorder from autism.

Case 7 (Adam) – a child with hearing impairment

A speech therapy examination confirms the lack of active speech development due to a hearing impairment of the investigated boy.

Adam does not communicate verbally with the environment. The contact is dominated by the gestural form and the production of inarticulate guttural sounds. He reacts well to his name, trying to locate the source of the sound. The speech apparatus is properly built, but needs to be improved functionally. Adam has a lot of vocalization that accompanies any activity. His voice is strong with no signs of nasalization. He reveals very poor understanding of speech, limited to a few familiar objects and activities, making numerous attempts to imitate sounds, but still to a very small extent.

Due to the lack of speech development and the inability to establish communication with the environment, speech therapy is recommended for the child, in which the following instructions should be followed:

- improvement of the speech apparatus, conducting breathing and voice exercises;
- performance of auditory exercises (sound localization, intensity, height);
- evoking and consolidating simple sounds, from vowels to onomatopoeic syllables;
- development of passive and active vocabulary;
- application of lip reading exercises;
- support and motivation to participate in therapy by grading difficulties, playing with the child and appropriate selection of exercise materials.

Case 8 (Julia) – child with hearing loss

The speech therapy examination of the patient (a girl) confirms the lack of active speech development due to bilateral sensorineural hearing loss.

The girl is currently showing auditory responses to her name, but has a big problem with locating the sound; speech understanding is limited to a few gestural-backed concepts. She does not repeat vowels, and the vocalizations that appear after the instrumentation have no meaning. The structure and efficiency of the speech apparatus are not an obstacle to the learning of speech sounds.

Due to the lack of development of active speech and significant limitations in the field of passive vocabulary, it is recommended to include the child in speech therapy classes in kindergarten, and actively institute the following instructions:

- improvement of the articulation apparatus, with effective practice of the respiratory and vocal functions necessary for the development of speech;
- gradual development of the sound repertoire from vowels to sound onomatopoeic syllables;
- conduct aural and language exercises (sound localization, intensity, height);
- support and motivation to practice purposefully designed activities by grading their difficulty, having fun and choosing materials appropriate to her age;
- development of the technique of reading speech from the mouth;
- works aimed at extending attention span.

Explanations, tips and suggestions

The development of electronic and electro-acoustic techniques has contributed to the improvement of many existing methods of measuring the degree of hearing loss. Young children, who are suspected of having such an impairment are most often unable to cooperate with a diagnostician for a long time, which makes it difficult to use many of the methods that enable recording reactions to acoustic stimuli, regardless of the interaction of the examined person. These methods are used in the case of young children and people with intellectual disabilities or autism, who have limited ability to systematically perform specific tasks. However, despite technical improvements, observing a person's behavior in hearing testing still remains valid. This approach refers to traditional methods in which the knowledge concerning conscious learning of the reactions evidencing the perception of auditory sensations is required.

Thinking about the treatment of hearing disorders, we accept the thesis that in most cases we have a situation that is a consequence of the damage that occurred some time ago. It is important to be able to start working on the systematic development of various language habits as early as possible, using everyday situations and playful and imitating tendencies of a child with hearing impairment. It is important to take into account the basic principles of developmental psycholinguistics, which analyzes linguistic activity together with social and cognitive development.

In order for the educational and rehabilitation effects to be fully effective, one should try to adapt them to the characteristic features of the developmental profile of the child with hearing impairment. Each of these children has specific and unrepeatable characteristics of psychomotor and cognitive development, to which we should properly adjust a set of therapeutic methods and rehabilitation programs. The assessment of a child's abilities is the task of a multi-specialist team that provides expert assistance.

Actions taken by speech therapists and/or other speech therapy specialists have a broader meaning – it is not only about correctness in terms of articulation, phonation, breathing and preventing the occurrence of speech defects but also the entirety of activities related to social communication, both in terms of the sender and these of the recipient. Thanks to the media, but also to various changes in the economy and social interactions, and in particular to progress in both medicine and education, it becomes possible to integrate children with various deficits into the overall social life. This is done thanks to greater social awareness; more specialized and more effective educational, pedagogical and psychological activities; and speech therapy care for people with various degrees and types of speech impediments or disabilities.

References

Gałkowski, T. (2005). Zdolności porozumiewania się w autyzmie i ich wspomaganie [Communication in autism and their suport]. In T. Gałkowski, E. Szeląg, G. Jastrzębowska (Eds.), *Podstawy neurologopedii* [Fundamentals of neurologopedia] (pp. 736–749). Opole University Pubishing House.

Herzyk, A. (2000). Afazja: mechanizmy mózgowe i symptomatologia [Aphasia: brain mechanisms and symptomatology]. *Logopedia*, *27*, 23–54.

Kawula, S. (2005). *Kształty rodziny współczesnej. Szkice familologiczne* [Shapes of the contemporary family. Families sketches]. Adam Marszałek Publishing House.

Kwaśniewska, M., & Żaba-Żabińska, W. (2015). *Arkusz obserwacji dziecka pięcioletniego/sześcioletniego* [Observation sheet of a five-year-old/six-year-old child]. Mac Education (brochure).

Paluch, A., Drewniak-Wołosz, E., & Mikosza, L. (2003). *AFA-Skala. Jak badać mowę dziecka afatycznego?* [AFA-scale. How to examine the speech of an aphasic child?]. Impuls Publishing House.

Tomczak, J., & Ziętara, R. (2009). *Kwestionariusz diagnozy i narzędzia badawcze w terapii pedagogicznej* [Diagnosis questionnaire and research tools in pedagogical therapy]. Impuls Publishing House.

4 On the application of selected tools useful in pedagogical and speech therapy diagnostics

Proposals of selected tools used in the diagnosis of a child's school readiness, with comments and practical tips

Testing a child in terms of readiness to start education at school is a complex process that requires many integrated activities. A process like this is aimed at finding out whether the child is intellectually, psychically and physically developed to meet and endure the school education hardships. In many countries, it is carried out by school teachers and sometimes also by specialists, for example speech therapists, psychologists, educators or other specialists employed in psychological and pedagogical counseling centers. In each country, however, this process relates to different areas of child development. And so, for example, a child's holistic development examination is conducted in Belgium, Denmark, Germany and Iceland, while in the Czech Republic, Estonia, Austria, Hungary or Cyprus, the diagnosis covers specific areas of child development, that is, his/her physical, psychological, social and mental (intellectual) spheres. In turn, other aspects of the diagnosis of a child's readiness to attend school are conducted in Liechtenstein, where the three leading areas concern the state of the child's development, school requirements and maturity of the family environment. In Luxembourg, on the other hand, the level of education determines the transition of children from kindergarten to primary school. In this country, 4-year-old children are obliged to attend preschool education. After two years, the child's progress is assessed. In case it has been assessed as insufficient, the child stays in kindergarten for another year. Postponement of compulsory education (at the request of the child's parents, or other parties) is possible in all countries besides Bulgaria, Ireland, Greece, Spain, France, Italy, Lithuania, Malta, the Netherlands, Portugal, England, Wales, Scotland, Northern Ireland and Norway. In Germany, Luxembourg and Austria, postponement is done without any involvement of the parents (EURYDICE, 2011, pp. 12–36). In Poland, however, the parent is allowed to submit an application to a psychological and pedagogical counseling center, which, as a result of the diagnosis, issues an opinion on the postponement of the child's obligation to start school.

DOI: 10.4324/9781003354758-5

It is the preschool and/or school institution – depending on where the child is preparing for school during a one-year-long preschool preparation – that is expected to prepare a diagnosis of the child's holistic development. In practice, this is often the first specialist (pedagogical) diagnosis a child experiences. As a result, the child's parents receive information on the level of psychophysical and social development (in Poland also emotional development) of the child. Often, such a diagnosis indicates that the child has behavioral problems and/or other disorders (e.g. pronunciation and/ or other language problems, fine or gross motor skills, socio-emotional problems, etc.) that make it difficult for the child to be ready to start school. Research conducted in the USA among 5-year-old children attending pre-school institutions, which are expected to prepare them to start school, indicates that many children with behavioral problems have lower speech development and/or other language skills, present various fine and motor skills delays, or even reveal insufficient involvement in play; generally, many of them show delays in those skills that are necessary to start learning at school (Montesa et al., 2012, pp. 541–548). These children require early screening tests (diagnosis) and interventions. Regardless of the type of disorder, psychophysical development delay or dysfunction, each child of a certain age (each country has a specific age of the child who is subject to the compulsory entry into school) is subject to diagnosis in terms of readiness to start education at school. **In order for this process to run smoothly, it is necessary to use many methods and diagnostic tools. The diagnosis of a child's readiness to start education at school requires the use of specialist (standardized) tools, which should take into account both the child's necessary knowledge and skills, as determined by the core curriculum in a given country, and the adopted developmental norms for a given child's age.** Sometimes the use of these tools in practical operation requires a completion of training and obtaining a certificate that authorizes the use of a given tool in practice (in Poland, for example, the SRAC (School Readiness Assessment Card) test or the SRS (School Readiness Scale) should be applied.

The first research on a child's school maturity (currently the term 'child's school readiness' is used) led to the emergence of two directions, the so-called 'German school' and 'Vienna school'. The representatives of the German school (including K. Penning, F. Krause and H. Winkler), as a result of research on the child's school readiness, considered the development of cognitive factors as mandatory to establish the needs and requirements of the school hardships in respect to a child. The Winkler Test (1930), translated into Polish by Fietz (1932) and adapted to the school's needs, enjoyed great interest among specialists (teachers) in the process of diagnosing children's readiness to start school. Winkler considered as the most important factors revealed by a child the ability to perceive shapes and numbers; the ability to observe; his/her manual dexterity of the hand; motor, visual and auditory memory; along with the ability to focus one's attention on a topic;

and one's level of perseverance (after: Szewczuk, 2014). On the other hand, the research on the school readiness carried out by the representatives of the 'Vienna School' (including K. L. Bühler and L. Schenk-Danzinger) included such factors as *[…] understanding the social situation, the ability to submit to the will of elders, intentional actions, concentration, cooperation and coexistence* (after: Wilgocka-Okoń, 1972, p. 102). Both indicated directions of research conducted by the representatives of the two schools aimed to answer the following questions: (a) Which features of a child's development determine their school maturity and at what age does she/he achieve it? (b) To what extent is intellectual development an important element of school maturity? and (c) Are the skills of purposeful and intentional action also important? (Wilgocka-Okoń, 1972). Information on the preceding tests, as the first diagnostic tools used in practice in the study of school readiness of a child to start education at school, along with a brief description of them, is included in Table 4.1, along with other diagnostic tools that are currently used in practice.

Pedagogical diagnosis of a child in terms of his/her readiness to start education at school should follow an interdisciplinary approach. The diagnostic material should be collected with the use of a multitude of methods and tools, including the accuracy of selection due to the studied phenomenon and the child's age. Therefore, in addition to the specialized tools presented in Table 4.1 concerning the diagnosis of a child in terms of his/her readiness to start school, the following may also be helpful in collecting diagnostic material:

1 Observation of the child. It plays a huge role in the diagnostic procedure. It allows a diagnostician to obtain knowledge about a child in natural conditions; learn about him/her; and determine the properties of his/her mental, physical, motor, social and emotional development, in order to be able to properly support him/her in therapeutic interventions. Child observation can be carried out in various educational and play situations (e.g. observation in terms of the child's approach to the task, communication and relations with peers). A child participating in various situations reflects the image of him/herself, his/her characteristic features and skills (Włoch & Włoch, 2009, p. 133). Each observation that is to provide reliable materials for the analysis must be very carefully prepared and properly carried out. If the teacher precisely defines the purpose of the observation, clearly and unambiguously formulating the topic and clarifying the manner of the recording, it will become effective and efficient (Kaleta-Witusiak et al., 2013, p. 52).

2 Conversation with the child. It should be planned in accordance with the assumed goal of the diagnosis. It may be a free conversation in terms of the discovery of the child's interests or the activities she/he is currently performing. It is important that the child feels comfortable during such a conversation.

Table 4.1 Proposals of selected tools used in the diagnosis of a child's readiness to start education at school

Tool name	General characteristics	Persons authorized to use the tool
Winkler Test (1930)	A test based on verbal scales, assuming that school maturity is primarily understood as maturity to start learning, and thus tests the ability to perceive shapes and numbers, the ability to observe, hand dexterity, motor and visual memory, remembering the content of a heard story, repeating words, pronunciation skills, fantasies, constructive combination and creating concepts as well as the ability to concentrate attention and persistence (Słyszowa, 1974, p. 28).	Teachers of preschool and/or school groups, in which children have one-year-long compulsory preparation for starting school.
Schenk-Danzinger Test (1932)	A test based on the assumptions of the Vienna school, examining social development (social attitudes, the ability to cooperate with a partner), learning abilities (visual and auditory memory), the ability to master the material (remembering by imitation, persistent completion of work), development of intellectual skills (numerical concepts, understanding numerical and cause–effect relationships expressed in verbal and pictorial forms and occurring in the course of the child's practical activity, speech development), constructional and manual skills, attention ability (children's age: 5–11) (Wilgocka-Okoń, 2002, pp. 70–80).	Teachers of preschool and/or school groups, in which children have one-year-long compulsory preparation for starting school.
The School Maturity Test by Wilgocka-Okoń (2002)	It is used to determine the level of preparation for compulsory schooling of children aged 6–7 years, as well as its environmental conditions and the method of compensating for developmental deficiencies in a child who exhibits them. The tasks of the test come down to assessing the level of physical, mental and social maturity of the child. The research is carried out in two stages: collectively (30–40 minutes) and individually (10 minutes). It precedes their assessment of the family and home conditions as well as the child's health based on an interview with parents and analysis of documents (child's health card). The examination is combined with the observation of the child's behavior during the course of the study research on the basis of a standardized observation sheet aimed at assessing: the child's attitude to fulfilling orders, understanding tasks, concentration, persistence, work pace, independence in performing tasks, use of school supplies, self-service, movement around school, making peer contacts, parting with parents/caregivers and overall assessment of behavior in terms of balance, and emotional and behavioral hyperactivity (after: Chojak, 2019, p. 22).	Teachers of preschool and/or school groups, in which children have one-year-long compulsory preparation for starting school.

(Continued)

Table 4.1 Proposals of selected tools used in the diagnosis of a child's readiness to start education at school (*Continued*)

Tool name	General characteristics	Persons authorized to use the tool
School Readiness Assessment Card (SRAC) (authorship: J. Gruby, B. Gubała)	The test consists of two parts: **part I**, the so-called autumn diagnosis should be carried out at the beginning of the school year (September/October), in which the child begins the compulsory one-year-long preschool preparation. The purpose of this diagnosis is to identify possible problems in the child's development and to provide him/her with appropriate educational and therapeutic, as well as psychological and pedagogical help during the day-to-day work in the kindergarten. **part II**, the so-called spring diagnosis should be carried out at the end of the school year (most often it is used at the turn of March and April), in which the child completes the annual compulsory preschool preparation. The purpose of this diagnosis is to collect materials on the psychophysical and social development of the child (in particular areas), on the basis of which the teacher prepares the diagnosis of school readiness. This diagnosis includes tasks related to the assessment of the child in the following areas: • self-service • great motor skills • emotional development • social development • auditory perception • visual perception • graphomotorics • mathematic skills • conceptual thinking • visual and auditory memory • environmental knowledge • orientation in time and space • communication and speech The diagnosis can be made individually with the child or in a group. (cf. https://www.komlogo.pl/index.php/kategorie/diagnoza/karty-oceny-gotowo%C5%9Bci-szkolnej-kogs–detail (accessed on 17/07/2022))	Teachers of preschool and/or school groups, in which children have one-year compulsory preparation for starting school. The teacher must be trained and certified to use the SRAC test in practice

(*Continued*)

Table 4.1 Proposals of selected tools used in the diagnosis of a child's readiness to start education at school (*Continued*)

Tool name	General characteristics	Persons authorized to use the tool
School Readiness Scale (SRS) by Koźniewska (2006)	SRS – consists of 72 items (subscales) (one item is in two subscales). It was assumed that the school readiness of a 6-year-old child should be considered through the child's activities in the preschool or school environment. The School Readiness Scale consists of five parts: A behaviors and skills related to the cognitive activity of the child; B child's behavior in a group of peers; C child's independence and his/her ability to cope with difficult situations; D child's task activity, demonstrated independently during spontaneous games or in the course of classes under the supervision of a teacher; E preparing the child to learn to read, write and count. The questions contained in the preceding parts are grouped into six subscales: SS – School Skills (20) CC – Cognitive Competences (12) ME – Motor Efficiency (8) I – Independence (12) NC – Non-Conflict (12) SA – Social Activity (9) For each of these subscales the number of items in the statements is indicated in brackets (Frydrychowicz et al., 2006).	Teachers of preschool and/or school groups, in which children have one-year-long compulsory preparation for starting school. The teacher must be trained and certified to use the SRS in practice.

(*Continued*)

Table 4.1 Proposals of selected tools used in the diagnosis of a child's readiness to start education at school *(Continued)*

Tool name	General characteristics	Persons authorized to use the tool
A set of tests to test the school readiness of Brejnak (2006)	The set developed by W. Brejnak (Brejnak et al., 2007) contains the criteria of school readiness and a list of 20 questions on the directed observation of the child ('Preschool' test), which allow to determine at what stage of development a child is. The set of samples for testing school readiness includes the following samples: • conversation with the child • picture description • pronunciation • sound analysis • reading test • learning a rhyme • counting • differences • similarities • recreating the text of the poem • mapping • physical activities • attempts to dominate the eye • child's behavior	Teachers of preschool (and/or school) groups, in which children have one-year-long compulsory preparation for starting school.

Source: Authors' own elaboration based on a literature review.

3 Tests (in the form of special questionnaires or in the form of specifically designed aids, such as blocks, labyrinths etc.) are used to study various aspects of a child's functioning at school. These are the so-called intelligence tests and special ability tests. Some other tests observed here are (a) personality tests, which include tests of features, attitudes, interests, as well as characterological and/or typological issues; (b) school tests (Robert L. Ebel pedagogical approach specifies the following school tests: vocabulary tests, knowledge tests, explanation tests, application tests and calculation tests); (c) psychological tests, often reserved for use by psychologists only (Kaleta-Witusiak et al., 2013, p. 58; Konarzewski, 2000). In diagnostic practice, the application of tests is usually perceived as a measurement that most strongly 'aspires' to the accuracy and objectivity of the information obtained.

4 Analysis of the child's products (e.g. drawings, art works, worksheets, etc.). It gives the possibility of insight into the child's psyche to extract various contents that determine his/her relationship to him/herself and to the surrounding reality. The analysis of the child's drawing provides the researcher (teacher) with knowledge about the child's internal conflicts, his/her fears, the nature of interactions with family members and/or internal and external experiences. Spontaneous drawing is usually considered as the child's own statement (see Bartoszeck & Przybysz-Zaremba, 2022; Braun-Gałkowska, 1985; Chermet-Carroy, 2005; Duksa, 2011; Fleck-Bangert, 2001; Rodríguez, 2011).

5 Interview and/or conversation with the child's parents or legal guardians. The teacher-diagnostician conducting such an interview should be prepared for such an interview/conversation. It is recommended that, in line with the stated purpose, she/he should prepare a set of questions that should be asked during an interview or conversation with the parents. In addition to preparing such questions in advance, the place is also important when conducting the interview. The teacher-diagnostician should choose a place that will be well-known to the child's parents – for example, a school or other institution attended by the child.

It should be emphasized that the pedagogical diagnosis of a child's readiness to start primary school education cannot be made solely on the basis of the above-mentioned methods of collecting diagnostic material, that is, observation, interview/conversation, tests, analyses of products, etc.; the key tool for making such a diagnosis is a tool developed by specialists in the field of examining a child's school readiness (suggestions for such tools are presented in Table 4.1). On the other hand, the methods and tools indicated here are treated as additional methods of collecting diagnostic material, supplementing and deepening the knowledge of the teacher-diagnostician about the child's development in his/her particular areas. Therefore, it is recommended that the diagnostic material collected with the use of specialized tools used in pedagogical diagnosis should be supplemented with the material obtained using other methods and tools.

Proposals of tools used in the diagnosis of selected areas of child development

The practical experience of the authors shows that for a pedagogical diagnosis to be holistic (comprehensive) and in-depth, it should be based on collecting diagnostic material using several research tools (see case studies in Chapter 3). Table 4.2 discusses the tools used in the study of selected spheres of child development. The use of these tools in practical operation allows the teacher-diagnostician to supplement the diagnostic material in terms of the child's school readiness. These tools provide an opportunity to gain in-depth knowledge about a given child in terms of his/her development in selected areas, for example general development and physical fitness, maturity of perception and/or visual-auditory coordination and so on. A detailed list of proposed tools along with their brief characteristics is included in the Table 4.2.

Proposals of selected tools used in the diagnosis of a gifted student

The materials include proposals of selected tools used in the diagnosis and identification of talents of schoolchildren (lower primary school level). The use of these tools in practice requires professional knowledge, appropriate preparation and sometimes specialist training, which ends with obtaining a certificate allowing for the right to use a given tool. The presented tools (Table 4.3) in practical operation are used by such specialists as psychologists, educators and/or special educators; some of them can be used by parents.

Various tools are used to diagnose pupils' abilities at the primary school level. Some of them are presented here together with a commentary concerning their application.

Proposals of selected tools used in the diagnosis of the causes of educational difficulties

The materials below present selected suggestions of tools useful in diagnosing the causes of a child's educational failure. The tools are used when working with zero level (6-year-old kindergarten) children, or at the level of early school education (grades 1–3), in a situation where the teacher noticed the first symptoms of problems in the child/learner that may lead to his/her educational failure. Listed in Table 4.4 are the tools that concern, among others, early detection of symptoms of developmental dyslexia; diagnosis of disorders in the psychomotor development of a child aged 5–6; diagnosis of

Table 4.2 Proposals of selected tools used in the diagnosis of selected areas of child development

Tool name	General characteristics	Persons authorized to use the tool
Bender-Koppitz test	The Bender-Koppitz test consists of nine figures – the tested child should redraw the indicated figures in the form in which they were designed. The examiner analyzes the figures redrawn by the child due to their shape and details in combination. When examining a child's emotional adaptation, the main emphasis is placed on the size of the drawings, their arrangement and size on paper and the thickness of the pencil lines. This test can be used for (a) tests to measure the maturity of child's perception and visual-auditory coordination; (b) research on the perception of cohesive systems as a result of brain damage; (c) research on the emotional adaptation of a child. This test is also used in screening for all children attending the so-called zero grade (used in Poland to prepare some children to start school education). The test result is one of the indicators of the so-called school maturity (Choynowski, 1971).	Teachers of preschool and/or school groups – selected parts of the test. Also educators, psychologists, neuro-psychologists
Edgard A. Doll's Social Maturity Scale	The scale is used to test the social maturity of children from 2 months of age. The tool consists of 117 questions. This scale was established in 1935 on the basis of research on mental retardation and IQ, assuming that often a person with a lower level of intelligence can cope better in life than another person with a higher IQ (after Kostrzewski, 1971, pp. 115–146).	Teachers, specialists
Kraus Weber's Physical Fitness Test	The American Kraus Weber test of (minimum) physical fitness is a proposition of an individual test of muscle strength. The test consists of six simple tests to check one's muscle strength. These are: 1　test of strength and endurance of the abdominal and lumbar muscles (spine) 2　test of strength and endurance of the abdominal muscles 3　test of the muscles of the loins and the lower parts of the rectus abdominals 4　test of strength and endurance of the upper back muscles 5　endurance test of the lower back muscles 6　test of the ability to lengthen the long muscles of the back and the back side of the legs Correct performance of all six attempts indicates minimal fitness for the muscular system (Gołąbek & Jasiak, 1986, p. 15; see also: Kulkarni et al., 2010, pp. 30–35; Prasad, 2013, pp. 60–62)	PE teachers, educators

(Continued)

(Continued)

Table 4.2 Proposals of selected tools used in the diagnosis of selected areas of child development *(Continued)*

Tool name	General characteristics	Persons authorized to use the tool
European Physical Fitness Test (EUROFIT)	The test is used to assess the indicators of physical activity, the level of functional–motor (psycho–physical) abilities related to health. The test can be used with both children and adults (see Heimer et al., 2004, pp. 223–233; Tomkinson et al., 2018, pp. 1445–1456).	PE teachers, educators
International Physical Fitness Test (IPFT)	The test consists of eight tests assessing motor skills, that is speed, jumping ability, endurance, hand strength, strength of arms and shoulders, agility, abdominal muscle strength, and flexibility (Pilicz et al., 2005).	PE teachers, specialists

B. Sekita's Wrocław Physical Fitness Test for Preschool Children	From this test, four basic motor characteristics can be determined: strength, power, speed and agility. The test consists of four samples.
	
	A Test of strength – throw a 1 kg medicine ball overhead.
	    The greatest distance at which the child made the throw in one of the three attempts was taken as the measure of the explosive force. The distance of the throws should be measured with an accuracy of 10 cm.
	B Power test – standing long jump.
	    The length of the farthest jump was taken as the measure of power. The length of the jumps made is measured with an accuracy of 1 cm.
	C Speed test – 20 m run from the high start.
	    The measure of the child's running speed is the time of the better attempt, that is the faster one (out of three attempts). The test time is measured with an accuracy of 0.1 s.
	D Agility test – 4 × 5 m pendulum run with carrying the block.
	    The time of a better, that is, faster attempt, is taken as the measure of agility. The duration of the test is measured with an accuracy of 0.1 s.
	
	External motor manifestations are assessed, expressed by the quantitative results obtained by the child in individual exercises based on natural forms of movement (Sekita, 1988, pp. 23–25).
		PE teachers, specialists

Table 4.2 Proposals of selected tools used in the diagnosis of selected areas of child development *(Continued)*

Tool name	General characteristics	Persons authorized to use the tool
Assessment of the lateralization of motor activities – a set of diagnostic tasks (authors: M. Bogdanowicz, J. Bala, E. Klima)	Proposals of diagnostic exercises (tasks) for the assessment of hand dominance concern: • stringing beads • fastening buckles • using blocks and peg • playing cricket • inserting pins • hammering the pegs • putting on sleeves • throwing in tokens • clapping • how high will you reach? Three diagnostic tasks are used to assess the eye dominance: • using a scope • using a kaleidoscope • using a cone When assessing the domination of the eye, the authors (Bogdanowicz et al., 2011, pp. 24–26) assumed that: • if the child makes all three attempts with the right eye – there exists right-eye dominance; • if the child makes all three attempts using the left eye – there exists left-eye dominance; • if in at least one of the trials the child performed the task with the use of a different eye than in the other tasks, it is binocularity, that is undetermined domination of each of the eyes.	People who have received appropriate training in the use of the text, for example teachers, educators, specialists.

(Continued)

Table 4.2 Proposals of selected tools used in the diagnosis of selected areas of child development *(Continued)*

Tool name	General characteristics	Persons authorized to use the tool
Intelligence Profile Scale 'Range of Possibilities'	This scale contains 48 statements about different behaviors. The task of the person performing his/her self-diagnosis is to define the degree of truthfulness of these statements in relation to him/herself on a five-point scale (5 – *I fully agree with a given statement*, 4 – *I rather agree with a given statement*, 3 – *It is difficult to say*, 2 – *I rather disagree with statement*, 1 – *I completely disagree with a given statement.*) After assessing the degree of truthfulness of all statements, the answers are entered in the appropriate places in the scoreboard and the results added up for a given type of intelligence. In this a range of one's own intelligences can be found (Kopik & Zatorska, 2011, pp. 43–48).	Teachers, educators, specialists
J.C. Progressive Matrix Test Raven in a color version	This test is a tool used to test intellectual abilities (according to Spearman it is the ability to educate, or the ability to think correctly). The test consists of 36 tasks, grouped into three series of 12 matrices. In each series, the dies are arranged in an order of increasing (i.e. progressive) difficulty. Each of the colors is used to sustain the attention and interest of children (after: Gardner et al., 2001, p. 72).	Psychologists
SPK-DP Scale of Sense of Control in Preschool Children	This scale is used to measure a personality variable known as the Sense of Reinforcement Control. SPK-DP consists of 18 questions describing various situations in the child's life. The child has two answers to each question. Half of the questions form the Success scale and half the Failure scale. A high score in the SPK-DP indicates a sense of external control (Szmigielska, 1996).	Psychologists
Columbia Mental Maturity Scale (CMMS) (Authors: Bessie B. Burgemeister, Lucille Hollander Blum, Irving Lorge)	A tool for examining the mental abilities of a child, understood as the ability to reason (making simple classifications based on perceptual data and manipulating symbolic concepts). This is a wordless scale that can be a valuable tool for examining children with hearing impairment, cerebral palsy, children with language communication disorders and children with mental retardation. This scale is used in work with children from 3 years and 6 months to 9 years of age (Dłużniewska & Szubielska, 2017, p. 33).	Psychologists

Source: Authors' own elaboration based on a literature review.

Table 4.3 Proposals of selected tools used in the diagnosis and identification of students' talents

Tool name	General characteristics	Persons authorized to use the tool
(CBQ III) Creative Behavior Questionnaire III	The first version of the CBQ III (Creative Behavior Questionnaire) was published in 1989. In Poland, it was modified based on the works of Bernacka (2003, 2004) and Karwowski (2006). The current version of CBQ III consists of 26 questions and includes two-dimensional (continuum) scales that diagnose 13 characteristics from the conformity–nonconformity scale (C–N–C) and 13 characteristics from the algorithmic behavior–heuristic behavior scale (A–H). The following answers were introduced: **A** – yes; **B** – rather yes; **C** – I have no opinion; **D** – probably not; **E** – no. The questionnaire was developed for both genders. (see Bernacka et al., 2016, pp. 33–57)	Psychologists, educators
Eby's & Smutny's Three Ingredients Talent Identification Sheet (1998)	The Three Ingredients Talent Identification Sheet was developed on the basis of the definition of abilities by JRenzulli & Reiss (1997), which recognizes school talent as a set of extraordinary abilities (general abilities and extraordinary (i.e. special) abilities), task commitment and creative abilities. The tool consists of 15 statements, five statements for each of the indicated aspects. The diagnosis of the degree of ability is carried out by marking the level of task performance on a four-point scale. (1 – below average, to 4 – outstanding) (see Eby & Smutny, 1998, pp. 23–24).	Psychologists, educators, teachers
APIS–P (R) Test Battery (Authors: Matczak et al., 1995)	The tool is used to test general intelligence. It consists of eight tests that refer to testing the child's behaviors, classification, squares, using pads, producing new words, creating stories, synonyms and number conversions. These tests diagnose various aspects of intelligence, that is abstract–logical, verbal, visual–spatial and social abilities (see Matczak et al., 1995).	Psychologists
Spionek's test for testing the level of manual dexterity and visual perception	This test consists of drawings containing geometric figures that are recreated by the child as a result of the diagnosis. The child recreates figures one at a time, from 1 to 14. The element of diagnosis is the way the child recreates figures, that is the level of his/her graphic abilities (visual analysis and synthesis processes). Child's drawings are assessed in terms of his/her manual dexterity (i.e. muscle tone, precision and hand–eye coordination),as well as his/her spatial and visual perception, analysis and synthesis (see Guziuk–Tkacz, 2011).	Psychologists, educators

(Continued)

Table 4.3 Proposals of selected tools used in the diagnosis and identification of students' talents *(Continued)*

Tool name	General characteristics	Persons authorized to use the tool
Child observation sheet for teachers and parents (Authors: Kopik, Zatorska)	The tool makes it possible to diagnose a child's intelligence profile, which can be determined using ten statements. The test consists in the targeted observation of the child during his/her stay at school (mainly during classes and games) or in a child-friendly environment. The task of the parent/teacher is to describe the child's reactions and behavior in accordance with the aspects specified in the tool sheet. During the diagnosis, the cooperation of the teachers and the child's parents/guardians is important, because the information obtained during the diagnosis may differ from each other and only when they are put together will give a full picture of the child's behavior (see Kopik & Zatorska, 2009).	Teachers, educators, parents
G. Lewis's check sets for recognizing the abilities	Control kits for recognizing the abilities elaborated by G. Lewis are used to diagnose general and specific predispositions. The check kits include aspects such as (a) scientific abilities; (b) creative talent; (c) linguistic talent (written and spoken language); (d) math talent; (e) sports talent; (f) artistic abilities; and (g) leadership and organizational talent. They consist of 12–28 statements presenting the child's behavior in the aspects just indicated. The answers are given on a scale of 1 to 5, where '1' means *never* and '5' *always*. The presence of a specific talent can be concluded on the basis of positive responses in defining a given ability (see Kamińska & Kowalczyk, 2014).	Parents, teachers
Emotional Understanding Test (EUT) (Authors: Matczak & Piekarska, 2011)	The tool is used to diagnose the level of the ability to understand emotions. It is one of the elements of the model by Salovey and Meyer (1990). With the help of the test, one can gain knowledge about the emotions of the child: the range of knowledge of the vocabulary related to emotions, connections between emotions, knowledge about emotional processes (changes, influence of external factors, causes, etc.). The tool consists of five components, with tasks constructed on the verbal material (see Matczak & Piekarska, 2011).	Psychologists, educators, HR specialists and career counselors (after training)

(Continued)

Table 4.3 Proposals of selected tools used in the diagnosis and identification of students' talents *(Continued)*

Tool name	General characteristics	Persons authorized to use the tool
Teacher's Creative Attitude Assessment Form by Szmidt	The tool is used to assess the creative attitude of learners, taking into account three spheres: cognitive, emotional–motivational and action. The tool is aimed at the teachers who, in the process of diagnosing a student by means of a number, determine the intensity of the described characteristic of the student, which in their opinion is the most visible in comparison with other students in the class. The scale of the Teacher's Creative Attitude Assessment Form is as follows: 1 – below average; 2 – at the average level; 3 – above average; 4 – to an outstanding degree (see Cybis et al., 2013, p. 94).	Teachers

Source: Authors' own elaboration based on a literature review.

Table 4.4 Proposals of selected tools used in diagnosing the causes of students' educational difficulties

Tool name	General characteristics	Persons authorized to use the tool
Dyslexia Risk Scale with standards for classes zero and 1 and the Dyslexia Risk Scale with standards for classes 1–2 (authorship: Bogdanowicz, 1990)	The tool is used for the early detection of symptoms of developmental dyslexia in a child in terms of (a) fine motor skills; (b) gross motor skills; (c) visual functions; (d) linguistic functions (perception and expression); (e) attention. The tool is aimed at learners in grades zero and 1 along with learners in grades 1–2 (see Bogdanowicz, 2011).	Teachers, parents
A battery of methods for the diagnosis of psychomotor development of 5- and 6-year-old children Revision 2015 (authors: Bogdanowicz, Sajewicz-Radtke, Radtke, Kalka)	The tool is used for the psychological and pedagogical diagnosis of the psychomotor development of a child aged 5–6 years. It can also be used in the diagnosis of school readiness. It consists of diagnostic tests in the following areas: (a) auditory-linguistic functions; (b) visual-spatial functions; (c) orientation in space; (d) fine motor skills; (e) gross motor skills; (f) cognitive development; (g) socio-emotional development (see Dłużniewska & Szubielska, 2017, pp. 34–37).	Psychologists and educators employed in psychological and pedagogical counseling centers. To use the tool in practice, qualification training in the use of the tool is required.
A battery of methods for diagnosing the causes of school failure in students aged 7–9, Battery-7/9 [B-7/9] (authors: Bogdanowicz, Kalka, Karpińska, Sajewicz-Radtke, Radtke)	A battery of methods for diagnosing specific reading and writing difficulties in children aged 7–9 years. It consists of several diagnostic tests, including visual-spatial functions (including visual-spatial perception and the speed of visual perception when working with visual material; eye-hand coordination, structuring perception; attention and visual-motor control when working with composite material; visual short-term memory capacity); auditory-linguistic functions; naming rate; perceptual-motor integration along with reading and writing (see Bogdanowicz et al., https://pracowniatestow.pl/pl/p/Bateria-metod-diagnozy-przyczyn-niepowodzen-szkolnych-u-uczniow-w-wieku–7–9-lat-B79-Protok.-badania/125 (accessed: 10.08.2022)).	Psychologists and educators employed in psychological and pedagogical counseling centers To use the tool in practice, qualification training in the use of the tool is required.

(Continued)

Table 4.4 Proposals of selected tools used in diagnosing the causes of students' educational difficulties *(Continued)*

Tool name	General characteristics	Persons authorized to use the tool
DYSLEXIA 3 – Diagnosis of dyslexia in third grade primary school students (authors: Bogdanowicz, Jaworowska, Krasowicz-Kupis, Matczak, Pelc-Pękala, Pietras, Stańczak, Szczerbiński)	The tool is used to investigate problems in the field of (a) reading, (b) writing, (c) phonology, (d) quick naming. It is intended for third-grade students of primary school (see Bogdanowicz et al., 2014).	Psychologists, educators, speech therapists University graduates with master's degrees in psychology or pedagogy
Aloud Reading Test – Marek's House (authorship: Bogdanowicz)	The test is designed to diagnose reading skills of students who complete the first year of reading education (children aged 6–7). It is used in individual examinations. It enables the diagnosis of the level of reading skills understood as the pace, technique and correctness of reading aloud. The test enables the assessment of the level of understanding of the text being read (see Bogdanowicz, https://pracowniaatestow.pl/pl/p/Test-czytania-glosnego-Dom-Marka.-DM/95 (accessed: 10/08/2022)).	Psychologists, educators, speech therapists University graduates with master's degrees in psychology or pedagogy
A set of methods for diagnosing reading difficulties. Decode Test. (authors: Szczerbiński and Pelc-Pękala)	The Toolkit for Diagnosing Reading Difficulty includes a toolkit for diagnosing word decoding and word recognition skills and related cognitive functions. These tools are intended for the diagnosis of first-grade students of primary school (students are 6–7 years old) (see Szczerbiński & Pelc-Pękala, 2013).	Psychologists, educators, specialists in pedagogical therapy

Source: Authors' own elaboration on the literature review.

specific reading and writing difficulties in 7- to 9-year-old children; diagnosis of dyslexia in third-grade primary school learners and a diagnosis of reading difficulties of such learners. The presented diagnostic tools should be treated as some suggestions only, which should be thoroughly studied before using them in practice; any person wishing to use them should have deepened knowledge about them, as some of them require having appropriate qualifications. The use of these tools by specialists from different countries requires their translation into the language of a given country and, in the scope of some tools, also specialist training.

Proposals of selected research tools used in speech therapy diagnosis

There are many methods and techniques used in speech therapy diagnostics. Some of the most commonly used are (a) methods of observation (with the help of an observation sheet); (b) exploratory methods (with the application of a conversation); (c) diagnostic examination (where an articulation test is used); (d) test methods (with the use of lateralization tests); (e) case studies (where research-based case studies are applied); (f) analyses of the results of selected activities (where school results may be analyzed, for example); (g) instrumental methods (with the examination of pupil's articulation, for example).

When using any of them, various principles should be followed. Some of them are the complexity of the study, looking for the most objective assessment possible, assessing the entire personality of the examined person, looking for the cause, continuity, etc.

In speech therapy, one can also use numerous methods assigned to other fields of knowledge, such as general pedagogy (for example the use of verbal method, practical classes and/or demonstration) and special pedagogy (where the application of the method of compensation or improvement may be observed) to mention only a few of them. It is absolutely necessary to differentiate between techniques and strategies of speech therapy and methods. While a method means a specific path to an end, a technique, in turn, is a process, an act by which one can reach the goal. This strategy should be understood as a specific plan or concept of deliberate use of particular techniques.

The research tools used in speech therapy entail various tests, questionnaires, trials, speech test cards, questionnaires and scales, computer programs. Whereas most of them are not standardized, some examine various aspects of speech, and some others only deal with the articulation side. There are also tests for phonemic hearing, auditory analysis and synthesis. The most commonly used diagnostic tools include:

- picture questionnaires (for articulation research);
- different tests (to test phonemic, phonemic and phonetic hearing, auditory synthesis and analysis, auditory perception);

- questionnaires to determine speech disorders in children (for the examination of speech);
- tests of linguistic proficiency (to test one's linguistic proficiency).

Some tools designed for diagnostic purposes can also be used during therapeutic activities.

As far as diagnostic tools are concerned, the following can be mentioned:

Articulation tests:

- different picture questionnaires – in Poland, the questionnaires designed by Bartkowska (1968), Demel (1994), Antos et al. (1978), Balejko (1994), Nowak (1993), and Michalak-Widera and Węsierska (2014) belong to these most often applied;
- pronunciation questionnaire for younger children (2 years of age or older) entitled *In the Land of Lolandia,* designed by Billewicz and Zioło (1992).

Tests of phonemic and phonemic hearing, auditory analysis and synthesis:

- various tests designed by Styczek (1982), Rocławski (2001), Muszyńska and Żarczyńska (1996), and/or Nowak (1993);
- a scale for measuring auditory perception of words by Kostrzewski (1981);
- a phonemic hearing test by B. Kaja (2001);
- a zetotest for testing phonological memory by Krasowicz-Kupis (2008);
- a test for reproducing rhythmic structures designed Stambak (1974).

Examination of various aspects of speech:

- a questionnaire for determining speech disorders in children designed by L. Kaczmarek (1955);
- a test entitled *From Picture to Word* by Rodak and Nawrocka (1993);
- a test *Check How I Speak,* designed by E. Stecko (2014);
- a picture and letter test for aphasia examination by J. Szumska (1980);
- AFA – scale by Paluch et al. (2003);
- a speech therapy screening test designed and offered by Z. Tarkowski (1992a);
- a speech disfluency and logophobia questionnaire also designed by Z. Tarkowski (1992b);
- Cooper questionnaire for stuttering assessment by M. Chęciek (1993);
- a Speech Therapy Screening Test for school-age children, whose authors are Grabias et al. (2007);

- a questionnaire of screening tests for detecting speech development disorders in 2-, 4- and 6-year-old children by Emiluta-Rozya et al. (1995);
- a language proficiency test proposed by Z. Tarkowski (1992a).

Visual perception can be tested with the help of:

- a visual perception test by Frostig (1999);
- a Bender-Kopittz test (5.0–10.0) (I give for: Choynowski, 1971).

Lateralization

- different tests by R. Zazzo (1974);
- a hatch test by M. Stambak (Gruba, 2012);
- a test of Matejck Zlab (1983);
- Harris Tests of Lateral Dominance (1985);
- Edinburgh Questionnaire lateralization (Gut, 2007).

Motor development

- Ozierecki's test by A. Barańska (for children 4–16 years of age) (Przewęda, 1973).

Perceptual-motor integration

- a Kephart's perceptual and motor development assessment scale (Kephart, 1970);
- tests measuring one's visual-auditory-motor integration by M. Bogdanowicz (1997);
- tests measuring one's transformation by M. Bogdanowicz (1990);
- a rhythm reproduction test by Z. Zlab (developed by Bogdanowicz, 1990).

Diagnosing phonological and articulation disorders is multidimensional. This means that during the entire process, the speech therapist is obliged to use several different methods and tools, the vast majority of which may be normative and/or standardized ones. Most often, these are picture questionnaires that do not have clearly defined norms but are helpful as tools to aid the diagnosis process. However, the speech therapist most often has to assess the correctness of articulation of the sound and its compliance with the age norm on the basis of his/her own professional experience. So far, the only tests standardized and normalized in Polish conditions, thanks to which articulation can be assessed, are:

- a speech therapy screening test for school-age children (Grabias et al., 2002);
- a speech therapy screening test (Tarkowski, 2002);
- the 100-word articulation test (Krajna, 2008).

Phonological competence is one of the subcomponents included in a much broader concept, which is linguistic competence. The components of phonological competence include:

- the ability to differentiate auditory phenomena (phoneme hearing);
- the ability to perform operations on syllables (analysis and synthesis);
- the ability to operate on phonemes (analysis and synthesis);
- the ability to perform operations on inter-syllabic elements (identifying rhymes).

Every educator, or teacher, dealing with children should be able to test their sense of hearing in an indicative way. An approximate hearing test is carried out in the form of simple commands given to the child in a voice that is increasingly soft or from greater distances. To test phonemic hearing, a letter test, a syllable test and a word test are used. All these tests are discussed in depth in the monograph *Researching and Shaping Phonemic Hearing* (Styczek, 1982); the linguistic material included in the work for the study of phonemic hearing, auditory analysis and synthesis of words along with visual analysis is a proposal that truly helps people dealing with the removal of speech disorders and difficulties in writing and reading. When assessing auditory perception, one can use such tools as the Auditory Perception Measurement Scale (Kostrzewski, 1981); the Auditory Differentiation Test of Phonemes (Nowak-Czerwińska, 1994); propositions to test the linguistic competence of 6- to 8-year-old children with hearing impairment (Krawiec, 2003); a program for developing and assessing the perception of the auditory sounds of the environment and speech (Szuchnik & Święcicka, 2003); an assessment of speech perception in children with hearing impairment (Kurkowski, 2003); or a test of 12 sounds from the environment and six sounds of speech (Szuchnik & Wojewódzka, 2003).

An excellent method used both in the prevention and treatment of psychomotor development disorders in children is the *Good Start Method* developed by Marta Bogdanowicz (1989), in which great emphasis is also placed on developing one's phonological competence. Its purpose is to not only improve the activities of three analyzers – motor, auditory and visual – but also to integrate them. Exercises conducted with the use of this method improve abnormally developing functions and activate their development. Early initiation of exercises with children to raise the level of skills included in the phonological competence could significantly reduce the number of children with problems in the first years of education, and thus reduce school failures.

During the diagnostic and therapeutic procedure, measures, that is all technical devices that can be used by a speech therapist, are also used; some of such devices are a computer, a tape recorder, an echo-corrector, a speech analyzer, speech indicators, audiometers, hearing aids, speech therapy instruments, a mirror, musical instruments, etc.

Table 4.5 Proposals of selected research tools used in diagnosing the causes of students' educational difficulties

Tool name	General characteristics	Persons authorized to use the tool
Speech screening test for preschool children (authors: I. Michalak-Widera & K. Węsierska, 2014)	A test for the initial speech evaluation in children from 3 to 6 years of age. The tool allows to roughly and easily check whether a preschool child has problems with speaking, and whether his speech is developing correctly. The purpose of the screening test is to initially assess a child's speech, detect possible speech problems, check the correctness of speech development, check speech understanding and assess the efficiency of the speech organs.	Speech therapists, teachers, educators, psychologists, pediatricians, nurses and other specialists who have a contract with preschool children in their professional practice
CSTAC – Child Speech Therapy Assessment Cards (author: Gruba, 2018)	Child Speech Therapy Assessment Card (CSTAC) is a test used to assess the most important areas of speech in a child from 1 month of age to 9 years of age. The structure of the CSTAC test allows for a quick and efficient assessment of the skills of children in individual age groups; the establishment of developmental norms allows one to find out whether the examined child develops correctly in particular areas of the speech therapy examination or shows abnormalities. Testing enables the diagnosis of children in 12 age groups in the following areas: (a) measurement of auditory reactions; (b) testing of speech organs; (c) understanding speech; (d) broadcasting speech; (e) articulation and efficiency of articulation organs (from 2 years of age); (f) testing pragmatic and social skills (from 3 years of age).	Speech therapists, neurologopedists
Comprehensive speech therapy examination (author: Emiluta-Rozya, Mierejewsja & Atys 2013)	A comprehensive speech therapy examination is a practical tool that is helpful during the first stage of speech therapy, that is, a diagnosis. The tool is a research method (a set of tests) that comprehensively allows for a comprehensive assessment of the use of language by a child, and for making a basic diagnosis in such a way as to facilitate the determination of the priority assumptions of the therapy.	Speech therapist

(Continued)

Table 4.5 Proposals of selected research tools used in diagnosing the causes of students' educational difficulties *(Continued)*

Tool name	General characteristics	Persons authorized to use the tool
Speech therapy test for children and adolescents (author: I. Michalak-Widera, & Węsierska (2008)	The pictorial questionnaire with the speech test card is a diagnostic and therapeutic test for children and adolescents with speech impediments, both intellectually normal and with reduced intellectual performance. The test is intended for testing small children – from 3 years of age to adolescence, those properly developing and those, whose psychophysical development is not harmonious – from the moment they can name the presented pictures. Thanks to the natural appearance of the designations presented on individual cards, it is possible to use the questionnaire also in the case of adults. The picture questionnaire can be successfully used during speech therapy, for example to repeat words with a practiced sound, to compose sentences with them, to tell imaginary stories or to ask questions and invent puzzles using the pictures on the boards.	Speech therapists
100-Word Articulation Test (author: Krajna, 2015)	The 100-Word Articulation Test is the first Polish standardized test for examining the pronunciation of preschool children, with tables of numerically expressed comparative norms. It consists of five parts: **the picture material** includes 84 color illustrations printed on double-sided laminated A5 cardboard; **the manual** is an instruction for conducting the test along with the analysis of the obtained results; **the theoretical assumptions** contain theoretical foundations necessary for the proper conduct of the test and standardization procedures. Additionally, the study includes examples of filling in research cards; **the speech test cards** are handy forms for entering the following test results: (a) speech test card qualitative assessment (IPA version); (b) speech test sheet quantitative assessment (IPA version); (c) speech test sheet quantitative assessment (Slavic version). The final component is **the hearing training**, that is a specially elaborated computer program that contains sample recordings of children's statements in the field of the tested vocabulary. The test has been standardized, thanks to which it provides the most objective speech evaluation. It is the only one containing transcriptions of phonetic notation in the Slavic standard and IPA (International Phonetic Alphabet); the picture material was made on a durable cardboard and stapled in a handy binder; the theoretical part was separated from the test procedure (test questions, interpretation of results), thanks to which a functional manual for carrying out the test was obtained; speech test cards including the phonetic notation of Slavic and IPA were developed and placed in a folder; exemplary realizations of children's pronunciation, which were the subject of the test, were taken and developed in the form of a computer program.	Speech therapists

(Continued)

Table 4.5 Proposals of selected research tools used in diagnosing the causes of students' educational difficulties *(Continued)*

Tool name	General characteristics	Persons authorized to use the tool
Speech test questionnaire (authors: G. Billewicz & B. Zioło, 2015)	The speech test questionnaire is an uncomplicated, precise tool supporting the process of examining a child's articulation. It works well when working in a kindergarten or early school group and fully reflects the child's articulation level, taking into account its natural development. It consists of pictures whose names contain vowels and consonants in three positions, in which they can appear in a word: on the forehead, in the mid-voice and in the final voice. The phonemes appearing in the names of the pictures are arranged in order according to how they appear in the child's speech development. The questionnaire takes into account labial, labio-dental, antero-linguistic–dental, antero–linguistic–gingival, middle–lingual, posterior–lingual and basic vowels. A speech test sheet is attached to the questionnaire, where the order of sounds is written in the order of the words appearing. The proper part is preceded by a speech card with a list of the desired labial, labio-dental, antero-dental, pre-lingual–gingival, middle–lingual, posterior–lingual and vowel sounds. Each group consists of several words containing a given sound in the word initial, middle and final position. The next part contains as many as 110 pictures of nouns. The pictures are so expressive and characteristic that even the youngest toddler should have no problem identifying and naming them.	Speech therapists
AFA SCALE – how to test the speech of an aphatic child? (authors: Paluch et al., 2003)	The scale is a specific proposal for a method of collecting material used to assess the linguistic and communicative skills of a child with speech impairment. Its main goal is to help speech therapists-practitioners to diagnose and plan therapy for children with aphasia.	Speech therapists, neurologopedists

(Continued)

Table 4.5 Proposals of selected research tools used in diagnosing the causes of students' educational difficulties *(Continued)*

Tool name	General characteristics	Persons authorized to use the tool
CLAC – AFA (Child Language Assessment Cards – AFA) (authors: E. Drewniak-Wołosz & A. Paluch, 2018)	Child Language Assessment Cards (CLAC) – AFA is the newest tool for diagnosing aphasia-type speech underdevelopment in children of preschool and school age. The tool is designed to test preschool children (with the easier version of the test) and school children (with its more difficult version). The tasks are adjusted to the cognitive abilities of these two age groups. CLAC-AFA is designed to diagnose the entire language system of a child, with particular emphasis on communication deficits. CLAC-AFA examines language in both the phonetic and phonological sphere (articulation, word structure), assessing the lexical resource, inflection, the ability to build declarative sentences, asking questions, understanding and carrying out commands, verbal memory, as well as the pragmatic aspect and communication skills of the child. The examination with the CLAC-AFA tool enables the diagnosis to summarize information about the child's language and communication. It allows to characterize not only articulation, but also the ability to repeat, name, independently create sentences and longer statements, confirm the understanding of words, sentences, texts, questions and commands. It helps to describe abnormal linguistic phenomena in the child's speech. It improves the assessment of making contact, commitment, and learning new skills. Entering data into the KomKOD computer program is a great help for a diagnostician.	Speech therapists, therapists who assess the child's speech, educators, psychologists
Language Proficiency Test (author: Tarkowski, 1992a, 1992b, 1992c)	The LST Language Skills Test is designed to assess the linguistic development of children and consists of seven subtests: (a) Understanding a fairy tale; (b) Dictionary; (c) Correction of sentences; (d) Inflection; (e) Asking questions; (f) Requests and orders; (g) Telling a fairy tale. It has sten standards for children aged 4–8. The test is used to: (1) assess the level of language development, (2) to identify delayed children, and (3) to direct the stimulation of therapy.	Speech therapists, educators

(Continued)

(Continued)

Table 4.5 Proposals of selected research tools used in diagnosing the causes of students' educational difficulties (*Continued*)

Tool name	General characteristics	Persons authorized to use the tool
Speech Therapy Screening Test – STST (author: Tarkowski, 1992a, 1992b, 1992c)	STTS Speech Therapy Screening Test is used to quickly select children with delay in speech development; it is modeled on similar American methods (Tarkowski, 1992b). It consists of four subtests: (a) Understanding; (b) Dictionary; (c) Grammar and (d) Pronunciation. It has developed sten standards for children aged 4–8 years. The test is used to (a) assess the level of language development, (b) identify delayed children, and (c) direct the stimulation of therapy.	Speech therapists
'Check how I speak' – speech therapy examination card with auxiliary materials (authoress: Stecko, 2009)	Articulation test – a set of tongue and lip exercises helpful in assessing their efficiency. The card consists of three parts and an interview, the collected results of which provides a picture of the child's possibilities and development from birth to the end of speech therapy exercises or the present moment. The overall picture of a child's speech development is made up of the results of all parts. Each part can be used independently of the others. The use of the whole card is of particular importance in the case of children with a burdened pregnancy–perinatal period, as it enables the registration of the child's condition, sets a plan for improvement and allows to track the obtained effects. It is intended for the diagnosis of children from newborns to children over 7 years of age (no upper age limit is specified). It is divided into three parts: for newborns, reflexes from the area of the face (from birth) are examined; in children up to the age of 3, the respiratory and swallowing functions, the structure and efficiency of the articulation apparatus, along with the development of speech and language (including understanding, naming, utterance, articulation), phonemic hearing, memory and auditory attention are assessed; older children (from the age of 3) are tested for the efficiency of the articulation apparatus (movement imitation), speech understanding and expression, articulation, articulation, auditory analysis and synthesis. The diagnostic material for this tool is adapted to the examination of children under and over seven years of age. It contains an interview card, an examination card for reflexes, a card for examining and recording nonlinguistic vocal behaviors, a card for examining the efficiency of articulation and speech organs (includes naming, storytelling, expressive speech – including articulation, analysis and synthesis of words), summary card for marking the number of points and colorful cards with illustrations for speech research.	Speech therapists

Table 4.5 Proposals of selected research tools used in diagnosing the causes of students' educational difficulties *(Continued)*

Tool name	General characteristics	Persons authorized to use the tool
Child's Dictionary Test – CDT (author: Z. Tarkowski, 1996)	CDT Child's Dictionary Test – is used to assess the development of the skills of defining, generalizing and categorizing. It consists of three subtests: (a) Formation of sub-words; (b) Defining terms; (c) Formation of parent words. Sten norms for children aged 4–9 have been developed. The test is used to (a) assess the level of language development, (b) identify delayed children, and (c) direct the stimulation of therapy.	Speech therapists, psychologists
From Picture to Word (authors: H. Rodak & D. Nawrocka, 1993)	The set titled *From Picture to Word* consists of a guide, picture materials, including language games and combinations of language exercises, and labels with captions for individual pictures. This material can be used as a diagnostic aid and as a basis for creating individual therapy programs for children with communication difficulties of various etiologies. The games also help to develop linguistic concepts in all children of preschool and young learners. The attached guide explains in detail the methods of using the materials that can be applied in the psychological and pedagogical help program, for example during specialist classes in grades 1–3 of primary school.	Speech therapists, educators, teachers of preschool and early childhood education
Screening questionnaire for detecting speech development disorders in children aged 2, 4 and 6 (authors: Emiluta-Rozya et al., 1995)	Articulation test – tongue and lip exercises helpful in assessing their efficiency. The examination is an element of speech therapy prophylaxis, which is aimed at early detection of abnormalities in the child's speech, along with providing speech therapy as soon as possible and preventing the disorder from becoming permanent.	Speech therapists, educators, preschool teachers

(Continued)

Table 4.5 Proposals of selected research tools used in diagnosing the causes of students' educational difficulties *(Continued)*

Tool name	General characteristics	Persons authorized to use the tool
Speech Influence and Logophobia Questionnaire (author: Tarkowski, 1992a, 1992b, 1992c)	The Speech Disfluency and Logophobia Questionnaire (SDLQ) is used to assess stuttering in various communication situations and to develop a therapeutic program. SDLQ consists of a textbook and test protocols. The handbook can be divided into two parts: diagnostic and therapeutic. The therapeutic part is supplemented by test protocols containing information about the patient and his stuttering, that is speech disfluency, logophobia, vegetative and psychological neuromuscular symptoms. The test can be repeated on the same person, using the same protocol. The test with the use of SDLQ is carried out with the child or his guardian (mother, father). SDLQ is used to test children, adolescents and adults; it can be used for both younger school-age children and preschool children over 5 years of age.	Speech therapists, balbutologopedists
Cooper questionnaire for stuttering assessment	The questionnaire for testing the degree of speech disfluency in children (3–10 years of age) allows the patient to assess four aspects of stuttering. The questionnaire examines the frequency of stuttering and allows you to analyze the severity of stuttering in: spontaneous speech (monologue and dialogue), verbal automatisms (counting, listing the days of the week and the names of months), recitation from memory, repeating individual words and sentences, answering questions with one word and reading.	Speech therapists, balbutologopedists

(Continued)

Table 4.5 Proposals of selected research tools used in diagnosing the causes of students' educational difficulties *(Continued)*

Tool name	General characteristics	Persons authorized to use the tool
Speech Therapy Screening Test for School-Age Children (authors: Grabias et al., 2002)	The Speech Therapy Screening Test for School-Age Children is used to test both 7- and 15-year-olds. The test consists of seven commands that examine in turn: (a) pronunciation (command 1 and 2); (b) semantic, grammatical and narrative skills (command 3 and 4); (c) motor skills of the speech organs (command 5); (d) perception of speech sounds (command 6 and 7). In terms of pronunciation, the child is recommended to name the displayed 20 pictures and repeat sentences that are difficult to articulate. Overall, in the pronunciation test, a child can score 46 points. Semantic, grammatical and narrative skill is tested by the child telling everything he knows about dwarfs (instruction 2) and telling a simple story based on the attached pictures (instruction four). Command 3 allows for asking auxiliary questions, but the respondent receives one instead of two points for the answer after asking the question. In command 4, the child's incorporation of all reference situations into the narrative, along with the structure and arrangement of events, is assessed. The linguistic assessment of both narrative statements concerns the fluency of the narrative and phonic waveforms, grammatical correctness, lexical skills and the ability to establish verbal interactions. In total, in orders 3 and 4, the child can get 53 points. The examination of the motor skills of the speech organs consists in the child making six movements of the tongue shown by the examiner. In this command, a correct move is 1 point, an incorrect move is 0 points. In terms of testing the perception of speech sounds, the respondent is given ten pairs of nonsense words, at the same time being instructed to indicate whether they are the same or different, while the child cannot look at the examiner's mouth (command 6) and asking them to syllabize five words of increasing difficulty (command 7). For each correctly performed command, one point is given, so in the study of the perception of speech sounds, the subject may receive 15 points. Overall, there are 120 points to be scored in the Speech Therapy Screening Test. Conducting the research allows to identify the least linguistically efficient units in the peer group and to determine the etiology of disorders through further research.	Speech therapists

(Continued)

Table 4.5 Proposals of selected research tools used in diagnosing the causes of students' educational difficulties *(Continued)*

Tool name	General characteristics	Persons authorized to use the tool
Picture–letter test for the examination of aphasia (author: Szumska, 1980)	The test consists of two parts. The first part focuses on the characteristics of the different types of aphasia. The second is the material for research. This material, consisting of drawings, letters and numbers, allows to identify and organize the symptoms of speech disorders and combine them with the brain injuries described in the first part. The research material includes (a) descriptive speech testing, (b) repeated testing, (c) naming test, (d) speech understanding test (e)reading test, (f) examination of the handwriting, (g) counting test, (h) spatial orientation study, (i) memory test and (j) praxia study.	Speech therapists, neurologopedists
Krakow Neurolinguistic Battery for Diagnosing Aphasia (KNBDA) (authors: M. Pąchalska –, 1995)	The Krakow Neurolinguistic Battery for Diagnosing Aphasia (KNBDA) is a standardized technique for assessing language disorders in patients with aphasia. The most important KNBDA assumptions are (a) differentiation of aphasia with other speech disorders; (b) determination of the type and depth of aphasia; (c) determining the type of aphasia within the four language modalities (understanding, speaking, reading and writing); (d) setting the goals of therapy; (e) evaluation of the results of conducted rehabilitation; (f) the forecast of the possibility of returning lost language functions.	Speech therapists, neurologopedists
Token Test, also known as the Token Test (1962) www.tokentest.eu/ (accessed: 12/03/2017)	The Token Test is a technique that allows to determine the state of language disorders in a child with aphasia. The test includes a set of geometric figures of different colors, sizes and shapes. The child's task is to indicate the appropriate figure. The degree of difficulty of the commands is adjusted to the patient's abilities. With the help of this test, it is possible to quantify the impaired understanding exclusively.	Speech therapists, neurologopedists
Boston Naming Test (authors: Kaplan et al., 1983)	The Boston Naming Test is used to test a patient's naming disorder and to assess their ability to understand and form utterances.	Speech therapists, neurologopedists

(Continued)

Table 4.5 Proposals of selected research tools used in diagnosing the causes of students' educational difficulties *(Continued)*

Tool name	General characteristics	Persons authorized to use the tool
The Comprehensive Aphasia Test (CAT) (authors: D. Howard, Swinburn & Porter., 2004)	The Comprehensive Aphasia Test (CAT) is used to assess the type and level of aphasia. Its task is to determine the level of existing language disorders, to assess the efficiency of cognitive functions and (using the Disability Level Questionnaire) to examine the impact of aphasia on the functioning of the patient. The test consists of materials for examining language disorders, materials for assessing the efficiency of cognitive functions, the Disability Level Questionnaire of the examined person and a guide that allows to determine the approximate pace of the patient's work during the therapy (based on the previous assessment of the patient's language condition). Due to the large number of tasks, CAT is performed over several sessions. Thanks to the large number of tasks of varying difficulty, CAT is one of the few tests on the market that allows the therapist to monitor the patient's progress on an ongoing basis.	Speech therapists, neurologopedists
BAT test – Bilingual Aphasia Test	BAT – Bilingual Aphasia Test – a test for examining aphasia in bilingual people; it was developed for the people who knew and used at least two languages before losing their language skills. By adjusting the questions to one of the two languages, a person who has lost the ability to communicate in one language as a result of aphasia, can undertake effective speech therapy in a language that is easier for them to communicate.	Speech therapists, neurologopedists
The Aphasia Dynamics Assessment Scale (ADAS) (authors: Puchowska–Florek et al., 2005)	The Aphasia Dynamics Assessment Scale (ADAS). It consists of three parts assessing consecutively: understanding speech, transmitting speech, naming objects.	Speech therapists, neurologopedists
FAST test (authors: M. Puchowska–Florek et al., 2005)	The FAST test is a simple test for finding the presence of aphasia. It is based on the study of comprehension, giving expression, reading and writing.	Speech therapists, neurologopedists
Tests and trials for phonemic hearing (author: I. Styczek, 1982).	The most popular picture questionnaires included in the publication: '*Badanie i kształtowanie słuchu fonematycznego (komentarze i tablice)*' [*Research and development of phonemic hearing (comments and tables)*], which allow to make a diagnosis with the use of tools and assess the functioning of phonemic hearing.	Speech therapists

(Continued)

(Continued)

Table 4.5 Proposals of selected research tools used in diagnosing the causes of students' educational difficulties *(Continued)*

Tool name	General characteristics	Persons authorized to use the tool
Phoneme Hearing Test (author: Rocławski, 2001).	The most popular picture questionnaires included in the Polish publication: '*Słuch fonemowy i fone-tyczny. Teoria i praktyka*' [*Phonemic and Phonetic Hearing. Theory and Pratice*] that allow one to make a diagnosis with the use of the tools indicated there and assess the functioning of a child's phonemic hearing.	Speech therapists
Communication Behavior Assessment Card (CBC) of a hearing impaired child (authors: K Krakowiak & M. Panasiuk, 1992)	The Communication Behavior Assessment Card (CPC) of a hearing-impaired child is a tool for a categorized assessment and description of the manner in which a hearing-impaired child communicates. The CBC is helpful in diagnosing the special developmental and educational needs of children and adolescents, and the standards, guidelines and guidelines contained therein are helpful for the preparation and adaptation of diagnostic tools for children and adolescents with selected special development and educational needs.	Speech therapists, surdologists
Dialogue Articulation Test (author: A. Majewska–Tworek, 2000)	The Dialogue Articulation Test is a test of child's articulation skills. The author used a spontaneous test, that is conducting research in such a way that the child him/herself (or with the help of a speech therapist) tells the story, and does not name only individual words shown in the drawings. Such guided examination of the pronunciation of a preschool child allows for obtaining better, that is more accurate and spontaneous results necessary to make a diagnosis.	Speech therapists
Auxiliary materials for diagnosis and therapy, examples of diagnostic tools (author: Minczakiewicz, 1997).	1. Logopaedic Card. 2. Questionnaire–interview. 3. Chart for examining articulation motor skills. 4. A logopedic card insert intended for mentally handicapped dyslexic (allal) children. 5. A speech therapy card insert for dyslexic children. 6. Insert for a speech therapy card intended for children with a hearing impairment. 7. Writing texts by listening and testing reading techniques. 8. Texts to rewrite or test the degree of its understanding. 9. Pronunciation card.	Speech therapists

Table 4.5 Proposals of selected research tools used in diagnosing the causes of students' educational difficulties *(Continued)*

Tool name	General characteristics	Persons authorized to use the tool
Picture questionnaire for speech examination and speech therapy (author: Balejko, 1994)]	The drawing questionnaire contains 44 pictures of objects known to the youngest children. Using pictures, the examined child makes articulation tests that allow to evaluate his/her pronunciation. Articulation attempts begin with vowels and, through the sounds that are easy to articulate, turn to the sounds of the highest degree of difficulty. Adopting such an order from the easiest to the most difficult sounds retains the principle of grading difficulty. The proposed questionnaire makes it possible to assess the development of speech and pronunciation in both nonreading and reading children, along with those whose speech has not yet developed. The questionnaire allows to test not only the articulation, but also the child's dictionary. It is used to examine young children (under 4 years of age); it allows to examine their active dictionary by asking the question: 'What is it?' and the passive dictionary by saying the request: 'Show where it is'.	School educators, kindergarten and early childhood education teachers, psychologists, speech therapists
The syllable test for the assessment of speech fluidity (IFPS) (author: Z. M. Kurkowski, 2003)	The syllable test for the assessment of stuttering designed by Zdzisław Marek Kurkowski (2003) contains material for testing a person with speech impedance in four age groups, including children under the age of 7. The test for this age group includes the following tests: naming pictures, repeating sentences, answering questions and telling a picture story.	Speech therapists, balbutologopediasts
Test for phonemic hearing in children and adults (authors: E. Szeląg & A. Szymaszek, 2006)	The tool is used to evaluate one of the elements of speech understanding, that is phonemic hearing. The sets of sentences included there, illustrated with appropriate drawings and sound material, help in the diagnosis of speech perception disorders that result from its deficits. The authors also propose a computer version of the tool.	Speech therapists, neuro-psychologists, educators

(Continued)

Table 4.5 Proposals of selected research tools used in diagnosing the causes of students' educational difficulties *(Continued)*

Tool name	General characteristics	Persons authorized to use the tool
Palin PCI Scale (authors: E. Kelman & A. Nicholas, 2013) and/or Palin PRS Scale (authors: S. Millard et al., 2009)	The strategies for diagnosing stuttering in children described in the *Palin PCI Handbook* include a set of questionnaires for screening, a full interview with the child and the parent and summary sheets of the results that additionally assess their interactions based on recorded parent–child play, which is used for further therapy planning. At the same time the Palin PRS Scale – *The Palin Scale for a Parent of a Stuttering Child* is a parental questionnaire that shows how a parent perceives each of the following situations: the impact of stuttering on the child; the severity of stuttering; the impact of stuttering on himself as a parent; and the parent's knowledge and level of coping with the problem of stuttering.	Speech therapists, balbutologopedists
DJ – Diagnosis of Stuttering in Preschool Children (authors: K. Węsierska & B. Jeziorczak, 2016)	The newest and most comprehensive tool is the DJ – *Diagnosis of Stuttering in Preschool Children*. The test is a standardized tool. It contains not only a set of questionnaires for interviewing a young child, but also expressive and pictorial material for the direct examination of a preschooler. The screening card can be used to assess the risk of stuttering. When diagnosing the risk of stuttering, the test includes further questionnaires for parents: a basic information sheet; an extensive interview with the child's parents (guardians); a card for describing the child's personality and behavior; a mother (father) child interaction assessment card (to be filled with the help of the parents). In addition, the test includes an observation sheet for the parents. The child is examined by an interview card (suitable for a preschooler) and a picture–word material that includes the following tests: understanding and naming pictures (both nouns and verbs); repeating sentences; answering questions with one word; finishing sentences; recreating a story told by a speech therapist; telling a picture story; finding differences in two pictures; finding a mismatched element in pictures; describing abstract pictures; changing colors for 30 seconds; and exchanging animals for 60 seconds.	Speech therapists, balbutologopedists

Source: Authors' own elaboration on the literature review.

This is mostly why speech therapy aids include the following materials (Table 4.5):

- language-related materials (speech therapy collections of words and sentences, stories, lyrics, poems, riddles, etc.);
- pictures (questionnaires and picture sets, games, stories, charts; instead of picture questionnaires, you can use multimedia programs currently available on the market);
- items, toys;
- phonograms, X-rays, labiograms.

Speech therapy is one of the most progressive scientific disciplines within the humanities. If we take into account the complicated social problems that may be related to one's impaired ability to communicate, the development of speech therapy in recent years is very justified and logical. However, the problem that remains to be possibly solved is still unclear terminology, large discrepancies between Polish and foreign nomenclature, along with an insufficient number of normative and standardized diagnostic tools.

References

Antos, D., Demel, G., & Styczek, I. (1978). *Jak usuwać seplenienie i inne wady wymowy* [How to correct lisp and other speech impediments]. PZWS Publishers.

Balejko, A. (1994). *Jak usuwać wady wymowy. Porady dla nauczycieli i rodziców* [How to remove speech impediments. Advice for teachers and parents]. Speech Therapy Publishers.

Bartkowska, T. (1968). *Rozwój mowy dziecka przedszkolnego jako wynik oddziaływań wychowawczych rodziny i przedszkola* [Speech development of a preschool child as a result of educational interactions of the family and kindergarten]. PZWS Publishers.

Bartoszeck, A. B., & Przybysz Zaremba, M. (2022, April 1). Dreams of Polish-Brazilian children with the spectrum of autistic disorders – based on the analysis of drawings. *Parana Journal of Science and Education (PJSE), 8*(3), 1–15. https://drive.google.com/file/d/1deWgnZRQw_VHCGhanNsSCra-AouJwhry/view.

Bernacka, R. (2003). "Struktura czynnikowa skal konformizm i nonkonformizm Kwestionariusza Twórczego Zachowania KANH" [Factor structure of the conformism and nonconformity scales of the KANH Creative Behavior Questionnaire] *"Annales UMCS", sec. J, Pedagogia–Psychologia, XVI*, 31–45.

Bernacka, R. (2004). *Konformizm i nonkonformizm a twórczość* [Conformism and non-conformism and creativity]. Maria Curie-Skłodowska University Press.

Bernacka, R. E., Popek, S. L., & Gierczyk, M. (2016). Kwestionariusz twórczego zachowania KANH III – prezentacja właściwości psychometrycznych [The creative behaviour questionnaire CBQ III – presentation of the psychometric characteristics]. *ANNALES UNIVERSITATIS MARIAE CURIE-SKŁODOWSKA LUBLIN-POLONIA, XXIX*(3), 33–57. https://doi.org/10.17951/j.2016.29.3.33.

Billewicz, G., & Zioło, B. (1992). *W krainie Lolandii* [In the land of Lolandia]. Impuls Publishing House.

Billewicz, G., & Zioło, B. (2001). *Kwestionariusz badania mowy* [Speech research questionnaire]. Impuls Publishing House.

Bogdanowicz, M. (1989). *Metoda Dobrego Startu w pracy z dzieckiem w wieku od 5 do 10 lat* [Good start method in working with children aged 5 to 10]. WSiP Publishers.

Bogdanowicz, M. (1990). *Integracja-percepcyjno-motoryczna. Metody diagnozy i terapii* [Perceptual-motor integration. Methods of diagnosis and therapy]. Centralny Ośrodek metodyczny poradnictwa wychowawczo-zawodoweg ministerstwa edukacji narodowej [Central Methodical Center for Educational and Vocational Counseling of the Ministry of National Education Publishing].

Bogdanowicz, M. (1992). *Leworęczność u dzieci* [Left-handedness in children]. WSiP Publishers.

Bogdanowicz, M. (1997). *Integracja percepcyjno – Motoryczna* [Perceptual and motor integration]. Methodological Center for Psychological and Pedagogical Assistance.

Bogdanowicz, M. (2011). *Ryzyko Dysleksji, dysortografii i dysgrafii. Skala ryzyka Dysleksji wraz z normami dla klas 1 i 2* [Risk of dyslexia, dysorthography and dysgraphia. The dyslexia risk scale with standards for grades 1 and 2]. Harmonia Publishers.

Bogdanowicz, M. *Test Czytania Głośnego – Dom Marka* [Reading aloud test – Mark's house]. https://pracowniatestow.pl/pl/p/Test-czytania-glosnego-Dom-Marka.-DM/95 (accessed 10.08.2022).

Bogdanowicz, M., Bala, J., & Klima, E. (2011). *Ocena Lateralizacji Czynności Ruchowych – Zestaw zadań diagnostycznych, broszura informacyjna* [Assessment of lateralization of movement activities – a set of diagnostic tasks, information brochure] (pp. 24–26). ZPH Pilch Publishers.

Bogdanowicz, M., Jaworowska, A., Krasowicz-Kupis, G., Matczak, A., Pelc-Pękala, O., Pietras, I., Stańczak, J., & Szczerbiński, M. (2014). *Dysleksja 3 – Diagnoza dysleksji u uczniów klasy III szkoły podstawowej* [Dyslexia 3 – Dyslexia diagnosis in 3rd grade students of primary school]. Pracownia Testów Psychologicznych Polskiego Towarzystwa Psychologicznego. Retrieved August 10, 2022, from https://www.practest.com.pl/stosowanie-baterii-dysleksja-3-i-5-po-reformie-edukacyjnej.

Bogdanowicz, M., Kalka, D., Karpińska, E., Sajewicz-Radtke, U., & Radtke, B. M. (2010). *Bateria metod diagnozy przyczyn niepowodzeń szkolnych u uczniów w wieku 7–9 lat* [A battery of methods for diagnosing the causes of school failure in students aged 7–9]. Pracownia Testów Psychologicznych i Pedagogicznych. Retrieved August 10, 2022, from https://pracowniatestow.pl/pl/p/Bateria-metod-diagnozy-przyczyn-niepowodzen-szkolnych-u-uczniow-w-wieku-7–9-lat-B79-Protok-badania/125.

Braun – Gałkowska, M. (1985). *Test rysunku rodziny* [Family drawing test]. KUL Publishing House.

Brejnak, W. (2006). *Czy twój przedszkolak dojrzał do nauki?* [Is your preschooler ready to learn?]. PZWL Publishers.

Brejnak, W., Kitlińska-Pięta, H., & Nowak, E. (2007). *Diagnozowanie osiągnięć edukacyjnych uczniów klas I-III* [Diagnosing the educational achievements of students in grades 1–3]. Żak Zofia Dobkowska Educational Publishing House.

Chęciek, M. (1993). *Kwestionariusz Cooperów do oceny jąkania* [Cooper questionnaire for stuttering assessment]. Orator Foundation Press.

Chęciek, M. (2000). *Kwestionariusz Cooperów do oceny jąkania. Zarys terapii* [Cooper questionnaire for stuttering assessment. Outline of therapy]. Orator Foundation Press.

Chermet-Carroy, S. (2005). *Zrozum rysunki dziecka czyli jak interpretować rysunki małych dzieci: Kolory, kształty, postacie* [Understand your child's drawings, or how to interpret toddlers' drawings: Colors, shapes, figures] [J. Kluza, Trans]. Ravi Publishers.

Chojak, M. (2019). *Rodzice a gotowość szkolna dzieci – Aspekt teoretyczny i praktyczny* [Parents and school readiness of children – Theoretical and practical aspect]. UMCS Publishing House.

Choynowski, M. (1971). *Test Bender Koppitz dla dzieci od 5 do 10 lat* [Bender Koppitz test for children from 5 to 10 years old]. Polish Society of Mental Hygiene.

Ciechanowicz, A., Jaworowska, A., Matczak, A., & Szustrowa, T. (1995). *Bateria Testów APIS-P (R)* [APIS-P (R) test battery]. Psychological Test Lab Publishers.

Cybis, N., Drop, E., Rowiński, T., & Cieciuch, J. (2013). *Uczeń zdolny – Analiza dostępnych narzędzi diagnostycznych* [Gifted student – Analysis of available diagnostic tools]. Center of the Development of Education Press.

Demel, G. (1994). *Minimum logopedyczne nauczyciela przedszkola* [Speech therapy minimum for a kindergarten teacher]. School and Pedagogical Publishers.

Demel, G. (1998). *Logopedia – kwestionariusz obrazkowy + karta badania mowy pakiet do badania mowy dzieci w przedszkolach i szkołach* [Speech therapy – picture questionnaire + speech test card package for testing the speech of children in kindergartens and schools]. WSiP Publishers.

Dłużniewska, A., & Szubielska, M. (2017). Diagnoza – Definicja, klasyfikacje, modele, narzędzia [Diagnosis – Definition, classifications, models, tools]. In K. Krakowiak (Ed.), *Diagnoza specjalnych potrzeb rozwojowych i edukacyjnych dzieci i młodzieży. Standardy, wytyczne oraz wskazówki do przygotowywania i adaptacji narzędzi diagnostycznych dla dzieci i młodzieży z wybranymi specjalnymi potrzebami rozwojowymi i edukacyjnymi* [Diagnosis of special developmental and educational needs of children and adolescents. Standards, guidelines and guidelines for the preparation and adaptation of diagnostic tools for children and adolescents with selected special development and educational needs] (pp. 20–44). Center of the Development of Education.

Drewniak-Wołosz, E., & Paluch, A. (2018). *KOJD-AFA Karty Oceny Języka Dziecka-AFA* [KOJD-AFA child language assessment cards-AFA]. Komlogo. Retrieved July 17, 2022, from https://www.komlogo.pl/index.php/kategorie/diagnoza/karty-oceny-gotowo%C5%9Bci-szkolnej-kogs-detail.

Duksa, P. (2011). Rysunek dziecka w diagnozie psychopedagogicznej [Drawing of a child in psycho-pedagogical diagnosis]. *Studia Elbląskie, 12,* 425–435.

Eby, J., & Smutny, J. (1998). *Jak kształcić uzdolnienia dzieci i młodzieży* [How to educate children and adolescents' talents]. School and Pedagogical Publishers.

Emiluta-Rozya, D., Mierzejewska, H., & Atys, P. (1995). *Badania przesiewowe do wykrywania zaburzeń rozwoju mowy dzieci dwu-, cztero- i sześcioletnich* [Screening tests for detecting speech development disorders in two-, four- and six-year-old children]. Wyższa Szkoła Pedagogiki Specjalnej im. Maria Grzegorzewska Publishing House.

EURYDICE. (2011). *Grade retention during compulsory education in Europe: Regulations and statistics* (pp. 12–36). Education, Audiovisual and Culture Executive Agency. https://doi.org/10.2797/50570.

Fietz, J. (1932). O dojrzałości dziecka do szkoły [On the child's school readiness]. *Kwartalnik Pedagogiczny* [Educational Quarterly], *2*(2), 10–21.

Fleck-Bangert, R. (2001). *O czym mówią rysunki dzieci* [What the children's drawings talk about]. Jedność Publishers.

Frostig, M. (1999). Test rozwoju percepcji wzrokowej [polska standaryzacja; E. Pietsch-Szurek, B. Szmigielska-Siuta, J. Siuta, 1990] [Visual perception development test <Polish standardization; E. Pietsch-Szurek, B. Szmigielska-Siuta, J. Siuta, 1990>] Pracownia Testów Psychologicznych Polskiego Towarzystwa Psychologicznego [Laboratory of Psychological Tests of the Polish Psychological Association].

Frydrychowicz, A., Koźniewska, E., Matuszewski, A., & Zwierzyńska, E. (2006). *Skala Gotowości Szkolnej (SGS)* [School readiness scale (SRS)]. Methodological Center for Psychological and Pedagogical Assistance.

Gardner, H., Kornhaber, M. L., & Wake, W. K. (2001). *Inteligencja. Wielorakie perspektywy* [Intelligence. Multiple perspectives]. School and Pedagogical Publishers.

Gołąbek, T., & Jasiak, H. (1986). *Trener domowy – Jesień* [Home trainer – Fall issue]. SPAR Publishers.

Grabias, S., Kurkowski, Z. M., & Woźniak, T. (2007). *Logopedyczny test przesiewowy dla dzieci w wieku szkolnym wyd. 2* [Speech therapy screening test for school-age children. Second edition]. Maria Curie-Skłodowska University Department of Speech Therapy and Applied Linguistics, Polish Society of Speech Therapy.

Grabs, S., Kurkowski, Z. M., & Woźniak, T. (2002). *Logopedyczny test przesiewowy dla dzieci w wieku szkolnym* [Speech therapy screening test for school-age children]. Maria Curie-Skłodowska University Department of Speech Therapy and Applied Linguistics, Polish Society of Speech Therapy.

Gruba, J. (2018). *Karty Oceny Logopedycznej Dziecka. Podręcznik* [Speech therapy assessment cards for a child. A textbook]. Komlogo Publishers. Retrieved July 17, 2022, from https://www.komlogo.pl/index.php/kategorie/diagnoza/karty-oceny-gotowo%C5%9Bci-szkolnej-kogs-detail.

Gruba, J. (2012). *Ocena słuchu fonemowego u dzieci w wielu przedszkolnym* (Assessment of phonemic hearing of preschoolers]. University of Silesia Publishing House.

Gut, M. (2007). Preferencja ręki – Rozwój, determinant i metody pomiaru [Hand preference – Development, determinants and methods of measurement], *Logopeda* [Speech Therapist], *1*(4), 30–77.

Guziuk-Tkacz, M. (2011). *Badania diagnostyczne w pedagogice i psychopedagogice* [Diagnostic research in pedagogy and psychopedagogy]. Żak Academic Press.

Harris, A. J. (1958). *Harris tests of lateral dominance.* The Psychological Corporation.

Heimer, S., Mišigoj-Duraković, M., Ružić, L., Matković, B., Prskalo, I., Beri, S., Tonković-Lojović, M. (2004). Fitness level of adult economically active population in the Republic of Croatia estimated by Eurofit System. *Collegium Antropologicum*, *28*(1), 223–233. Retrieved August 22, 2022, from https://hrcak.srce.hr/file/7946.

Iskra, L., & Szuchnik, J. (2005). *Diagnoza logopedyczna* [Speech therapy diagnosis]. In T. Gałkowski, E. Szeląg, & G. Jastrzębowska (Eds.), *Podstawy neurologopedii. Podręcznik akademicki* [Fundamentals of neurologopedics. Academic textbook] (pp. 297–299). Opole University Publishing House.

Kaczmarek, L. (1955). *Kwestionariusz do ustalania zaburzeń mowy u dzieci* [Questionnaire for determining speech disorders in children]. PWN.

Kaja, B. (2001). *Zarys terapii dziecka* [Outline of child therapy]. Akademia Bydgoska im. Kazimierza Wielkiego Publishing House.

Kaleta-Witusiak, M., Kopik, A., & Walasek-Jarosz, B. (2013). *Techniki gromadzenia i analizy wiedzy o uczniu. Casebook ze wskazówkami dla praktyków* [Techniques for collecting and analyzing knowledge about the student. A casebook with tips for practitioners]. Staropolska Szkoła Wyższa w Kielcach Publishing House.

Kamińska, A., & Kowalczyk, A. (2014). Metody i techniki diagnozowania uczniów zdolnych na tle tworzonego przez nauczycieli środowiska sprzyjającego diagnozie [The methods and tools of diagnostic assessment of gifted learners, considered in relation to the creation of an environment conducive to diagnosis by teachers]. *Edukacja Elementarna w Teorii i Praktyce: Kwartalnik Dla Nauczycieli* [Elementary Education in Theory and Practice: Quarterly for Teachers], *33*(3), 207–220.

Kaplan, E., Goodglass, H., & Weintraub, S. (1983). Boston Naming Test (BNT), *APA PsycTests*. https://doi.org/10.1037/t27208-000.

Karwowski, M. (2006). Intuicja jako zdolność, wymiar osobowości i styl funkcjonowania. Syntetyzujący przegląd niektórych stanowisk psychologicznych [Intuition as an ability, dimension of personality and style of functioning. A synthesizing review of some psychological position]. *Studia Psychologica: Theoria Et Praxis*, (6), 189–206.

Kelman, E., & Nicholas, A. (2013). *Praktyczna interwencja w jąkaniu wczesnodziecięcym* [Practical intervention in early childhood stuttering]. Harmonia Universalis Press.

Kephart, N. C. (1970). *Dziecko opóźnione w nauce szkolnej* [Child with school retardation]. PWN.

Konarzewski, K. (2000). *Jak uprawiać badania oświatowe. Metodologia praktyczna* [How to do educational research. Practical methodology]. WSiP Publishers.

Kopik, A., & Zatorska, M. (2009). *Wielointeligentne odkrywanie świata. Program edukacji wczesnoszkolnej (maszynopis)* [Multi-intelligent world discovery. Early school education program (typescript)]. Center of the Development of Education Press.

Kopik, A., & Zatorska, M. (2011). *Wielointeligentne odkrywanie świata w przedszkolu. Program wychowania przedszkolnego* [Multi-intelligent discovering the world in kindergarten. Pre-school education program]. European Agency of Development Publishers.

Kostrzewski, J. (1971). Wyniki badań dojrzałości społecznej 1530 dzieci w wieku od 2 do 30 miesięcy dokonanych polskim przekładem skali Edgara A. Dolla [The results of the social maturity survey of 1,530 children aged 2 to 30 months using the Polish translation of The Edgar A. Doll scale]. *Roczniki Filozoficzne* [Annals of Philosophy], *19*(4), 115–146.

Kostrzewski, J. (1981). Problem rzetelności i trafności testu pomiaru słuchu fonematycznego [The problem of reliability and validity of the phonemic hearing test]. *Zagadnienia Wychowawcze a Zdrowie Psychiczne* [Educational Issues and Mental Health], *11*(1/1981), 56–85.

Koźniewska, E. (2006). *Skala Gotowości Szkolnej* [School readiness scale]. Methodical Center for Psychological and Pedagogical Assistance Publishers.

Krajna, E. (2015). *100-wyrazowy test artykulacyjny* [100-word articulation test]. Komlogo Publishers.

Krajna, E. (2008). *100-wyrazowy test artykulacyjny* [100-word articulation test]. Komlogo Publishers.

Krakowiak, K., & Panasiuk, M. (1992). *Umiejętności komunikacyjne dziecka z uszkodzonym słuchem* [Communication skills of a hearing-impaired child]. Maria Curie-Skłodowska University Press.

Krasowicz-Kupis, G. (2008). *Psychologia dysleksji* [The psychology of dyslexia]. PWN Publishers.

Krawiec, M. (2003). *Próby do badania kompetencji językowej dzieci 6–8-letnich z uszkodzeniami słuchu* [Attempts to test the language competence of 6–8-year-old children with hearing impairments]. SODiR-PZG Publishers.

Kulkarni, S. D., Desai, H. R., Sharma, C. S., & Bhatt, P. J. (2010, Oct–Dec). Assessment of muscular fitness in school children using Kraus-Weber tests. *NJIRM*, *1*(4), 30–35. Retrieved August 10, 2022, from http://njirm.pbworks.com/f/6muscular+fitness.pub.pdf.

Kurkowski, Z. M. (2003). *Próba sylabowa do oceny niepłynności mówienia* [The syllabic test for the assessment of speech fluidity]. IFPS Publishers.

Kurkowski, Z. M., Szuchnik, J., & Kurkowska, E. (2013). *Audiogenne uwarunkowania zaburzeń komunikacji językowej* [Audiogenic determinants of language communication disorders]. Maria Curie-Skłodowska University Press.

Majewska- Tworek, A. (2000). *Dialogowy test artykulacji* [Dialogue test of articulation]. Orator Foundation Publishers.

Matéjček Žlab, Z. (1983). *Test lateralizacji. Psychdiagnostické a didaktické testy* [Lateralization test. Psychdiagnostic and didactic tests]. NP Publishing House.

Matczak, A., & Piekarska, J. (2011). *Test Rozumienia Emocji (TRE)* [Emotional understanding test (EUT)]. Retrieved August 10, 2022, from https://www.practest.com.pl/tre-test-rozumienia-emocji.

Michalak-Widera, I., & Węsierska, K. (2014). *Test do badań przesiewowych mowy dla dzieci w wieku przedszkolnym* [Speech screening test for preschool children]. Unikat 2 Publishers.

Millard, S. K., Nicholas, A., & Cook, F. M. (2009). Is parent-child interaction therapy effective in reducing stuttering? *Journal of Speech, Language, and Hearing Research.* 2008 Jun;51(3):636–50. https://doi.org/10.1044/1092-4388(2008/046).

Minczakiewicz, E. M. (1997). *Logopedia. Mowa. Rozwój-zaburzenia-terapii* [Speech therapy. Speech. Development-therapy-disorders]. Scientific Publishers of the Pedagogical Academy in Cracow.

Montesa, G., Łotyczewski, B. S., Halterman, J. S., & Hightower, A. D. (2012). School readiness of children with behavioral problems when entering kindergarten: Results of a US national survey. *European Journal of Pediatrics, 171,* 541–548. https://doi.org/10.1007/s00431-011-1605-4.

Muszyńska, J., & Żarczyńska, A. (1976). *Rozpoznawanie trudności w nauce czytania i pisania uczniów klas pierwszych szkoły podstawowej. Zeszyt do indywidualnych badań* [Identifying difficulties in learning to read and write in first grade students of primary school. A book for individual research]. UWM Publishing House.

Nowak, J. (1993). *Piosenka w usprawnianiu wymowy dzieci z trudnościami w uczeniu się* [Song in improving the pronunciation of children with learning difficulties]. UKW Publishers.

Nowak-Czerwińska, M. (1994). Test słuchowego różnicowania głosek (TSRG) [Auditory differentiation Test (TSRG)]. In *Mowa głośna i pismo. Materiały z Konferencji Naukowej Sekcji Logopedycznej Towarzystwa Kultury Języka* [Loud speech and handwriting. Materials from the scientific conference of the speech therapy section of the language culture society]. Bialystok University Publishing House.

Pąchalska, M. (1999). *Afazjologia* [Aphasiology]. PWN.

Paluch, A., Drewniak-Wołosz, E., & Mikosza, L. (2003). *AFA SKALA – jak badać mowę dziecka afatycznego?* [AFA SKALA – how to study the speech of an aphatic child?]. Impuls Publishing House.

Pilicz, S., Przewęda, R., Dobosz, J., & Nowacka-Dobosz, S. (2005). Punktacja Sprawności Fizycznej młodzieży polskiej wg Międzynarodowego testu Sprawności Fizycznej. Kryteria pomiaru wydolności organizmu testem Coopera [Scoring of the physical fitness of Polish youth according to the international physical fitness test. Criteria for measuring the body's efficiency with the cooper test]. *Studia i Monografie* [Studies and Monographies], II(94), 6–137. http://www.zs9.bydgoszcz.pl/sites/default/files/MTSF%20opis%20AWF.pdf.

Prasad, S. (2013). A survey of minimum muscular strength on school children in Pune district. *IJMESS, 2*(2), 60–62. Retrieved August 11, 2022, from http://www.ijpehss.org/admin/image/99b4fd319900a0354aa107b4852616241495129939361.pdf.

Przewęda, R. (1973). *Rozwój somatyczny i motoryczny* [Somatic and motor development]. PZWS Publishers.

Puchowska-Florek, M., Książkiewicz, B., & Nowaczewska, M. (2005). Ocena przydatności wybranych skal i testów do oceny afazji u pacjentów w ostrym okresie udaru mózgu [Evaluation of the usefulness of selected scales and tests for the assessment of aphasia in patients with acute stroke]. *Udar Mózgu* [Brain Stroke], *VII*(2), 39–47.

Renzulli, J., & Reis, S. (1997). *The schoolwide enrichment model* (2nd ed.). Creative Learning Press.

Rocławski, B. (2001). *Słuch fonemowy i fonetyczny, Teoria i praktyka* [Phonemic and phonetic hearing, Theory and practice]. Glottispol Publishers.

Rodak, H., & Nawrocka, D. (1993). *Od obrazka do słowa. Poradnik dla pedagogów, logopedów i rodziców dzieci z trudnościami w porozumiewaniu się* [From picture to word. A guide for educators, speech therapists and parents of children with communication difficulties]. WSiP Publishers.

Rodriguez, N. (2011). *Co nam mówią rysunki dzieci* [What the children's drawings tell us] (K. Schmidt, Trans). Jedność Publishers.

Salovey, P., & Meyer, J. D. (1990). Emotional intelligence. Imagination. *Cognition and Personality*, *9*, 185–211.

Sekita, B. (1988). Rozwój somatyczny i sprawność fizyczna dzieci w wieku 3–7 lat [Somatic development and physical fitness of children aged 3–7]. In S. Pilicz (Ed.), *Rozwój sprawności i wydolności fizycznej dzieci i młodzieży* [Development of fitness and physical efficiency of children and adolescents] (pp. 23–25). Academy of Physical Education Press.

Słyszowa, S. (1974). *Poznawanie dzieci rozpoczynających naukę i kierowanie ich rozwojem* [Getting to know children starting learning and managing their development]. WSiP Publishers.

Stambak, M. (1974). Test odtwarzania struktur rytmicznych [Rhythm structure playback test]. In R. Zazzo (Ed.), *Metody psychologicznego badania dziecka* [Methods of psychological examination of children] (transl. M. Maniecka, E. Lewicka). PZWL Publishers.

Stecko, E. (2009). *Sprawdź, jak mówię – Karta badania logopedycznego z materiałami pomocniczymi* [Check how I speak – Speech therapy examination card with auxiliary materials]. ES Publishers.

Stecko, E. (2014). *Sprawdź, jak mówię. Karta badania logopedycznego z materiałami* [Check, how I speak. Speech therapy examination card with materials]. E. S. Dr Stecko Publishers.

Styczek, I. (1982). *Badanie i kształtowanie słuchu fonematycznego (komentarz i tablice)* [Research and development of phonemic hearing (commentary and tables)]. WSiP Publishers.

Szczerbiński, M., & Pelc-Pękala, O. (2013). *Zestaw metod diagnozy trudności w czytaniu: Test Dekodowania – Podręcznik* [A set of methods for diagnosing Reading difficulties: Decoding test – Textbook]. SEBG Laboratory of Psychological and Pedagogical Tests Publishers.

Szeląg, E., & Szymaszek, A. (2006). *Test do badania słuchu fonematycznego u dzieci i dorosłych* [Test for phonemic hearing in children and adults]. Gdańsk Psychological Publishers.

Szewczuk, K. (2014). Gotowość szkolna dzieci 5-i 6-letnich w zakresie kompetencji matematycznych – Analiza porównawcza [School readiness of 5 and 6-year-old children in the field of mathematical competences – A comparative analysis]. *Edukacja Elementarna w Teorii i Praktyce* [Elementary Education in Theory and Practice], *9*(33), 25–48. doi: https://doi.org/10.14632/eetp_33.2.

Szmigielska, B. (1996). *Skala Poczucia Kontroli u Dzieci Przedszkolnych SPK-DP*. Publishing House of the Psychological Test Lab of the Polish Psychological Association.

Szuchnik, J., & Święcicka, A. (2003). *Program rozwijania i oceny odbioru słuchowego dźwięków otoczenia i mowy* [A program for developing and evaluating auditory perception of ambient sounds and speech]. Papers issued by the Institute of Physiology and Pathology of Hearing.

Szumska, J. (1980). *Metody badania afazji* [Methods of examining aphasia]. PZWL Publishers.

Tarkowski, Z. (1992a). *Kwestionariusz niepłynności mówienia i logofobii* [Speech disfluency and logophobia questionnaire]. Orator Foundation Publishers.

Tarkowski, Z. (1992b). *Przesiewowy test Logopedyczny* [Speech therapy screening test]. Orator Foundation Publishers.

Tarkowski, Z. (1992c). *Test sprawności językowej* [Language proficiency test]. Orator Foundation Publishers.

Tarkowski, Z. (2002). *Przesiewowy test logopedyczny* [Speech therapy screening test]. Orator Foundation Publishers.

Tomkinson, G. R., Carver, C. D., Daniell, N. D., Lewis, L. K., Fitzgerald, J. S., Lang, J. J., & Ortega, F. B. (2018). European Normative values for physical fitness in children and adolescents aged 9–17 years: Results from 2 779 165 Eurofit performances representing 30 countries. *British Journal of Sports Medicine*, *52*, 1445–1456. https://doi.org/10.1136/bjsports-2017-098253.

Węsierska, K., & Jeziorczak, B. (2016). *DJ – Diagnoza jąkania u dzieci w wieku przedszkolnym* [DJ – Diagnosis of stuttering in preschool children]. Komlogo Publishers.

Wilgocka-Okoń, B. (1972). *Dojrzałość szkolna dzieci a środowisko* [School maturity of children and the environment]. PWN Publishers.

Wilgocka-Okoń, B. (2002). Gotowość szkolna w perspektywie historycznej: O pomyślny start ucznia w szkole [School readiness in a historical perspective: For the successful start of a student at school]. In W. Brejnak (Ed.), *Biuletyn informacyjny PTD* [PTD information bulletin] (*Vol. 23*, pp. 70–80).

Włoch, S., & Włoch, A. (2009). *Diagnoza całościowa w edukacji przedszkolnej i wczesnoszkolnej* [Comprehensive diagnosis in preschool and early childhood education]. Żak Academic Press.

Zazzo, R. (1974). *Metody psychologicznego badania dzieci* [Methods of psychological examination of children]. PZWL Publishers.

5 Suggestions for exercises and games used in pedagogical and speech therapy in improving disturbed areas

How to deal with a child's emotions? – A survey of selected exercises and games

The exercises and games presented here are intended for children in preschool and early school age (grades 1–3). They can be conducted in kindergarten, school, therapy institutions and at home. Their goal is to help children recognize positive and negative emotions and teach them to feel better when they experience difficult feelings triggered by unfavorable situations. The included exercises/games have been developed based on the practical experience of the authors of the book.

How to tame anxiety?

Due to the situation related to the outbreak of the pandemic caused by the SARS-CoV-2 virus (a virus belonging to the coronavirus group) experienced by the whole world, many children are afraid of wearing a mask. The aim of this exercise is to help the children to tame the fear associated with wearing the mask and, above all, to persuade them to wear it.

What you need: a piece of fabric (preferably cotton), a patch with a favorite hero or a motif from a child's favorite fairy tale, an elastic band, a needle, and thread.

The course of the exercise: tell the child what will be performed during the exercise, emphasizing its cognitive values and stressing on fun. Encourage the child to make two masks: one for him/her and another one for his/her favorite toy together. It should be ensured that the material from which the mask will be made is pleasant to the touch, delicate, preferably made of cotton. It is advisable that the material includes a motif from the child's favorite fairy tale; in the absence of such material, you can use a patch that will contain the said motif or your favorite fairy tale hero. After the child has made a mask with the help of a teacher, encourage them to also make the mask for their favorite mascot, soft toy, doll, etc. It is important that the child actively participates in both the design of the mask and its implementation. After making the mask, you could instruct/teach the child how to properly and

DOI: 10.4324/9781003354758-6

safely put the mask on, wear it and take it off. When teaching how to wear the mask, you can refer to the child's favorite fairy-tale characters, whose heroes wear masks (e.g. superheroes); it should be emphasized that every child who wears a mask is such a superhero. This type of exercise can also be carried out during joint workshops in which not only children and teachers but also the learners' parents will participate.

Illustration of emotions

The aim of the exercise is to help the child recognize and name such feelings as happiness, fear, sadness, nervousness. Preschool (and early school) children express their emotions through drawing and talk about them willingly.

What you need: paper, crayons, felt-tip pens, pencils (or other writing tools), paints will be helpful in this exercise.

The course of the exercise: encourage the child to make drawings that will show a happy boy, a scared girl, a sad gentleman and a nervous woman. Drawings can be made in any technique, preferably the one that gives the child the most joy (the child is eager to do the job). By asking questions, encourage the child to discuss each of the prepared drawings (tell you what each of them represents). Some examples of the questions you may ask are: (a) How do you think you can tell when a boy is happy? (b) Why do you think this boy is happy? (c) What do children do when they are happy? (d) What is happiness, can you tell us about it? (e) Are you a happy child? (f) When was the last time you felt happy? (g) How do you think you can tell when a girl is scared? (h) Why do you think this girl is scared? (i) What do children do when they are scared? (j) What is fear, can you tell us about it? (k) Have you felt scared lately? What happened then? (l) Who can a child talk to if he or she has become scared? (m) How do you think you can tell when you are sad? (n) Why do you think this gentleman is sad? (o) What do children do when they are sad? (p) What is sadness, how does it manifest itself, tell me about it? (q) Have you felt sad lately? (r) What happened then, tell me about it? (s) Who can a child talk to when he or she is sad? (t) How do you think you can tell if the lady is upset? (u) Why do you think this lady is upset? (v) What do children do when they are upset? (w) What is nervousness, can you tell us about it? (x) Have you experienced any nervousness? What was the situation? Can you tell us about it? (y) Who can a child talk to if he or she is upset?

The definition of anger

The purpose of this exercise is to equip the child with knowledge about the emotions of anger. The exercise is perfect for working with children from grades 1–3 of primary school.

What you need: paper, pencil, pen, or other writing tool will be helpful in this exercise.

The course of the exercise: children and adults (one of the parents, the legal guardian, or the child's teacher) take part in the exercise. The exercise takes the form of the so-called unfinished sentences that are completed by both adults and children. After completing the sentences, you should conduct a joint conversation with the child and their parent(s) regarding the information that they have supplemented, and ask what they learned about each other and what it resulted from. An exemplary set of sentences to be possibly completed may look as follows:

1 I feel angry when you .... and that's why I'm asking you to ....
2 I don't like when you get angry because then ....….......…
3 Through anger you express ....….....
4 Anger gives me ....…....
5 Anger helps me in ....…....…
6 Anger takes away from me ....…......…
7 Anger disturbs me in ....…..........…
8 I will replace anger ....…....

Suggestions for exercises and games to improve a child's concentration and attention

The following suggestions for exercises and games are aimed at improving young learners' concentration and attention in the older preschool age (5–6 years) and early school age (grades 1–3). They can be conducted in a kindergarten or primary school. All the exercises and games have been designed by the authors of this book.

Inverted letter

The aim of the exercise is to improve a child's concentration and attention related to reading a written letter in a form other than the traditional one.

What you need: an adult (preferably a parent) or a teacher, a child, a stick or a pencil.

The course of the exercise: the child turns his back to the parent, on which the parent writes a letter to the child with a finger, a stick or the opposite side of the pencil, with any content. The child, focusing his attention, reads the text written on his back – word after word. When the reading has been found correct, the roles may be changed – now the child writes a letter to the parent on the parent's back. The game can be repeated several times. Students themselves can also participate.

Juggler (Cheater)

The aim of the exercise/play is to shape and improve concentration of attention.

The course of the exercise: at least two people take part in the game (playing in pairs). One of the players uses certain gestures and/or movements (in the case of preschool children, it may be an activity determined by the teacher, and in the case of older children, that is, from grades 1–3, it may be an activity invented by themselves), for example, scratching my head and at the same time incorrectly (falsely) naming this activity, saying, for example 'I am combing my hair'. The task of the second person is to determine what activity was performed (shown) by the first person and name it (saying: 'she was scratching her head') as well as by showing another activity with a gesture, for example, scratching the cheek – deceiving the opponent. The fun continues until one of the players is the first to make a mistake. The game can be expanded to include more children (players), but it should be remembered that each child should play the role of both the showman and the guesser.

A champion of remembering

The purpose of the exercise/play is to improve concentration. Taking part in this play requires a lot of concentration of attention.

The course of the exercise: all children of a given preschool group (or school group, i.e. a given class) can participate in the game. The chosen child leaves the class for a moment, and the other children choose partners and make pairs. Each pair determines a specific sign or movement, such as tapping their hands on their thighs, clapping their hands, stamping their feet, etc. Then the children scatter all over the room and invite the child waiting outside the door to come back into the room. After entering the room, the child looks around, carefully observing his/her peers, their behavior, activities and movements. The child's task is to pair up those children who perform the same activity or movement. Those children who will be paired go aside. The fun ends when all the children are joined in pairs.

Selected exercises and/or games to improve learning the skill of reading, with comments and practical tips

The presented suggestions for exercises and games aimed to improve learning the skill of reading take into account the way of mastering the skill of reading as soon as possible. These are selected exercises and games that can be used in working with preschool children, those attending the so-called 'zero' classes and those of early school education (grades 1–3). It is important that, when selecting exercises and games, the teacher takes into account the abilities of children (i.e. their level of psycho-social and motor development) and also refers to the core curriculum applicable at the indicated level of education in a given country. Some of the proposed exercises and games have been developed by the authors and take into account the phonetics and the knowledge of the letters that are used in the alphabet of the Polish language. They can be used to practice the skill of reading taught in preschool and school institutions in Poland (mainly at the level of early childhood education). However, most of the proposed exercises can be used by teachers working in different countries with children of a certain age.

Before we go over to refer the readers to study the suggestions for games and exercises, the question concerning the age a child could start learning how to read ought to be asked and answered. We will not find an unequivocal answer to this question, but while being with a child, playing with them, we are able – as parents or kindergarten teachers – to notice the child's first interest in a book – this, obviously, is not learning to read. In order for a child to develop the skill of reading, their brain must develop gradually, which will enable them to use the abstract thinking, analysis and synthesis of information that is necessary for this learning. If this stage is not yet visible in the child's development (it has not come), the child will not be interested in reading anything. However, actions can be taken to redirect a child's attention to letters and 'test' their readiness to read. If the child does not react to the situation, we should not force them to do so. Many teachers claim the age at which every child should be ready to learn to read can be called the so-called 'school readiness', which most often appears at the age of 6 or 7. As parents, we should not force a child to learn to read too early, but instead create situations for them to reach for books and be in contact with books on a daily basis – this is one way of attracting a child to a book.

The processes of learning to read and write are quite strongly integrated with each other. In some cases, these processes run simultaneously. A child who starts playing with letters, in practice, often grabs a writing tool (pen, crayon or pencil) and begins to draw the first letters, which at this stage are poorly formatted (lopsided, hardly legible). Therefore, some of the exercise suggestions presented next apply to both reading and writing.

Exercises helpful to improve the auditory and language functions

- all forms of exercises and games with the use of music, for example listening to musical fairy tales (often repeated), as well as active participation in different forms of storytelling and/or independent creation of story ends;
- nursery rhyme games, for example choosing rhyming names based on pictures (the teacher places different pictures in front of the child; the teacher names each picture and asks the child to pair the pictures that rhyme, (e.g. *pee – tree, class – glass*, etc.);

- rhyming games: the teacher presents the child with a set of sentences with gaps, and the child's task is to complete them in such a way that the sentence ends in a rhyme, for example:

  - Round a tree flies a .... (bee).
  - Jack and Jill went up the .... (hill).
  - Old Mother Hubbard went to the .... (cupboard).
  - If you want to take a trip, climb aboard my rocket .... (ship).

- creating rhymes yourself: the teacher shows the child a word and his/her task is to create a rhyme to it, e.g. **hill** – *mill, pill, ill,* etc.;
- guessing on words broken down into syllables, for example *Pe-ter; Mar-tin; can-dy,* etc.;
- the play called *Chain of Words*: the teacher says the word aloud, and the child's task is to propose a word that begins with the letter that ends with the word said by the teacher, for example, when the teacher says the word *sad*, the child can say the word *dad*, etc.;
- activities based on listening and solving puzzles;
- creating rebuses out of selected words;
- creating words with the use of different syllables, transforming words by changing the sounds in different positions, for example *ear – are, pale – peal*);
- creating stories with the help of pictures;
- creating comic-like stories.

Exercises to help consolidate the knowledge of letters

- matching the same letters in pairs;
- searching for a given letter in the text;
- matching lowercase letters to uppercase letters and vice versa;
- matching printed letters to written letters;
- exercises in distinguishing letters with a similar graphic shape. In the Polish alphabet such letters are, for example, *b-d-g, m-n-u, l-ł-t*;
- searching for the letter indicated by the teacher in the words scrambled around, e.g. looking for all the vowels /a/, or /o/;
- matching the description to the picture, for example, the learner's task is to find the word *lemon* in the scrambled groups of letters scattered around, after she/he has been given a picture of a lemon.

Exercises to prepare for the introduction of basic concepts in the field of language science

- recognizing nouns as words describing the names of people, things, plants, animals;
- recognizing verbs as words describing the names of activities;

- indicating words with the opposite meaning;
- creating a family of words;
- arranging the alphabetical order of the words in concord with their first letters;
- recognizing types of sentences: affirmative, interrogative, exclamation;
- division of sentences into words, or paragraphs into sentences – counting letters, syllables, words, sentences.

Exercises in writing and reading sentences

- exercises in writing capital letters at the beginning of a sentence, in first and last names;
- matching sentences to pictures;
- arranging sentences from given words;
- completing missing words in sentences;
- independent production of answers to questions;
- composing questions to the text;
- arranging a picture story to the topic indicated by the teacher.

Exercises in reading and understanding short texts

- illustrating the text;
- searching for answers to the questions asked by the teacher that are hidden in the text;
- individual forming questions to the text read by the learners;
- free comments on the text just read by the learners.

Learning to read while having fun

Fun with the text

The child reads the text indicated by the teacher in a given period of time: next, the child divides it into segments, that is counts how many sentences, words and/or even sounds (both vowels and/or consonants) there are in the text. Additionally, the child may be asked to indicate in the text words that begin with a capital letter; or those that begin with the same letter (e.g. with the letter /a/); or how many identical words can be found there; etc.

This game can be developed by going further, for example asking the child to indicate in the text words that end with the same letter; or the same bound morpheme (e.g. -ed or –ing, etc.). The child can also be asked to search for words that begin and end with the same syllable; or the words that have the same second syllable indicated by the teacher, etc.

Word – answer

The role of the child in this game is to indicate in the text a word that is the answer to the question posed by the teacher, for example *What is the name of the main character of the story? Who is the main character of the story (boy or girl)? What animal is in the story?* etc.

Sentence – answer

The teacher asks the child a question, for example *What did Mum say to Alex?* The child's task is to indicate in the text the sentence that answers this question.

Selected exercises and games to improve the technique of writing, with comments and practical tips

The exercises and games in this section are about improving the learners' writing technique. All of them can be applied when working with 6-year-old children expected to be annually prepared for their school activities in the kindergarten and/or lower primary school students (grades 1–3) in attending their primary schools. The presented suggestions for exercises were developed by the authors on the basis of literature review and practical experience.

Before we move on to the proposal of exercises and games, it should be noted that improving the technique of writing requires the introduction of many exercises (the so-called warming up activities included), as well as improving the learners' gross and fine motor skills. Graphic exercises should observe the principle of gradation of difficulty, that is the work should begin on a large sheet, so as to gradually move on to a smaller format. Also, when choosing patterns, one should start with an activity based upon drawing straight lines, gradually moving to drawing diagonal lines, then waves and finally loops. Similar actions should be taken when writing in the ready-made ruler: start with wide lines, gradually moving to narrower ones. It is also important to choose the right writing tool. Pencils or crayons should be well sharpened and of appropriate hardness. Children with weak muscle tone should use pencils with a high hardness (H) – they mobilize the child to use more effort while drawing. Children with excessive muscle tension should work with soft tools, such as felt-tip pens or type B pencils. Below are some exercises and games to improve gross and fine motor skills. Exercises and games can be undertaken in different places the children like to be: in the playground, at home, in the preschool or school institution.

Games and exercises to improve gross motor skills

Backyard games: all kinds of movement games with the use of balls, scooters, skipping ropes; games on the playground with the use of swings, carousels, slides, etc.

Exercises to improve gross motor skills related to performing daily activities: independent dressing and undressing, fastening buttons, tying shoes, threading clothes to the other side; activities related to taking care of physiological needs (activities with self-service in the toilet); activities related to self-consumption of meals (of this type); such activities also affect the improvement of fine motor skills).

Fun-producing exercises with props: the child holds a ribbon or a scarf in his/her hands and, to the rhythm of the music, makes sweeping movements with his/her hands – once with one hand, then with the other and then with both hands.

Games and exercises with rubber: children, to the rhythm of the teacher's (guardian) indications, stretch the rubber while standing in a circle – raise their hands up, pull out to the sides, backwards.

Playing with large pieces of foil or other various materials: playing with a large surface area, or Klanza animation scarf – they are perfect for group games; for making sweeping movements, they allow one to fan, lift, wrap, run under them, toss objects, etc. These materials can also be used to construct houses or tents; one can perform various movements that imitate performing certain activities, such as washing clothes, shaking off, folding, etc. These types of games can be additionally made more attractive with music when the children perform the activities indicated by the teacher, to the rhythm of the music.

Playing with large surfaces, for example large sheets of gray paper, large boards, a playground with a hard (asphalt) surface: children draw with chalk (in the case of gray paper with a felt-tip pen) on a large surface, making sweeping movements, putting a lot of energy into this activity, discharging some tension.

Games and exercises to improve fine motor skills

Games and exercises with the use of various objects, for example playing with yarn (wool) – children arrange various patterns using a bench or a yarn rug, connect them with each other and freely move them around.

Placing puzzles: one can use self-made puzzles, for example colorful newspapers or postcards cut into large pieces. By arranging elements, the child exercises precision. In the case of older children, it can be difficult, for example, to cut the pictures into smaller pieces.

Playing with shoelaces: prepare a template made of thick cardboard, in which we make holes arranged in various patterns. Children thread the shoelaces through the holes, in this way creating various compositions. They can also learn how to tie shoelaces in bows.

Play with the use of thin wire: the child bends the wire according to the pattern/template specified by the teacher or creates his/her own compositions/shapes. This exercise improves the efficiency of the fingers and wrist, and shapes the child's imagination.

Painting with ten fingers: the child has at his/her disposal a large sheet of paper (or a large surface of white cloth) and a collection of paints, which should be muddy, placed in bowls, where the child can easily put both hands. With this kind of play, the child is allowed complete freedom and the initiative to paint. Painting is done with the child's hands and fingers. Before starting the game, you can present the child with instructions, such as: *There's paint in these cups. We will not use brushes, we have ten fingers – five on one hand and five on the other hand, so we will paint with our fingers. You can paint whatever you want, tell me when the painting is done.*

In a situation where children are afraid of getting their hands in the paint, encourage them, show them how to do it and slowly introduce them to the painting process. There should be a bowl of water and a towel nearby so that children can wash themselves immediately after the work is done.

According to Bielska (2001, pp. 32–33), the method of finger-painting with the use of colored paints, in addition to improving fine motor skills, eye-hand coordination and spatial orientation, strengthens the child's faith in his/her abilities, stimulates fantastic expression, relieves the child from all kinds of inhibition and/or overcomes anxiety. This method is also used in shaping attention concentration, logical thinking skills and relieving emotional tension.

Jakubczyk (2012, pp. 193–202) finds this method to be successfully used when working with preschool and early school children; it can take various variants, among which the following can be mentioned:

- painting with the back of the hand and then finger painting individual elements (fruit, leaves, flowers, geometric patterns);
- finger painting various shapes, later outlined with colored chalk;
- spilling paint on the paper and putting your fingers in it;
- painting hands with paints and imprinting their traces on paper;
- rubbing the paint with the wrist clockwise.

Playing with sticks, thread, wire: the game consists in threading various objects, such as buttons, beads of different sizes, or even pasta that has the shape of a tube, on the thread (stick or wire); this kind of game trains the learners' fingers and helps them learn to count.

Games and exercises with the use of a handkerchief: for example tying knots, arranging, rolling, etc. These kinds of games improve the efficiency of the fingers and wrist.

Games consisting in twisting and unscrewing screws, gluing models: for example, ships, cars, airplanes, creating buildings from small blocks (e.g. Lego). These kinds of games improve fine motor skills, especially the tips of the fingers.

Exercises to help one learn the correct grip and the way of holding a pencil or a crayon

- making balls, plasticine snakes;
- crushing paper balls;
- tearing out small papers;

- 'salting', that is crushing and sprinkling salt, groats or sand on the tray with small movements of the learner's fingers;
- drawing in a horizontal plane: on the paper lying on the bench, when the child is standing and his/her hand hangs down freely;
- drawing on a vertical plane: on a piece of paper stretched on a wall or blackboard, when the child stands with his hand raised at the level of the lower part of his face;
- using plastic caps for writing tools (Rafał-Łuniewska, 2010, p. 7).

Graphomotor exercises

The following exercises/games can be practiced:

Drawing differently shaped lines on the blackboard with chalk;

Drawing along the lines with dry-erase felt-tip pens: children have at their disposal various patterns on which they draw. Begin this type of exercise with simple patterns and gradually move to more complex patterns;

Drawing with tracing paper: children put the tracing paper on the picture, outline its shapes with a pencil, color them. In the absence of carbon paper, this exercise can be performed using parchment. The child puts parchment on the picture and draws a pencil around its shape; subsequently, it is colored with crayons;

Independent drawing or supplementing drawings.

When performing graphomotor exercises, special attention should be paid to whether the child holds the writing instruments properly (they cannot be held too lightly or too tightly), and whether the muscle tone is adequate (if the tension is too strong, the child's hand gets tired quickly, which can discourage him/her from writing) and whether the child writes from left to right and with which hand. In a situation where the child is left-handed, the teacher (or parent) should not force the child to transfer the writing tool to the right hand – **such a procedure is not acceptable**!

It is important to improve the smoothness of movements of the dominant hand (Bernacka, 2001; Przepióra, 2014). Before using the exercises (especially in the case of the so-called manual exercises), the teacher should show the children the correct way to perform the exercise, and even guide the child's movements, holding his/her hand in hers. It is important that the exercises chosen by the teacher bring joy to the children and are perceived by them as fun. Children should have fun with this type of activity, and their work (although it may not always be perfect) should be accepted by the teacher. In this situation, the final result does not count as the result of the child's work; what is of key importance here is the process of improving the child's manual skills.

Exercises strengthening eye–hand coordination (hand–eye cooperation)

- Cutting out shapes out of napkins or shapes out of newspapers: children use scissors to cut out the shapes indicated by the teacher;
- Cutting out elements from paper and pasting them into compositions: designing a collage (from French: *sticking*; *wrapping with paper*). Collage is an artistic technique consisting in forming compositions from various materials, such as newspapers, fabrics, photographs, small everyday objects, etc.; objects are glued onto canvas or paper and combined with traditional artistic techniques, for example with oil paint, acrylic paint, gouache (Bloom, 2006, pp. 4–5);
- Adding missing elements to a drawing or a pattern;
- Drawing lines on designated points: after combining them, a specific figure or form can be created;
- Drawing under dictation (the so-called graphic dictation): the teacher tells the learners aloud what figure and where on the piece of paper it is to be drawn; only lines can be used when drawing the said figure;
- Coloring small spaces, such as figures or mandalas (for information on mandala, see Tucci, 2001);
- Drawing different types of lines: vertical, horizontal, diagonal, wavy, looped, semicircular, or circular lines;
- Drawing various patterns in the air, or on sand trays (non-graphic techniques): with the use of various tools, such as chalk, drawing charcoal, markers, crayons, pencils, pen (graphic techniques), the children are requested to draw various shapes and/or patterns.

Exercises to develop orientation in the body and space schema

The following exercises can be applied:

- Outlining various parts of the body and naming them (e.g. the child draws an outline of his hand or foot on a piece of paper);
- Sending messages to the peer(s): for example, *Give me your right hand. Raise your left hand up*, etc.;
- Pointing a finger at objects in the picture and determining their location;
- Movement games based on the teacher's instructions, for example, *Jump on the right leg. Take a step forward*, etc.

The presented samples of exercises and games that can be used to improve the writing technique should be conducted systematically, in an atmosphere of peace and without rush. They should not be too much of a burden for the child as it may discourage them from working. Great attention should be paid to the learners who have writing difficulties, for example, the ones diagnosed with dyslexia. In the case of such children, their work should be assessed qualitatively, that is the assessment should be descriptive in terms of the mistakes made. Children's writing exercises should be checked by an adult, preferably a teacher or other specialist such as a speech therapist (for children with dyslexia). They should be carried out systematically and persistently; sometimes they may last for several or even more than several months. Only effective and systematic cooperation between the learner and the teacher determines a child's success.

Selected exercises and games to improve the breathing appartus, phonation, articulation and auditory perception devices

Selected exercises and games to improve the breathing apparatus and phonics

Proposals of exercises and games to improve the breathing apparatus and phonation processes are aimed at (a) developing the habit of proper breathing, extending the expiratory phase; (b) increasing lung capacity; (c) improving the volume of voice and muscle tension; (d) reducing excessive muscle tension; (e) shaping the uniformity of the force of exhalation; (f) implementing the economic use of air; (g) developing attention span; and (h) reducing stress. Breathing exercises are designed to prevent speaking while inhaling, respiratory arrhythmia, discrepancy between the spoken text and the rhythm of breathing. This is because children are not yet able to manage their breathing properly and therefore maintain the correct rhythm of speech. All the proposals presented below have been taken from (or modelled on) the ideas suggested by the following speech therapists or speech therapy researchers: Dembińska (1994), Morkowska (1998), and Siedlaczek-Szwed and Jałowiecka-Frania (2016).

The speech therapist shows and briefly explains the essence of proper breathing. The child places one hand on the speech therapist's abdomen (lower chest) and the other hand on the upper chest. The diaphragm, moving downwards when inhaled, exerts pressure on the abdomen, which bulges out; on exhalation, the diaphragm returns to its previous position, that is it rises and the abdomen falls. Examples of exercises and games:

- *Bear's swing* – children lie down in a comfortable position on their backs. They put one hand on the upper chest and the other on the stomach. They try to feel their bellies rise as they breathe in, and feel how their bellies drop as they exhale (they gradually lengthen this activity). They then place the mascots on their stomachs and watch them 'swing'.
- *Walk in the meadow* (playing with relaxing music) – the participants imagine a walk in the meadow, breathe fresh air through their noses, smell the flowers, blow their petals.

- *Inflating the balloons* – children imitate the act of blowing up a balloon, draw air through their nose and inflate the balloon. The air is escaping from the balloon with a hissing sound *sss* …
- *Blowing on hot soup* – children produce the sound *fff* …
- *Blowing on feathers* – children blow on colorful feathers and balls made of cotton wool.
- *Fun with a candle* – blowing out a lit candle, blowing the candle flame with varying intensity so that it does not go out.
- *Colorful bubbles* – releasing soap bubbles.
- *Hit the goal* – blowing a celluloid ping-pong ball so that it hits the target.

Attention! *Children with upper respiratory tract diseases do not participate in breathing exercises.*

Breathing exercises with arm and torso movements

- Children inhale while bringing their arms to the side quickly, and exhale while moving their arms slowly forward until they cross them completely.
- Children breathe in while lifting their arms sideways, then slowly lower their arms while exhaling.
- Children place their hands on the back of their necks, and while inhaling, move their elbows sharply back, and while exhaling, slowly return their elbows forward until the elbows touch.
- Children perform a quick inhalation while turning their torso to the side, while exhaling slowly – they return to normal posture.
- Children lean their torso forward, let their arms hang freely, then breathe in as they straighten their torso and raise their arms up, then slowly repeat the bend, and exhale.
- In the kneeling position (palms resting on the floor), children raise their head while inhaling and look at the ceiling, slowly lowering when exhaling.

Breathing exercises focusing on relaxation

- While lying freely, try to imagine that you are a sheet of water-soaked cloth lying on the floor.
- In the supine position, stretch in all directions (like waking up in bed in the morning). Stretch your arms, legs, neck, the entire body. Stretching, yawn loudly, saying *a a a a* … Yawn wide, freely, like a waking lion.
- Lying on your back with your legs curled up, take a deep breath and in an undertone count: *one, two, three etc.* making an attempt to keep the air in. Repeat the exercise, trying to get to the higher figure each time.
- In the same supine position, lift your legs straight up at your knees and take a deep breath. Then exhale as you lower your legs at the same time. When exhaling, pronounce the sounds *ssss* … and *s. … s … s … s …*

- Lying on your back, raise your right leg straight at the knee. Breathe in as you lift, and then breathe out with the very slow lowering of your leg. Repeat the same exercise with your left leg and then with both legs simultaneously.
- Lying on your back, inhale and at the same time raise your joined legs to a height of approximately 20 to 40 cm. Then hold your breath and stay that way for a while. Then, as you exhale, slowly lower your legs to a lying position, with your heels gently resting on the ground.
- Lying on your back, say with one exhalation: *One crow cannot go, the other crow cannot go...* Try to count as many crows on one exhalation as you can.
- Change to a standing position. Pull the invisible rope toward you. Inhale quickly as you stretch your arms forward for the rope, and while pulling the rope toward you at a slow pace (the rope resists), breathe out slowly. Repeat the exercise several times, each time changing the position of the body (e.g. kneeling position, light squat, your arms extended upward instead being stretched in front of you). Do the same exercise with a single vowel tone sound: /a/, /o/, /u/, etc.
- Murmuring activities – connecting vowels with the consonant [m]; pronounce syllables slowly and effortlessly: *aaammmaaa, eeemmmeee, yyymmmyyy,* etc.

Selected exercises and games to improve the articulation apparatus

The exercises and games to improve the articulation apparatus presented here are aimed at improving the tongue, sublingual frenulum, lips, soft palate and mandible; developing skillful and purposeful movements of the articulation organs; developing the sense of movement and position of the articulation organs; sensitizing places and movements in the oral cavity necessary for proper pronouncing sounds; improving motor coordination in terms of the articulation apparatus; developing natural auditory sensitivity; and training perceptiveness and concentration of attention. All the exercises and/or games presented below can be found in very stimulating books written by the following eminent speech therapists: I. Michalak-Widera (1998, 2003); Skorek (2001a, 2001b); E.J. Lichota (2005); and K. Kozłowska (2008).

Tongue and sublingual frenulum exercises

- *Whose tongue is longer?* – we stick our tongue out over our chin.
- *Who will reach higher?* – we raise the tip of the tongue toward the nose.
- *Clock pendulum* – the tip of the tongue touches the corners of the lips (alternately).

- *Licking lips* – we lick jam-smeared lips with the tip of the tongue (mouth wide open).
- Licking with the tip of the tongue the places under the lower lip, along its entire length (dry, smeared with jam, honey etc.).
- Using the tip of the tongue to lick the places just above the upper lip, along its entire length (dry, smeared with jam, honey etc.).
- *Spoon* – raise the front part of the tongue in such a way that its tip and sides form a spoon.
- *Roll* – we stick the tongue out of our mouth, arranged in a roll.
- *Cat's back* – place the tongue in such a way that there is a bulge in its center; we do the so-called hill from the tongue.
- *A mill* – we circle the tongue in the mouth to the right and left (with the mouth closed).
- *Balls* – we close our lips and push the inside of our cheeks with our tongue.
- *Face painting* – the tongue imitates the painter's movements – paints the ceiling (palate) and walls, that is, the inside of the cheeks.
- *Wizard-tongue* – the tongue turns into a brush and makes brush-like movements while painting a picture.
- *Teeth cleaning* – we 'clean' the outer and inner surfaces of the teeth with the tongue.
- *We count the teeth* – we touch each tooth with the tip of the tongue.
- *Grasshopper's clawing* – mobile tongue imitates the sounds produced by a grasshopper.
- *Imitation of viper tongue movements* – the tongue quickly moves out in all directions.
- The tongue touches repeatedly each of the following: lower lip, upper lip, right corner of the mouth, left corner of the mouth.

Lip exercises

- *Kisses* – we send out 'kisses' to our reflection in the mirror.
- *Window* – we arrange the lips in the shape of a circle (teeth closed and visible).
- *A smile-beak* – we pull our lips together, as in the case of the articulation of a vowel, and then flatten them, withdrawing the corners of the mouth, as in the case of articulating the sound of /*u*/.
- *Lip application* – we alternately apply the lower lip to the upper lip and vice versa.
- *Lip massage* – lower teeth make an attempt to massage (biting it slightly) the upper lip, then upper teeth does similar massage to the lower lip.
- *Happy and sad faces* – we mimic happy and sad faces alternately.
- Mimicking selected noises produced by: owls (*hu, hu*), fire engine when on signal (*e-o-e-o*) etc.

Soft palate exercises

- *Snoring* – we inhale and exhale the air imitating the sounds produced when snoring.
- *A sick kitten* – we imitate the activity of yawning, coughing, gargling, swallowing pills, drinking syrup etc.
- *Pig* – we imitate the sounds made by a pig.

Lower jaw exercises

- *Crocodile* – a motionless tongue, stuck to the roof of the mouth – next we snap our teeth (we vigorously lower the jaw).
- *Drawer* – we rhythmically extend and retract the lower jaw.
- *Storm* – we move the lower jaw rhythmically to the sides.
- *Cow* – we make circular and lateral movements of the mandible with the closed crevice of the lips.

Selected exercises and games to improve auditory perception

Suggestions of exercises and games to improve auditory perception are aimed at (a) training the ability to recognize acoustic signals through the auditory path; (b) developing the ability to differentiate and identify sounds of human speech; (c) developing a correct analysis and synthesis of auditory sounds; (d) implementing proper identification of sounds in various positions of the word; and (e) improving phonemic hearing in specific phonological oppositions (Spałek & Piechowicz-Kułakowska, 1996). While performing the exercises, children (a) distinguish acoustic phenomena, their presence or absence; (b) distinguish the duration of the acoustic signal (long – short); (c) give the number of sounds emitted; (d) indicate the pace of the acoustic signal (fast – slow); (e) recognize the intensity of the sound (loud – quiet) and its frequency (high – low); (f) locate the source of the sound; (g) recreate the sound structures according to the given pattern; (h) sort pictures according to the first sound in a word; (i) distinguish sounds in individual words and signal this fact; (j) differentiate words audibly; (k) isolate words in a sentence, (l) divide words into syllables and syllables for sounds; (m) build a rhythm to a selected text or create a text to a given rhythm.

Auditory exercises are the most difficult, and therefore they are introduced only after articulation, breathing and phonation exercises have been completed (Rodak, 2002; Słodownik-Rycaj, 2000). It is not easy for a child to extract words from the speech stream, syllables in words and sounds in syllables. In the case of inability of differentiation or poor differentiation of sounds, speech disorders and difficulties in learning to read and write are usually present. This is why so much importance is attached to auditory exercises conducted in a targeted and intended manner. Following are selected suggestions of exercises aimed at the improvement of auditory perception:

1 *Listening to the silence* – catching sounds from the environment, for example water dripping, clock ticking, car humming, radio playing, etc.
2 *Recognition of instruments* by sound (different CDs can be used here).
3 *Recognition of animal voices and sounds characteristic of different motor vehicles* (different CDs can be used here).
4 *Recognizing sounds made by objects* – a glass, a can, a box, a spoon, etc. – the speech therapist hits objects, children have to recognize a sound by seeing the objects hit at first, then they are blindfolded and have to do the same.
5 *Differentiation of sounds* – a coin, a ping-pong ball, a pebble, etc. – we throw objects on the table, the participants recognize sounds by seeing the objects at first, then the speech therapist blindfolds them.
6 Spoons, blocks, two glasses (one empty, the other one with water), a sheet of paper – the speech therapist keeps tapping with spoons and/ or blocks, pouring water from one glass to another, tearing a sheet of paper – children have to recognize sounds by seeing them, then they are blindfolded.
7 Chestnuts, acorns, groats, peas, rice – put them in a box and shake them – the participants are to guess what they hear. We do the same exercise blindfolding the children.
8 Mimicking the number and pace of strokes (using a pencil hitting the table, clapping) – we start with a combination of two or three strokes. Children observe and repeat the beats, when they understand the essence of the exercise they repeat the beats they hear, blindfolded.
9 *Duration of the acoustic signal* (opposition: long – short): We unfold a blank sheet of paper. Then we recommend drawing a circle (the sun). Children draw the 'face' of the sun. The therapist turns her/his back to them and whistles. If they hear a long sound, they draw a long sunbeam; if the sounds heard by them are short, they draw a short sunbeam.
10 *Number of transmitted acoustic signals*: After the instructions for the course of the task and the rehearsal, the children perform the following exercise. It consists of several stages. Initially, the therapist puts two coins into the jar with an interval of about five seconds and counts the number of strokes of the coins hitting the bottom of the jar with the participants. The test should be repeated at least two times to consolidate the exercise. At the second stage, the speech therapist increases the number of coins thrown in, but remembers the five seconds between each coin put down. The children count aloud when they hear the sound of the coin being thrown in. When increasing the difficulty of this exercise the therapist is reducing the time distance between the signals, for example to three seconds. At first, the children see the coin being tossed in and hear the sound of it hitting the bottom of the jar, then they turn around and only use their hearing.

11   *Rate of the transmitted signal* (opposition: fast – slow): Children receive cards with pictures symbolizing the two opposite concepts: *fast* and *slow*. They spread them on opposite sides of the table. The children are given pictures of various animals and they are to determine which ones walk slowly and which ones are fast (with the help of the therapist). Next, the therapist stands behind the children and taps out the rhythm at a fast or slow pace. The participants' task is to select the animal to the pace heard and place it under the appropriate picture.

12   *Sound intensity* (opposition: loud – soft): We familiarize the children with 'loud' and 'soft' hitting the instruments, or we agree that hitting the drum is 'loud' and hitting the cymbal is 'quiet'. During each stroke, we show a red or blue strip of paper respectively, and place it on the half of the sheet. We agree with the children that, for example, the blue half of the card is 'loud' (blue strip), red is 'quiet' (red strip). At the beginning, we perform an exercise rehearsal in order to familiarize participants with the course of the task. When we see that the children are coping with the exercise, they turn around and make an attempt to place the correct strips of paper on the piece of paper only through the auditory pathway.

13   *Sound frequency* (opposition: high – low): We put two boxes of different sizes (small and large) in front of the children. Next we take the illustrations of animals and divide them into small and large ones. We explain that small animals make low sounds, while large animals make high sounds, for example, a large dog barking is 'high' and a small dog is 'low'. The therapist makes the same sounds as the animals; the task for the children is to recognize the frequency of the sound and place the illustration in a small or large box.

14   *Location of the sound source*: The therapist first introduces the children to the sound of the alarm clock. We take three (or more) boxes with covers and place them at a distance of one meter from each other. At first the participants' faces are located at the middle box in the distance of approximately 0.5 meter. Then the children turn around, and the speech therapist puts the filmed alarm clock in one box. After turning around and listening, the participants have to tell the therapist in which box the alarm clock is ringing. Then we put the alarm clock in other boxes and ask the children to do the same. When a number of trials of this exercise are done correctly, we can reposition the boxes, reduce the distance between them, or increase the children's distance from the boxes.

15   *Recognizing the presence or absence of sound*: The children are to tell or show the speech therapist that they have heard the sound produced by the therapist, for example by raising their hands upwards. At the beginning, the exercise is performed in front of the children, then the participants turn around, and finally hide behind the screen.

16   *Recreating sound structures according to given patterns*: The speech therapist taps out any rhythms, for example (.), (. ...), (... ...), (... ... ...), etc. The

children try to repeat them. There are short and longer time intervals in these systems. The teacher arranges any rhythm using the blocks, the participants tap it out, then the roles change.

17 Building a rhythm to the given text: for example, *The teacher asks for a book*, or *Peter has a large umbrella*.

18 *Creating a text to a specific rhythm*: The therapist (first) and the children (next) tap out the rhythm e.g. (.. . ...), clap it out and next make an attempt to put a text on it.

19 *Extracting words in a sentence*: The children are requested to do the following:

- How many words do you hear in this sentence?

  Ola is playing with her doll.
  Adam is reading the book.

- 'Convert' words in sentences using blocks. Each block is one word.
- Listen carefully and count 'in your memory' how many words there are in the sentence:

  Tomek and Ewa have their toys.
  The dog is sitting in front of the kennel.

20 *Lengthening words* by adding bound morphemes /-s/ or /-es/ at the end of a word, for example fox – fox*es*, cat – cat*s*, hive – hive*s*, house – house*s*, hiss – hiss*es*, fence – fence*s*, bus – bus*es*, etc.

21 *Division of words into syllables*: Look at the picture, give its name, and then break the word into the syllables: *eye, ear, bridge, birds, brick, tractor, umbrella, planes, refrigerator*, etc.

22 *Sorting pictures according to the first sound*: The children are requested to do the following:

- Look for items whose names begin with the letters/k/,/g/,/p/, /b/,/t/,/d/,/f/,/w/;
- Group the pictures according to the initial sound, for example under /ʃ/ – *shelf, show*, etc.; under /s/ – *scarf, smile*, etc.; under /z/ – *zebra, zip*, etc.

23 *Distinguishing sounds in words* and signaling this fact by raising a hand: The speech therapist gives different words; if she/he says a word that starts with, for example, the letter /p/, the children should raise their hand up.

24 *Auditory differentiation of words* – with the help of picture scatter: The children are requested to do the following:

- Point to the pictures: *bear – beer, line – pine, roll – ball, rat – cat, knives – knife, ship – shop, knee – key, play – pray, land – hand, rower – tower, three – tree*;

- Match the picture to the name spoken by the speech therapist: *knight – fight, pen – pan, writer – rider, bees – peas, path – bath, peach – beach,* etc. How are these pairs of words different?

Selected exercises and games used during speech therapy – disturbed articulation of sounds

The child prepares the articulation organs for speaking activities from the earliest months of life. In the second or third year of life, the child achieves motor skills that allow her/him to pronounce the easiest sounds without much effort. The constantly developing kinetic functions enable the appearance of sounds requiring more precise articulation at the age of 3 or 4. The most difficult sounds appear only at the age of 4 or 5 and are often difficult for children. Improving the articulation process is then based only on the act of speaking. At each of these stages, speech can be supported with appropriate exercises of the articulation, respiratory, phonation and auditory organs, in this way helping to increase their efficiency.

Proposals of exercises and games used during speech therapy have been designed by a number of experienced speech therapists (Chmielewska, 1997; Chrzanowska, 2002; Gawęda & Łazewski, 1995; Michalak-Widera & Węskierska, 2001; Minczakiewicz, 1997; Morkowska, 2000; Morkowska & Żmuda-Trzebiatowska, 2000; Rodak, 1999; Sachajska, 1992; Skorek, 2001a; Słodownik-Rycaj, 1998; Sołtys-Chmielowicz, 2008). All the selected games and exercises that are presented below are aimed at (a) strengthening the habit of proper breathing, articulation apparatus gymnastics; (b) training the skills of correct phonetic pronunciation; (c) recording the evoked sound in syllables; (d) introducing the correct articulation of sounds in the earpiece, voice and mid-voice of words, two-word expressions, sentences, texts. An experienced speech therapist, knowing all methodological approaches, most often chooses an eclectic position. The speech therpist has a flexible approach to the methodology (Pluta-Wojciechowska, 2013; Siedlaczek-Szwed & Jałowiecka-Frania, 2009; Węsierska, 2013; Zaorska, 2009). She/he uses various methods and their own modifications at different stages of work. Improvement methods consist in exercising the speech organs. Exercises conducted for some time improve oral somesthesia and make the child aware of the motor skills of her/his speech organs. Selected examples of exercises and games follow:

1   *Playing 'a hissing snake'* – we recommend that children imitate the sounds produced by a snake [sss. . . s], while running their fingers along the lines of a speech therapy spiral, which is played by the drawing of an animal.
2   *Naming individual pictures and grouping them according to the sound position,* for example the position of the sound /s/ in a word produced by the therapist:

- /s/ (at the beginning of the word) – *smile, sledge, sandals, celery, salt, stairs, skipping-rope,* etc.;

- /s/ (middle of the word) – *master, missus, policeman, wasp, plaster, rooster, moustache, passerby, sportsman*, etc.;
- /s/ (at the end of a word) – *hiss, miss, fox, plus, house*, etc.

3 *Solving rebuses*: The speech therapist shows the children and names the number four, then gives the end of the word, the participants are to give the full word: for example 4 + (square); 4 + (fold); 4 + (teen); 4 + (eyed); 4 + (ball); 4 + (chette).

4 *Composing sentences by children* (with the help of the teacher) to the presented illustrations.

5 *Drawn poems* – the speech therapist slowly gives the text of the poem, the children repeat the content they hear, taking care of the correct pronunciation of the sounds and together with the teacher they try to illustrate the poem.

6 *Talking parrot* – movement game with a ball. The speech therapist throws a ball to the child and pronounces the syllable at the same time. The child discards the ball and repeats the same syllable, for example [*for*-]. We can make the game more attractive by changing the way of throwing the ball: to the children's hands, bouncing it on the floor or wall, making a rotation after throwing the ball and repeating a syllable, etc.

7 *Echo*: The children are to repeat a series of syllables following the speech therapist. We start with easy, two-syllable lines, and then we offer children three- and four-syllable ranks, for example *za – zo, aza – ozo, za - za - za - zo - za – zo*, etc.

8 *Crossword*: The speech therapist reads the content of the entries, the children give the answer and try to determine the position of the letter [s] etc. in the word, then paint over the appropriate box in the crossword placed on large, gray paper:

- *The king lives there.* (castle)
- *Used for having fun in winter.* (skis)
- *A person who helps other people.* (servant)

9 *Saying two-word expressions* in which one of the words is presented by means of an illustration (the speech therapist gives one of the phrases, children name the picture, then repeat the whole expression using the appropriate grammatical form), for example *healthy tooth; kiss miss; clean cloth; excellent eyesight; hot pot; please police; crystal bristle*, etc.

10 *A board game with cards* with the following syllables: [ca], [co], [cu], [ce], [cy], [aca], [oco], [ucu], [ece], [ice], [ac], [oc], [uc], [ec] (the syllables selected should follow those that exist in a given language). The participant moves her/his pawn as many places as there will be spots on the thrown dice. The speech therapist pronounces the syllable, the child repeats it as many times as there were dots on the dice. The first person to reach the finish line receives a prize.

11 *Block tower*: The children build towers from blocks (or bricks). They place one block and say a word, including, for example, the sound /c/.

The words given cannot be repeated. The award is given to the person who has built the highest tower, that is produced the greatest number of words with the /c/ sound.

12   *Playing with a ball*: The speech therapist throws a ball to the child and says a specific word; the child throws the ball back by giving the plural of the word; the speech therapist gives the plural verb (3rd person plural – *they*, e.g. *catch*) and throws the ball; the child who has caught it and now has to throw it away, gives the same verb, but in the singular (3rd person singular – *he, she, it*, e.g. *catches*), etc.

13   *Enchanted picture*: The children have to find people, animals and objects in the pictures, in the names of which the sound/c/ is hidden (or any other voluntarily selected by the therapist).

14   *Arranging logically correct sentences*: The therapist is saying 'Jacek confused some words in sentences. Arrange them so that they make sense':

   •   How many *gusts* are we having for dinner today? *(guests)*
   •   Suddenly she felt overpowered by repeated *guests* of anxiety. *(gusts)*

15   *Tinkerbell*: The speech therapist rings a bell; the child's task is to repeat the indicated syllable as many times as the bell rang.

16   *Eliminating words* that do not match the rest. Justifying the choice:

   •   *scrabble, rabble, grabble,* **juggle**
   •   *bell,* **money**, *bell ringer, belfry*

17   *Contests*, e.g. solving puzzles – the person who gives the most correct answers receives a prize.

18   Saying two-word expressions in which one of the words is presented by means of an illustration (a speech therapist gives two of the elements of the expression, children name the picture, then repeat the whole expression using the appropriate grammatical form): *false teeth; fine vine; shop sheep; boring bowling*; etc.

19   *Actors and prompter*: The speech therapist suggests a drama-like exercise; the participants take on the role of actors who have forgotten the text and use the prompter to repeat the following tongue-twisting sentences:

   •   *Sheila sells seashells by the seashore.*
   •   *They saw a kitten eating chicken in the kitchen.*
   •   *Nine nice night nurses nursing nicely.*
   •   *Which wrist watches are Swiss wrist watches?*
   •   *She sees cheese.*

20   *Associative star*: The children match the pictures to the pictures inside the star and call them: for example, *clock – hand; satellite – astronaut; goat – cabbage*, etc.

21   *Completing sentences*: The children choose the correct picture, name it, and then repeat the sentence using the correct grammatical form, for example:

- Fog has hung over the pond.
- The car is parking on the road.
- The vase stands on the table.

22 *Playground*: This exercise aims at deciphering the names of children on the basis of given sentences and telling pictures with their use:

- The boys are playing soccer on the field.
- Zenek and Stach play tennis.
- Lucyna trains jumping rope.
- Zuzanna took Celina's pram and Celina is sad.
- Wicek and Wacek build a barrier of stones on the stream.
- Little Sabina is making a sand castle.
- There is a moat around the castle and a drawbridge above it.

23 *The Wawel[1] Dragon*: The children cut out individual pictures referring to the legend of a dragon inhabiting a cave underneath the castle and arrange them in the order of events, then color and stick them on separate sheets. Subsequently, they tell a picture story on their own or use the sentences provided.

24 *Look, tell, arrange*: The children choose pictures and place them on the free fields of large thematic cards; then they tell the picture.

25 *Playing with a doll*: The children, when dressing a doll, name the activities performed according to the following scheme:

- predicate ± object: *I am putting on* (what?) ………………; *I am taking off* (what?) ………………; *I am folding* (what?) ……………… ;
- predicate ± adverbial of manner: *I am* ………………… *putting on* (how?) – for example carefully, exactly ……………………………………;
- predicate ± adverbial of place: *I am putting it on* …………… (where?) – for example on arms, legs, head, torso, feet, hands, back;
- object ± direct object: (what?) for example, long pants, thick sweater, buttoned blouse, sports tracksuit, zipped suit, cotton socks, small headscarf, leather gloves, low boots, mountain heart, bathing suit, tied sandals, formal dress, pleated skirt;
- single sentence with a default subject: for example, *I am putting leather gloves on the doll's hands. I am taking off the cotton socks from its feet. I am folding a small handkerchief. I am putting on low boots. Now I am putting a thick sweater on the doll's back. And now I am putting on a pleated skirt on the doll.*

26 *The owl plays words*: The players place the board on the table. They sort the cards with pictures into groups according to a specific sound, which contains the word presented in a given picture. This way, four groups are created – for sounds /s/, /z/, /c/, /dz/. The teacher chooses one of the groups and shows the children each picture in turn. The participants

---

1 *Wawel* [wawel] is the name of a hill in Cracow with the Royal Castle upon it.

repeat the word when looking at the picture. The speech therapist places the picture on one of the six colored fields on the board so that the background color of the picture matches the color of the board field. In this way, she/he arranges all the pictures from the four groups. The person who starts the game rolls a colored die, and then selects and names a picture that lies on the board space in a color matching the color of the die. If the child pronounces the word correctly, she/he takes the picture and scores a point. If the player utters a word incorrectly, she/he puts the picture back where she/he has taken it from. The game continues until all the cards on the board have been removed. The winner is the child who has collected the most picture cards.

27 *Zoo* (a board game): The game starts with the child who shoots the greatest number of dice. The players, standing on the fields marked with arrows, collect pictures of 'watched' animals. When they stand on the marked field, they take one of the cardboards with the picture of the animal in the right place and name it. The winner is the person who collects the most cards and crosses the finish line first.

28 *We are shopping* (drama scenes): One person acts as a seller, the other children are 'buyers'. Together with the group, the speech therapist develops the rules of role-playing. The children are expected to use:

- phrases, when saying 'hello' and 'goodbye': *Good morning; Goodbye; Good evening; Good night* etc.
- such questions as: *How much does …?, Are there …?, Is there …?, Do you have …?, Where is ….?*
- answers, such as: *I'm afraid there is no … ; We don't have (… red), but there are …,* etc.

The products to be sold are shown in the appropriate pictures. When the role-playing is over, the 'seller' and the place of shopping are changed, for example grocery gets changed into a vegetable store, pet store, sports store, supermarket etc.

29 *What kind of sound is that?*: The children, looking at the drawings placed on the boards, call them loudly; they search for pictures and words containing sounds, the pronunciation and distinction of which is difficult for them: /sh/–/s/; /ż/–/z/; /cz/–/c/, /j/–/dz/. Then they extract the indicated sounds in the beginning, middle or end of the words, and then distinguish all the sounds that make up the given word. At the end, they arrange the given words, for example using LEGO blocks.

30 *Speech therapy fish*: The participants use a fishing rod to catch a 'fish', name the pictures on them and arrange them on individual boards in dependence on the sound found in the word:

- /sh/ – ship, shoulder, sheriff, shampoo, shoreline, shark;
- /z/ – zero, jazz, zebu, maze, zone, quiz, zebra;
- /cz/ – wristwatch, sketchbook, stretcher, witch, butcher;

- /th/ – throw, thief, moth, mother, broth, father;
- /s/ – stick, present, classes, August, artist, cost, smile;
- /ts/ – nuts, pants, fists, sets, nets, lists, pots.

31 *Skipping one* unnecessary word and then pronouncing correctly sounding sentences:

- A coat hanged (hang) in the wardrobe.
- There are glasses on the disc (desk).
- Giraffes (live) life in Africa.
- There a dock (dog) near the cherry tree.
- The teacher (thatcher) collected students' notebooks.

32 *Playing train*: The 'engine' (the speech therapist) and the 'carriages' (the children) are going on a long journey. Along the way, they encounter various stops and stations. They have practiced sounds in their names. These names can get more and more difficult.

33 *Inventing objects that contain the sound indicated*, e.g. /z/, in their names and drawing them. Presentation and evaluation of drawings made by children.

34 *Searching the local environment for the objects with the indicated sound*: The children give the name of the item they have found to be placed near them, then divide the word into syllables, specifying the position of the indicated sound in the word (e.g. they were requested to look for the words with the sound /ts/ in them; now they have discovered a 'wrist-watch'; they should divide this word into syllables and find out the position of the sound /ts/ in it).

35 *Speech therapy memory*: The cards with the pictures are placed face down; the therapist can arrange them in rows or lay them loosely on the table. Each player (clockwise) reveals two cards and says their name out loud. The child who discovers two of the same pictures picks up the pair from the table. The person with the most cards wins.

36 *Fictionalized games based on prepared scenarios*: The exercise assumes covering a given topic and taking into account the creative active work of the participants, for example *At the seaside*; *In the mountains*; etc.

Consolidation of the newly learned sound should take place in the form of games with the use of all didactic means making the exercises more attractive, activating the child, encouraging and motivating to work (Bernacka, 2001; Sachajska, 2002). For this purpose, for example, colorful pictures, puzzles, crosswords, sliders, riddles, poems, etc. are used. Poems should be short, easy to remember, with interesting and fun content. Children's literature abounds in this type of suggestion; you just need to choose a piece so that the practiced sound is repeated in it often (Skorek, 2010; Wójtowiczowa, 1993). In addition to stories and poems, speech therapists willingly use riddles. Riddles stimulate children to pronounce sounds spontaneously, which therapists can use to control the degree of automation of articulation movements.

References

Bernacka, D. (2001). *Od słowa do działania* [From word to action]. Żak Academic Press.

Bielska, B. (2001). Malowanie rękami jako niekonwencjonalna forma ekspresji [Painting with hands as an unconventional form of expression]. *Szkoła Specjalna* [Special School], *1*, 32–33.

Bloom, S. R. (2006). *Digital collage and painting. Using photoshop and painter to create fine art* (pp. 4–5). Focal.

Chmielewska, E. (1997). *Zabawy logopedyczne i nie tylko. Poradnik dla nauczycieli i rodziców* [Speech therapy games and more. A guide for teachers and parents]. Kielce Publishing House.

Chrzanowska, A. (2002). *Zabawy i ćwiczenia logopedyczne /s/, /z/, /c/, /dz/. Poradnik dla logopedów, nauczycieli i rodziców* [Speech therapy games and exercises /s/, /z/, /c/, /dz /. A guide for speech therapists, teachers and parents]. Academic Publishers.

Dembińska, M. (1994). *Domowe zabawy logopedyczne* [Home-practising speech therapy games]. WSiP Publishers.

Gawęda, K., & Łazewski, J. (1995). *Uczymy się poprawnej wymowy. Ćwiczenia usprawniające mówienie* [We learn the correct pronunciation. Exercises to improve speaking]. Alfa" Publishers.

Jakubczyk, K. (2012). Metoda malowania dziesięcioma palcami (finger-painting) [The ten finger painting method]. *Nauczyciel i Szkoła* [Teacher and School], *2*(52), 193–202.

Lichota, E. J. (2005). *Terapia wad wymowy* [Speech impairment therapy]. Impuls Publishing House.

Michalak-Widera, I. (1998). *Śmieszne minki dla chłopczyka i dziewczynki. Ćwiczenia usprawniające wymowę* [Funny faces for a boy and a girl. Exercises to improve pronunciation]. UNIKAT-2 Publishers.

Michalak-Widera, I. (2003). *Miłe uszom dźwięki. Ćwiczenia narządów artykulacyjnych przygotowujące do wymawiania głosek języka polskiego i metody prawidłowej realizacji dźwięków* [Sounds pleasant to the ears. Articulation exercises to prepare for pronouncing the sounds of the Polish language and methods of the correct implementation of sounds]. UNIKAT-2 Publishers.

Michalak-Widera, I., & Węsierska, K. (2001). Syczące wierszyki. *Materiał językowy (wierszyki, wyliczanki, powiedzonka wyrazowo-obrazkowe i rebusy fonetyczne) do utrwalania wymowy głosek syczących, zebrały i opracowały* [Hissing rhymes. The linguistic material (poems, rhyming, expressive and pictorial sayings and phonetic rebuses) for recording the pronunciation of sibilants]. UNIKAT-2.

Minczakiewicz, E. M. (1997). *Rysowane wierszyki i zagadki w rozwijaniu sprawności mówienia, czytania i pisania* [Drawing rhymes and riddles to develop speaking, reading and writing skills]. Educational Publishing House.

Morkowska, E. (1998). *Uczymy się chuchać, dmuchać i oddychać prawidłowo. Ćwiczenia logopedyczne dla dzieci* [We learn to breathe, blow and puff properly. Speech therapy exercises for children]. WSiP Publishers.

Morkowska, E. (2000). *Wąż syczy pod szumiącym drzewem. Ćwiczenia logopedyczne dla dzieci* [The snake hisses under the rustling tree. Speech therapy exercises for children]. WSiP Publishers.

Morkowska, E., & Żmuda-Trzebiatowska, K. (2000). *Szedł żuczek do szkoły się uczyć. Ćwiczenia logopedyczne dla dzieci* [A beetle was going to school to learn. Speech therapy exercises for children]. WSiP Publishers.

Pluta-Wojciechowska, D. (2013). Strategiczna metoda usprawniania realizacji fonemów. Motywacje i główne założenia [A strategic method of improving the realization of phonemes. Forms of motivation and principal assumptions]. *Logopedia* [Speech Therapy], *42*, 45–60.

Przepióra, A. (2014). Edukacja małego dziecka – Zabawy i ćwiczenia przygotowujące do pisania [Education of a young child – Games and exercises preparing for the skill of writing]. *Forum nauczycieli* [Teacher forum] (Vol. 2, pp. 53–54). Regional Teacher Training Center WOM in Katowice.

Rafał-Łuniewska, J. (2010). *Propozycje ćwiczeń do wykorzystania w pracy z dzieckiem z grupy ryzyka dysleksji w edukacji wczesnoszkolnej* [Samples of exercises to be used in work with a child at risk of dyslexia in early school education] (pp. 1–12 [pdf]). ORE. file:///C:/Users/user/Downloads/Propozycje_ćwiczeń_dla_dzieci_z_grupy_ryzyka_dysleksji_1.pdf.

Rodak, H. (1999). *Uczymy się poprawnie mówić. Poradnik logopedyczny z ćwiczeniami, wydanie II* [We learn to speak correctly. Speech therapy handbook with exercises] (2nd ed.). WSiP Publishers.

Rodak, H. (2002). *Terapia dziecka z wadą wymowy* [Therapy of a child with a speech impediment]. Warsaw University Publishing House.

Sachajska, E. (1992). *Uczymy poprawnej wymowy, wydanie IV zmienione* [We teach correct pronunciation, 4th edition amended]. WSiP Publishers.

Sachajska, E. (2002). Z metodyki pracy nad wymową [From the methodology of working on pronunciation]. *Logopedia* [Speech Therapy], *31*, 227–257.

Siedlaczek-Szwed, A., & Jałowiecka-Frania, A. (2009). *Polisensoryczne oddziaływanie logopedy* [Polysensory influence of a speech therapist]. Publishing House Stanisław Podobiński Academy of Jan Długosz in Częstochowa.

Siedlaczek-Szwed, A., & Jałowiecka-Frania, A. (2016). *Zaburzenia dyslaliczne w wymiarze teoretyczno-praktycznym* [Theoretical and practical dyslalic disorders]. SIM" Poligraphic and Publishing House.

Skorek, E. M. (2000a). *Ćwiczenia w wymowie samogłosek nosowych* [Exercises in the pronunciation of nasal vowels]. Impuls Publishing House.

Skorek, E. M. (2000b). *Samogłoski. Profilaktyka, diagnoza, korekcja nieprawidłowej artykulacji* [Vowels. Prevention, diagnosis, correction of incorrect articulation]. Impuls Publishing House.

Skorek, E. M. (2001a). *Reranie. Profilaktyka, diagnoza, korekcja* [Rhotacism. Prevention, diagnosis, correction]. Impuls Pubishing House.

Skorek, E. M. (2001b). *Oblicza wad wymowy* [Faces of speech impediments]. Żak Academic Press.

Skorek, E. M. (2010). *100 tekstów do ćwiczeń logopedycznych, wydanie VI* [100 texts for speech therapy exercises] (6th ed.). Harmonia Publishers.

Słodownik-Rycaj, E. (1998). *Rozwijanie mowy komunikatywnej dziecka* [Developing the child's communicative speech]. Żak Academic Press.

Słodownik-Rycaj, E. (2000). *O mowie dziecka, czyli jak zapobiegać powstawaniu nieprawidłowości w jej rozwoju* [The way a child speaks, or how to prevent abnormalities in his development]. Żak Academic Press.

Sołtys-Chmielowicz, A. (2008). *Zaburzenia artykulacji. Teoria i praktyka* [Articulation disorders. Theory and practice]. Impuls Publishing House.

Spałek, E., & Piechowicz-Kułakowska, C. (1996). *Jak pomóc dziecku z wadą wymowy* [How to help a child with a speech impediment]. Impuls Publishing House.

Tucci, G. (2001). *The theory and practice of the mandala.* Dover Publications, Inc.

Węsierska, K. (2013). *Opieka logopedyczna w przedszkolu. Profilaktyka – Diagnoza – Terapia* [Speech Therapy in kindergarten. Prevention – Diagnosis – Therapy]. Akapit Publishers.

Wójtowiczowa, J. (1993). *Logopedyczny zbiór wyrazów, wydanie II rozszerzone* [Speech therapy word collection, 2nd edition, extended]. WSiP Publishers.

Zaorska, M. (2009). *Wskazówki do działań logopedycznych w pracy logopedy szkolnego. Wybrane zagadnienia* [Tips for speech therapy activities in the work of a school speech therapist. Selected issues]. Akapit Publishers.

Conclusion

Pedagogical diagnosis is currently one of the important dimensions and, at the same time, tasks that are incumbent on teachers, pedagogues, speech therapists, psychologists, special educators and other specialists working with children and adolescents at school. (In the case of elementary schools in Poland, this is especially true for students who have an evaluation of the need for special education, or an opinion issued by a psychological–pedagogical clinic.) These tasks are all the more important because, currently, teachers/pedagogues and other specialists are burdened with relevant regulations that normalize the conduct of (pedagogical) diagnosis.

The process of diagnosis is organized by the standards and rules of diagnostic procedure, which the authors refer to in the monograph. It is quite a complex process, since it is not just a recording of data but also requires from the teacher/developer/diagnostician the necessary knowledge, skills and relevant competencies, including in the acquisition of diagnostic material, its processing, interpretation and also the ability to think, infer, seek and apply – often in cooperation with other specialists – appropriate methods and forms of assistance and support for the student. The teacher/pedagogue/logistician/diagnostician is required to have key diagnostic competencies, which consist primarily of theoretical as well as methodological knowledge, abilities and practical skills, as well as self-awareness of one's personal competencies. This is a difficult process, not only because of the amount of necessary knowledge and professional competence a speech therapist/diagnostician must possess, but above all because of the emotional and social difficulties they experience when engaging in relationships with various types of entities (e.g. specialized institutions, parents of the child, educator, etc.). These relationships can sometimes interfere with the diagnostic processes, which may thus result in the appearance of a superficial, unreliable diagnosis, preventing effective and purposeful action.

As indicated in the monograph, pedagogical and speech therapy diagnoses can have different scopes and dimensions. Diagnoses can be partial (selective) or holistic (general). But regardless of these characteristics, as well as many other external/internal conditions, the principal features that characterize a professional diagnosis are always strongly linked with

DOI: 10.4324/9781003354758-7

the notions of accuracy, reliability, thoroughness, objectivity and impartiality, as well as comprehensibility. It should be in the nature of practical but also comprehensive actions; the former should take into account both the 'strengths' and 'weaknesses' of the individual-focusing decision-making actions, constituting the undertaking of intervention tasks; the latter are related to the multidirectionality and multifacetedness of diagnostic activities.

Many of the studies presented in the monograph also indicate the issues of permanence, dynamism and interdisciplinarity strongly linked with both speech therapy and diagnostic activities. Thus, from the pedagogical point of view, a diagnosis should be evaluative – allowing the assessment of an individual's capabilities in relation to accepted norms and standards. It should also be descriptive and explanatory, in this way consisting of an evaluative description of the facts, as well as an explanation and interpretation of the data. It is also indicated that any diagnosis-connected activity (as well as any activity observed in the field of speech therapy) should also be hypothetical, insightful, predictive and characterized by reflexivity. The diagnostician/ speech therapist should act in such a way that she/he not only evaluates but more so also understands what has been evaluated.

What any professionally carried out diagnosis requires from the teacher/ researcher/speech therapist or other specialist is to use appropriate methods, techniques and, above all, tools. As indicated, methodological triangulation in the process of pedagogical and/or speech therapy diagnosis provides the opportunity to more fully understand the studied reality and often eliminate cognitive errors. Such features, and the necessary elements associated with the conduct of diagnosis, not only provide a key basis for planning and designing assistance activities, but also for constructing various types of remedial-assistance-support programs. This is mostly because support is (and has always been) a key category in the – generally perceived – educational process and teaching practice, strongly connected with it.

When reading the presented materials, one could come to the conclusion that they stress that many important issues in the field of pedagogical and speech therapy diagnostics still remain open, despite the ongoing interdisciplinary research. The work is not very extensive in quantity and volume, and therefore it cannot be said that in this set of texts a saturation state in any field has been reached. The limited volume also required significant condensation of the materials. We believe that the advantage of the presented materials will be an inspiration to a wider interest in the problems of pedagogical and speech therapy diagnoses in their various forms and possible aspects. What we primarily mean is transgressive education that goes beyond the current theoretical and praxeological framework of the areas of pedagogical and speech therapy practice. We see the tasks of the pedagogue and speech therapist as a necessity to influence all development spheres, not only as work on shaping communication competences or educational skills. This work cannot be based on algorithms that are perceived as a set of features and behaviors, but should focus on an individual living in educational environments. It also obliges educators, speech therapists, therapists and other specialists working with children to prepare diagnostic and therapeutic programs that must be modified and transformed to adapt them to individual needs and psychophysical abilities.

The intention of the authors was a multi-threaded and multifaceted presentation of the issues related to the diagnostic processes. The multifaceted nature of the issue prompts researchers specializing in various fields of knowledge to deal with the discussed phenomenon, therefore the presented volume includes interdisciplinary works. We believe that the views and research results presented here will be an interesting supplement to the discourses conducted on the basis of domestic scientific disciplines, often inspired by various examples observed in the research, referring to the descriptions found in a number of English-written topical books and papers. We hope that the proposed work will contribute to taking up the subject of creative approach related to different stages of diagnostic processing understood not as a challenge to the present day but as a vision and mission of the communities responsible for the education of future generations. By placing speech therapy among the pedagogical sciences, we adhere to the principle of noticing a person first, and only then his/her developmental problems. Such thinking requires a strong subjective approach during both diagnostic and therapeutic activities. The presented diagnostic tools and methods allow to proceed working with many developmental problems, such as, for example, autism, mutism or dyslexia.

Index

Note: Page numbers with *italics* refer to the figures and **bold** the tables.